STO

ACPL ITEM
DISCARDED

THE COMPLEAT
MOTION PICTURE
QUIZ BOOK

By the authors

The Compleat Motion Picture Quiz Book

SON OF
THE COMPLEAT
MOTION PICTURE
QUIZ BOOK

◎

Or 60,000 More Points
About Motion Pictures
30,000 for Buffs—30,000 for Duffers

◎

HARRY D. TRIGG
YOLANDA L. TRIGG

DOLPHIN BOOKS
DOUBLEDAY & COMPANY, INC.
GARDEN CITY, NEW YORK
1977

ALLEN COUNTY PUBLIC LIBRARY
FORT WAYNE, INDIANA

The quiz "Chicago, Chicago" is reprinted with the permission of the Chicago *Daily News,* Field Enterprises, Inc.

"La Ronde" artwork by Ed Hansen.

Library of Congress Cataloging in Publication Data

Trigg, Harry D
  Son of the compleat motion picture quiz book.

  1. Moving-pictures—Miscellanea. I. Trigg,
Yolanda L., joint author. II. Title. III. Title:
The compleat motion picture quiz book.
PN1993.85T73   791.43′076
ISBN: 0-385-12386-8
Library of Congress Catalog Card Number 77–74313

Copyright © 1977 by Harry D. Trigg and Yolanda L. Trigg
All Rights Reserved
Printed in the United States of America
First Edition

To . . .

Jules Herbuveaux and Bob Lemon, to whom we
owe so much for making so much happiness possible . . .
Sister Anthony and Father John Banahan, to whom
we owe so much for enriching our happiness . . .
and to Dr. Joseph Caprini, Sheldon Cooper,
Jack Jacobson, and Dan Pecaro—to whom we owe so
much for preserving that happiness . . .

The Authors

7022304

A NOTE FROM THE AUTHORS

QUESTION: Name a 1961 movie starring Debbie Reynolds, Andy Griffith, Thelma Ritter, and Juliet Prowse.

If you answered "The Second Time Around," you get no score, but you have opened the door for this Foreword to *our* second time around in the movie-trivia milieu. A couple of years ago, our perverse minds came up with *The Compleat Motion Picture Quiz Book*. Putting that book together was fun, and was—we hope—entertaining for our readers . . . though we know that for some there was more frustration than entertainment. As we told our good publisher at the time, we doubted if any motion picture quiz book could be considered "complete" . . . or even "compleat." And we were right! Or at least we felt there was still an ever-growing mass of movie minutiae which demanded our attention.

And so, in an effort to stay off the streets and out of trouble, as well as perhaps to get a payment or two ahead on the mortgage of the house we refer to as "Xanadu North" (fans of "Citizen Kane" will appreciate that one), we have made it the *second time around*.

For those of you who might like to do your own book, we offer this secret: as you may have discovered, *procrastination* is the worst enemy of the writer. To combat this, do as we did—announce to the entire free world that you're going to do another book. You'll find this startling announcement is received with reactions ranging from "So what?" through "Who cares?" to that poorly disguised look of disbelief which clearly says: "Just because you got lucky once, what makes you think you can deliver another one?" Key to this devil-may-care laying of your head on the block is a *working title*. This enables your skeptical friends not merely to needle you with "How's it coming?" or "How's the book going?" or even "How's the *second* book progressing?" By giving them a working title to use in such sadistic questioning, you enable them to transmit that they *know* the title you're expected to deliver, and you can bet your boots that they won't let up until they find it on the shelf at Kroch's & Brentano's or Nydle's Nook. (Side note to Carl Kroch and Fred Nydle: please give this one shelf space, and thereby take the heat off! Thanks!)

Coming up with the title for this one was easy. After tromping through cinema memorabilia for years, we winnowed possible titles down to three—and were able to discard two of those without hesitation. First to go was *The Return of The Compleat Motion Picture Quiz Book*. After all, it had never really been away, and there are those of literal mind who might've thought this edition was merely a reissue of the first one. Though our son, Christy, liked the second title, and we admit there was a catchiness to it, we didn't feel that we could live with the limitations imposed by a title like *Abbott & Costello Meet The Compleat Motion Picture Quiz Book*.

And so, more by elimination and default, we have entitled this second exercise in movie memory manipulation **Son of The Compleat Motion Picture Quiz Book.**

For those of you who fondly remember the original (and we challenge you to whistle the music from it), let us point out that this book is also done in two versions: again, the Buffs' version is the toughie, but should offer a good challenge for the dyed-in-the-wool movie fan! And for the more casual movie-goer, we offer a slightly easier version for the Duffer. If you feel you are ready for the Buffs' version, then good for you—and we wish you luck! For those more faint in heart, don't automatically head for the Duffers' Tee—rather examine the Buffs' version and see if you can't cut this slightly more difficult course.

So, head 'em up and move 'em out—you're going out a nobody, but you're coming back a star—and let's win one for the Gipper!

POSSIBLE SCORE

	BUFFS	DUFFERS	Your Score
1. Consumables	180	180	_____
2. Very Important Props	300	300	_____
3. Look Who's Dancing with Mr. Smooth	225	225	_____
4. Saturday Night at the Flicks	150	150	_____
5. Broth-er	100	50	_____
6. Link-ups	50	50	_____
7. Careers in Common	200	200	_____
8. Name the Star	400	400	_____
9. Penciled In	150	200	_____
10. Play Ball!	150	150	_____
11. Quotables	150	150	_____
12. Potshots	100	150	_____
13. Unique Characters	250	200	_____
14. Chicago, Chicago	370	375	_____
15. Anything You Can Do, I Can Do Better	350	300	_____
16. The "They Went Thataway" Crisscross	500	350	_____
17. The Big Bulb	180	180	_____
18. Hail to the Chief	150	150	_____
19. Spot the Bio: Show Biz	150	150	_____
20. Type-casting?	500	500	_____
21. Durable, and Darling	200	200	_____
22. Almost a Legend	150	150	_____
23. Who Was That Lady?	625	600	_____
24. Films in Common	225	225	_____
25. All We Need Is a Title	180	180	_____
26. The Big Bulb Part II	225	225	_____
27. Tell Us Who	250	250	_____

WHAT YOUR SCORE MEANS

BUFFS

30,000 points	So you're some sort of genius, too!
27,500–29,999 points	Oh, that was close. Get another book and give it another go.
25,000–27,499 points	Hang onto your Shirley Temple doll—you're a comer!
20,000–24,999 points	Even this score is fair for a Buff. Not good —fair!
12,750–19,999 points	So it's not a smash winner—it's no loser, either!
5,000–12,749 points	Still it's a lot less strenuous than jogging!
1,000–4,999 points	This score should not be bandied about. Just forget it.
Under 1,000 points	Imagine—you could've spent the money on football cards!

DUFFERS

30,000 points	Let's hear it for the Duffer champ.
27,500–29,999 points	Little bit of work, kid, and you can come back a Buff!
25,000–27,499 points	Above average, definitely. Not much, but still "above."
20,000–24,999 points	Perhaps you'd do better with woodworking or nuclear physics.
12,750–19,999 points	Rest awhile—change your name, and give it another go!
5,000–12,749 points	It might be wise to seek another leisure-time pursuit.
1,000–4,999 points	Chess, maybe? Needlepoint? Mah-jongg? Mugging?
Under 1,000 points	Keep at it. Who knows, losers might be the next "in" thing!

SON OF
THE COMPLEAT
MOTION PICTURE
QUIZ BOOK

1. CONSUMABLES

This exercise asks you to fill in the blanks and thus complete the film titles. A clue for you: each missing word has to do with something which is *consumed*. Take 15 points for each film title correctly completed.

1. "The C _ _ _ Is Green"
2. "Animal C _ _ _ _ _ _ _ _"
3. "One P _ _ _ _ _ _, Two P _ _ _ _ _ _"
4. "The D _ _ _ _ _ girls"
5. "T _ _ for Two"
6. "The C _ _ _ _ _ _ _ _"
7. "D _ _ _ _ _ _ at Eight"
8. "Three Bites of the A _ _ _ _"
9. "B _ _ _ _ _ _ _ _ _ at Tiffany's"
10. "D _ _ _ S _ _ _"
11. "The G _ _ _ _ _ _ of Wrath"
12. "T _ _ _ _ _ _ _ Road"

_____points

(*Answers on page 201*)

1. CONSUMABLES—DUFFERS' TEE

This exercise has to do with things which are consumed. Select the proper words from Column Two, insert them into the proper spaces in Column One, and take 15 points for each film title properly completed.

1. "The _____ Is Green"	a. Duck
2. "Animal _____"	b. Apple
3. "One _____, Two _____"	c. Tobacco
4. "The _____ girls"	d. Soup
5. "_____ for Two"	e. Dinner
6. "The _____"	f. Corn
7. "_____ at Eight"	g. Crackers
8. "Three Bites of the _____"	h. Grapes
9. "_____ at Tiffany's"	i. Dough

10. "_____ _____"   j. Potato
11. "The _____ of Wrath"   k. Breakfast
12. "_____ Road"   l. Tea
                                         m. Potato
                                         n. Coconuts

                                        _____points

                                        (*Answers on page 201*)

2. VERY IMPORTANT PROPS

A good property man, such as Irving Sindler was for many Goldwyn films, will search the script diligently, looking for those properties he must supply which are most important to the story. Of course, many of these are included right in the title of the film (though, we admit, frequently they are not really *used* in the picture itself). See how good a property man you are by naming the Very Important Props we've omitted from the following titles. You may add 15 points to your score for each Very Important Prop you supply correctly.

1. Errol Flynn, Maureen O'Hara,
   and Anthony Quinn
   in . . .   "Against All _____"
2. Rex Harrison and Lilli Palmer
   in . . .   "The _____ _____"
3. Carole Landis, Kay Francis,
   Mitzi Mayfair, and
   Martha Raye in . . .   "Four Jills in a _____"
4. Arlene Dahl, Fernando Lamas,
   and Gilbert Roland
   in . . .   "The _____ Queen"
5. John Hodiak, Gene Tierney,
   and William Bendix
   in . . .   "A _____ for Adano"
6. Gary Cooper, Phyllis Thaxter,
   and David Brian in . . .   "Springfield _____"
7. John Wayne, Joanne Dru, and
   John Agar in . . .   "She Wore a _____
                                           _____"
8. Nelson Eddy and Ilona Massey
   in . . .   "_____"

2

9. Spencer Tracy, Richard Widmark, and Katy Jurado in . . . "Broken _ _ _ _ _"

10. Sterling Hayden, Coleen Gray, and Keith Larsen in . . . "_ _ _ _ _ in the Dust"

11. Gene Kelly, Frank Sinatra, and Kathryn Grayson in . . . "_ _ _ _ _ _ _ Aweigh"

12. Ingrid Bergman, George C. Scott, and Rex Harrison in . . . "The Yellow _ _ _ _ _ _- _ _ _ _ _"

13. Sean Connery, Dyan Cannon, and Martin Balsam in . . . "The Anderson _ _ _ _ _"

14. Sir Laurence Olivier, Robert Donat, and Michael Redgrave in . . . "The Magic _ _ _"

15. Lew Ayres, Gene Evans, and Nancy Davis in . . . "Donovan's _ _ _ _ _ _"

16. Fess Parker, Jeffrey Hunter, and Claude Jarman, Jr., in . . . "The Great _ _ _ _ _ _ _ _ _ _ _ Chase"

17. Michael Moriarty, Robert De Niro, and Vincent Gardenia in . . . "Bang the _ _ _ _ Slowly"

18. Walter Matthau, Elaine May, and Jack Weston in . . . "A New _ _ _ _ _"

19. Rock Hudson, Doris Day, and Tony Randall in . . . "_ _ _ _ _ _ Talk"

20. Hurd Hatfield, George Sanders, and Donna Reed in . . . "The _ _ _ _ _ _ _ _ of Dorian Gray"

_____points

(*Answers on page 202*)

2. VERY IMPORTANT PROPS—DUFFERS' TEE

A good property man, such as Irving Sindler was for many Goldwyn films, will search the script diligently, looking for those properties he must supply which are most important to the story. Of course, many of these are included right in the title of the film (though, we admit, frequently they are not really *used* in the picture itself). See how good a property man you are by naming the Very Important Props we've omitted from the titles below. If you need some help, we have provided a list for you to shop from. Select carefully, and add 15 points to your score for each Very Important Prop you place in the appropriate title.

1. Errol Flynn, Maureen O'Hara, and Anthony Quinn in . . . "Against All _____"   a. Drum

2. Rex Harrison and Lilli Palmer in . . . "The _____"   b. Leaf

3. Carole Landis, Kay Francis, Mitzi Mayfair, and Martha Raye in . . . "Four Jills in a _____"   c. Box

4. Arlene Dahl, Fernando Lamas, and Gilbert Roland in . . . "The _____ Queen"   d. Anchors

5. John Hodiak, Gene Tierney, and William Bendix in . . . "A __ for Adano"   e. Arrow

6. Gary Cooper, Phyllis Thaxter, and David Brian in . . . "Springfield _____"   f. Picture

7. John Wayne, Joanne Dru, and John Agar in . . . "She Wore a _____"   g. Brain

8. Nelson Eddy and Ilona Massey in . . . "_____"   h. Flags

9. Spencer Tracy, Richard Widmark, and Katy Jurado in . . . "Broken _____"   i. Pillow

10. Sterling Hayden, Coleen Gray, and Keith Larsen in . . . "_____ in the Dust"   j. Yellow Ribbon

11. Gene Kelly, Frank Sinatra, and Kathryn Grayson in . . . "_____ Aweigh"   k. Four Poster

12. Ingrid Bergman, George C. Scott, and Rex Harrison in . . . "The Yellow _____"   l. Jeep

13. Sean Connery, Dyan Cannon, and Martin Balsam in . . . "The Anderson _____"   m. Balalaika

14. Sir Laurence Olivier,
    Robert Donat, and
    Michael Redgrave   "The Magic
    in . . .   ____"   n. Rolls-Royce
15. Lew Ayres, Gene Evans,
    and Nancy Davis
    in . . .   "Donovan's ____"   o. Rifle
16. Fess Parker, Jeffrey Hunter,
    and Claude Jarman,   "The Great ____
    Jr., in . . .   Chase"   p. Bell
17. Michael Moriarty, Robert
    De Niro, and Vincent   "Bang the ____
    Gardenia in . . .   Slowly"   q. Diamond
18. Walter Matthau, Elaine
    May, and Jack
    Weston in . . .   "A New ____"   r. Lance
19. Rock Hudson, Doris Day,
    and Tony Randall
    in . . .   "____ Talk"   s. Locomotive
20. Hurd Hatfield, George
    Sanders, and Donna   "The ____ of
    Reed in . . .   Dorian Gray"   t. Tapes

                                          _____points

(*Answers on page 202*)

3. LOOK WHO'S DANCING WITH MR. SMOOTH

This quiz is dedicated to one of the great Hollywood stars of all times—indeed, a legend: Mr. Fred Astaire. Perhaps a movie quiz book is the wrong place to recount his many talents and attributes, but as dyed-in-the-wool film buffs, we have to acknowledge his great contributions to the cinema as well as the many hours of enjoyment he's provided for us over the years. Just to repeat titles of his films evokes many pleasant memories, and we thought it would be in line to review the many films he's done, and remember some of his dancing partners. Below, in Column One, we list some Astaire films. Your task is to fill the blanks in Column Two with his dancing partner from that film. Take 15 points for each lady's name you can peg. One tip: these are not chronologically listed.

1. "Let's Dance"   ————— —————————
2. "Three Little Words"   ————-—————
3. "Easter Parade"   ——— ————————
4. "Holiday Inn"   ——————— ———————————
5. "Yolanda and the Thief"   ————— ———— ————————
6. "The Sky's the Limit"   ———— ————————
7. "Broadway Melody of 1940"   ———————— ——————————
8. "Easter Parade" (again!)   ———————— —————————
9. "You Were Never Lovelier"   ———————— —————————
10. "The Band Wagon"   ——— —————————
11. "Royal Wedding"   ———— ——————————
12. "Dancing Lady"   ———— ——————————
13. "Second Chorus"   —————————— ——————————
14. "Daddy Long Legs"   —————— ———————
15. "Top Hat"   —————— ———————

—————points

(Answers on page 202)

3. LOOK WHO'S DANCING WITH MR. SMOOTH— DUFFERS' TEE

This quiz is dedicated to one of the great Hollywood stars of all times—indeed, a legend: Fred Astaire. Perhaps a move quiz book is the wrong place to recount his many talents and attributes, but as dyed-in-the-wool film buffs, we have to acknowledge his great contributions to the cinema as well as the many hours of enjoyment he's provided for us over the years. Just to repeat titles of his films evokes many pleasant memories, and we thought it would be in line to review the many films he's done, and remember some of his dancing partners. Below, in Column One, we list some Astaire films. Your task is to select Mr. Astaire's dancing partners from the list we've provided, out of order, in Column Two, and pair the appropriate actress with each title. You may have 15 points for each correct pairing. Good luck!

1. "Let's Dance"   a. Joan Leslie
2. "Three Little Words"   b. Paulette Goddard
3. "Easter Parade"   c. Rita Hayworth
4. "Holiday Inn"   d. Betty Hutton
5. "Yolanda and the Thief"   e. Vera-Ellen
6. "The Sky's the Limit"   f. Leslie Caron

7. "Broadway Melody of 1940" g. Ginger Rogers
8. "Easter Parade" (again!) h. Ann Miller
9. "You Were Never Lovelier" i. Marjorie Reynolds
10. "The Band Wagon" j. Joan Crawford
11. "Royal Wedding" k. Lucille Bremer
12. "Dancing Lady" l. Eleanor Powell
13. "Second Chorus" m. Jane Powell
14. "Daddy Long Legs" n. Cyd Charisse
15. "Top Hat" o. Judy Garland

_____points

(*Answers on page 202*)

4. SATURDAY NIGHT AT THE FLICKS

American films were not made for the American audience only. An impression of America was created throughout the world for years by the exportation of Hollywood-made feature films. The English-speaking market was most important to movie-makers after the advent of sound, and—of course—a success in Great Britain was key to the worldwide receipts of American films. For the most part, films were exported without change; however, it seemed to be the rule, rather than the exception, that the title was changed for British consumption. In Column One below, we have listed a number of titles of American films that were used in British release. From your knowledge of the films—and from whatever other instincts you can bring to bear—use the clues we provide, and come up with the original American title of the film. Take 15 points for each title you complete correctly.

1. "His Other Woman" "T _ _ D _ sk S _ _"
2. "Unconventional Linda" "H _ _ _ _ _ _ y"
3. "Melody of Youth" "T _ _ _ Shall H _ _ _ M _ _ _ _"
4. "Harmony Parade" "P _ _ sk _ _ P _ _ _ _ _"
5. "The Big Heart" "M _ _ _ _ _ _ _ o _ 34 _ _
    S _ _ _ _ _"
6. "The Modern Miracle" "T _ _ S _ _ _ _ _ o _
    A _ _ _ _ _ _ _ _ _ G _ _ _ _ _
    B _ _ _"
7. "If You Feel Like
    Singing" "S _ _ _ _ _ S _ _ _ _"

8. "Everybody's Cheering"   "T _ _ _ M _ O _ _ t _ t _ _
                              B _ _ _ G _ _ _ _"
9. "The Affairs of Sally"   "T _ _ _ F _ _ _ _ _ _ B _ _ _ _
                              G _ _ _"
10. "Man of Bronze"   "J _ _ T _ _ _ _ _ _ —A _ _ _ -
                              A _ _ _ _ _ _ _"

_____points

(*Answers on page 203*)

4. SATURDAY NIGHT AT THE FLICKS—DUFFERS' TEE

American films were not made for the American audience only. An impression of America was created throughout the world for years by the exportation of Hollywood-made feature films. The English-speaking market was most important to movie-makers, especially after the addition of sound and—of course—a success in Great Britain was key to the worldwide receipts of American films. For the most part, films were exported without change; however, it seemed to be the rule, rather than the exception, that the title was changed for British consumption. In Column One below, we have listed a number of American films, while in Column Two (out of order) we have listed the titles these films were shown under during their British exposure. Your task is to match the original American title in Column One with the title used in Great Britain in Column Two. Take 15 points for each pairing you get correct. Cheerio now, ducks—it's a possible 150 more points!

1. "The Desk Set"   a. "Melody of Youth"
2. "Holiday"   b. "The Big Heart"
3. "They Shall Have Music"   c. "His Other Woman"
4. "Pigskin Parade"   d. "The Modern Miracle"
5. "The Story of Alexander Graham
      Bell"   e. "Man of Bronze"
6. "Miracle on 34th Street"   f. "Unconventional Linda"
7. "Take Me Out to the Ball Game"   g. "Harmony Parade"
8. "Summer Stock"   h. "The Affairs of Sally"
9. "The Fuller Brush Girl"   i. "If You Feel Like Singing"
10. "Jim Thorpe—All-American"   j. "Everybody's Cheering"

_____points

(*Answers on page 203*)

5. BROTH-ER

Family relationships in films have long been important in plot-building. Here we're looking at brothers, and in each of the films below, a "brother" relationship was most important to the plot. Below, we have provided a film title and the name of the actor who played one brother. You must tell us the actor who played the part of the other brother in the film. Take 10 points for each correct answer:

1.	"Lust for Life"	Kirk Douglas	_____
2.	"Sabrina"	Humphrey Bogart	_____
3.	"The Brotherhood"	Kirk Douglas	_____
4.	"Invisible Stripes"	George Raft	_____
5.	"Blaze of Noon"	Sterling Hayden	_____
6.	"On the Waterfront"	Marlon Brando	_____
7.	"Viva Zapata"	Marlon Brando	_____
8.	"Jesse James"	Tyrone Power	_____
9.	"The Cardinal"	Tom Tryon	_____
10.	"Champion"	Kirk Douglas	_____

_____points

(*Answers on page 203*)

5. BROTH-ER—DUFFERS' TEE

We're looking now at family relationships as depicted in films—and particularly at brothers. In each of the films in Column One below, a brother relationship was part of the film, and in Column Two, we have listed the name of the actor who portrayed one of the brothers in question. You have a multiple choice in Column Three from which you must select the actor who played the other brother. Take 5 points for each correct answer.

1.	"Lust for Life"	Kirk Douglas	a. Jeffrey Lynn b. James Donald c. James Craig
2.	"Sabrina"	Humphrey Bogart	a. John Lund b. John Howard c. William Holden

9

3. "The Brotherhood"	Kirk Douglas	a. James Donald b. Alex Cord c. James Caan
4. "Invisible Stripes"	George Raft	a. William Holden b. James Cagney c. Marc Lawrence
5. "Blaze of Noon"	Sterling Hayden	a. Alan Baxter b. Tom Brown c. William Holden
6. "On the Waterfront"	Marlon Brando	a. Lee J. Cobb b. Karl Malden c. Rod Steiger
7. "Viva Zapata"	Marlon Brando	a. Joseph Wiseman b. Anthony Quinn c. Lou Gilbert
8. "Jesse James"	Tyrone Power	a. Don Ameche b. Wayne Morris c. Henry Fonda
9. "The Cardinal"	Tom Tryon	a. John Huston b. Bill Hayes c. John Saxon
10. "Champion"	Kirk Douglas	a. Arthur Lake b. Arthur Kennedy c. Edgar Kennedy

_____points

(*Answers on page 203*)

6. LINK-UPS—BUFFS AND DUFFERS

Here's an exercise for Buffs and Duffers alike—and it should be no great obstacle for you if you'll just concentrate on the screen credits you've been watching for years. In *The Compleat Motion Picture Quiz Book,* we dredged up about half a hundred such examples as you'll find here, and it is simply a matter of *identification* of players. Below in Columns One and Three are two names—first names and surnames respectively. Into Column Two, you're asked to insert the one name which will act as a surname for the personality suggested in Column One *and* as a first name for the personality suggested in Column Three. The example we provided in *The Compleat Motion Picture Quiz Book* was

Benjamin _____ Roosevelt

By the insertion of "Franklin" you'd come up with Benjamin Franklin and Franklin Roosevelt. This is simple enough that the Duffers can play right along with the Buffs—and for that reason, we're only giving 5 points for each correct answer.

1.	Susan _____	Reed
2.	Leslie _____	Beatty
3.	Skye _____	Mather
4.	Heather _____	Tompkins
5.	James _____	MacLane
6.	Tina _____	Allbritton
7.	Virginia _____	Methot
8.	Christopher _____	Segal
9.	Jean _____	Beery
10.	Alex _____	Williamson

_____points

(*Answers on page 204*)

7. CAREERS IN COMMON

In Column One below, we list two players and films in which they appeared. In the films, these players pursued the same career. In Column Two, we list another player who pursued the same career in one of his (or her) roles. Tell us both the career and the film in which the actor in Column Two pursued that career. Answers, then, are in two parts, and you'll receive 10 points for each correct part, or a possible 20 points per question.

1. Robert De Niro–"Taxi
     Driver"
   James Cagney–"Taxi"   Dan Dailey   _____ _____
2. Lionel Barrymore–
     "Captains
     Courageous"
   Gregory Peck–"The Big   Warner
     Country"   Baxter   _____ _____

3. Fredric March–"One
   Foot in Heaven"
   David Niven–"The
   Bishop's Wife"   Orson Welles   _____ _____
4. Glenn Ford–"Trial"
   Humphrey Bogart–
   "Knock on Any   James
   Door"   Stewart   _____ _____
5. Ellen Burstyn–"The
   Exorcist"
   Lana Turner–"The
   Bad and the
   Beautiful"   Bette Davis   _____ _____
6. Walter Connolly–"The
   Adventures of
   Huckleberry Finn"
   Paul Newman–"The   George C.
   Sting"   Scott   _____ _____
7. Joan Crawford–
   "Mildred Pierce"
   Ann Sheridan–"They
   Drive by Night"   Marie Wilson   _____ _____
8. Charlie Grapewin–
   "The Wizard of Oz"
   John Phillip Law–
   "Hurry Sundown"   Zachary Scott   _____ _____
9. Max von Sydow–
   "Three Days of the
   Condor"
   Alastair Sim–"The   Frank
   Green Man"   Sinatra   _____ _____
10. Roosevelt Grier–
    "Skyjacked"
    Philip Dorn–
    "Ziegfeld Girl"   Jack Lemmon   _____ _____

                                           _____points

(Answers on page 204)

7. CAREERS IN COMMON—DUFFERS' TEE

In Column One below, we have listed pairs of stars and given the titles of films in which both had the same occupation. In Columns Two and Three, we list three players and films in which they appeared. One of these three had the same occupation as the players of Column One. Your task is to select the actor or actress of Column Two who matches the pair of Column One by virtue of "occupation," and also to name that occupation. Take 10 points for each correct answer, for a total of 200 points.

1. Robert De Niro– "Taxi Driver"
   James Cagney– "Taxi"

   Douglas Dumbrille
   Dan Dailey
   George Macready

   "Broadway Bill"
   "Taxi"
   "Alias Nick Beal"

2. Lionel Barrymore– "Captains Courageous"
   Gregory Peck– "The Big Country"

   Telly Savalas
   Everett Sloane
   Warner Baxter

   "Cape Fear"
   "Murder, Inc."
   "Slave Ship"

3. Fredric March– "One Foot in Heaven"
   David Niven– "The Bishop's Wife"

   Farley Granger
   Arthur Kennedy
   Orson Welles

   "The North Star"
   "The Desperate Hours"
   "Moby Dick"

4. Glenn Ford– "Trial"
   Humphrey Bogart– "Knock on Any Door"

   James Stewart
   Henry Fonda
   Tony Curtis

   "Anatomy of a Murder"
   "The Big Street"
   "Mr. Cory"

5. Ellen Burstyn– "The Exorcist"
   Lana Turner– "The Bad and the Beautiful"

   Bette Davis
   Ellen Corby
   Virginia Christine

   "The Star"
   "I Remember Mama"
   "Guess Who's Coming to Dinner"

6. Walter Connolly– "The Adventures of Huckleberry Finn"
   Paul Newman– "The Sting"

   William Holden
   Mel Tormé
   George C. Scott

   "Apartment for Peggy"
   "Good News"
   "The Flim Flam Man"

7. Joan Crawford– "Mildred Pierce"
   Ann Sheridan– "They Drive by Night"

   Marie Wilson
   Debra Paget
   Bella Darvi

   "Boy Meets Girl"
   "Stars and Stripes Forever"
   "Hell and High Water"

8. Charlie Grapewin–	Zachary Scott	"The Southerner"
"The Wizard of Oz"	Robert Mitchum	"Angel Face"
	Robert Mitchum	"River of No Return"
John Phillip Law–"Hurry Sundown"		
9. Max von Sydow–	Dana Andrews	"The Fallen Angel"
"Three Days of the Condor"	Frank Sinatra	"Suddenly"
	Ralph Richardson	"Exodus"
Alastair Sim– "The Green Man"		
10. Roosevelt Grier–	Richard Conte	"Whirlpool"
"Skyjacked"	Walter Brennan	"Centennial Summer"
Philip Dorn–	Jack Lemmon	"Some Like It Hot"
"Ziegfeld Girl"		

_____points

(*Answers on page 204*)

8. NAME THE STAR

On each line below, we have listed the names of two of the characters played by the same star. Either one should be sufficient for an old movie buff like you to make instant identification. Do so, and add 10 points to your score for each star you are able to identify. Of course, if this trail is too rough for a tenderfoot, then mosey on over there to the Duffers' Tee. *But* . . . if you can also name the titles of the films suggested below—in addition to the naming the star—we'll let you take 15 points for each title you get correct. That's a possible 40 points per question, or 400 points for a direct hit on the whole quiz!

1. Joe January   John Breen
2. Pinkie Peters   Pvt. Aloysius "Smacksie" Randall
3. Robert Lomax   "Boots" Malone
4. Dolly O'Brien   Joanne LaMarr
5. Hattie Maloney   Rita Phipps
6. Jack Andrus   Richard Dudgeon
7. Katina Jonadottir   Kristina Nielsen

8. Cherry Malotte   Teresina Vidaverri
9. Emily Blair   Carolyn Grant
10. John Palmer Cass   "Boots" Mulcahey

_____points

(*Answers on page 205*)

8. NAME THE STAR—DUFFERS' TEE

If you found the Buffs' version of NAME THE STAR a wee bit too difficult, then be our guest and try the Duffers' version. It's really quite simple, if you keep an eye open for those pesky sidewinders. On each line below, we've listed two characters, both of which were limned by the same player. The stars involved are the same ones used in the Buffs' version, but these characters they played are probably better known. For each star you identify, you may add 10 points to your score. However, if you can also name the titles of the films suggested, you may have 15 points for each title correctly identified.

1. Taw Jackson   Col. Mike Kirby
2. "Buzz" Wanchek   Det. Lou Brody
3. MacDonald Walling Pike Bishop
4. Rose Mapen   Margo Martin
5. Crystal Carpenter   Maisie Ravier
6. Midge Kelly   Col. Dax
7. Chris Linden   Karen Benson
8. Nefretiri   Eve Harrington
9. Claire Blake   Julia Brougham
10. Elder Wiggs   Fr. Peter Lonergan

_____points

(*Answers on page 205*)

9. PENCILED IN

From the producer's first thoughts of casting through to the film's completion, there are often a number of changes in the cast of a film. Sometimes, the initial casting is little more than an idea, perhaps followed by a test. On the other hand, there have been occasions when

15

someone is cast and signed, and has even begun shooting—only to be replaced along the way. Below, in Column One, we list a player who was originally cast for the film listed in Column Two. Obviously, this player did not appear in the film, and we ask you to tell us the name of the player who finally did play the role. Take 15 points for each name you can supply correctly.

1. Paulette Goddard	"Destry Rides Again"	_____
2. Ann Sheridan	"Casablanca"	_____
3. Judy Garland	"Annie Get Your Gun"	_____
4. Miriam Hopkins	"To Be or Not to Be"	_____
5. Lee Remick	"Goodbye, Mr. Chips"	_____
6. Tallulah Bankhead	"Macbeth"	_____
7. Ann Sheridan	"Strawberry Blonde"	_____
8. Betty Grable	"Guys and Dolls"	_____
9. Vera Zorina	"For Whom the Bell Tolls"	_____
10. Alice Faye	"Greenwich Village"	_____

_____points

(*Answers on page 205*)

9. PENCILED IN—DUFFERS' TEE

From the producer's first thoughts of casting through to the film's completion, there are often a number of changes in the cast. Sometimes, the initial casting is little more than an idea, perhaps followed by a test. On the other hand, there have been occasions when someone is cast and signed, and even begins shooting—only to be replaced in midstream. Below in Column One, we provide a list of features which did undergo some casting change. In Column Two, we list the personality who was originally cast for the part. In Column Three, out of order, we provide a list of players who subsequently did play the parts referred to in Columns One and Two. Your task is to match the player from Column Three with the correct film title and the player *originally* contemplated for the part. Take 20 points for each correct match you make.

1. "Destry Rides Again"	Paulette Goddard	a. Vivian Blaine
2. "Casablanca"	Ann Sheridan	b. Petula Clark
3. "Annie Get Your Gun"	Judy Garland	c. Carole Lombard

4. "To Be or Not to Be"	Miriam Hopkins	d. Ingrid Bergman
5. "Goodbye, Mr. Chips"	Lee Remick	e. Marlene Dietrich
6. "Macbeth"	Tallulah Bankhead	f. Betty Hutton
7. "Strawberry Blonde"	Ann Sheridan	g. Ingrid Bergman
8. "Guys and Dolls"	Betty Grable	h. Jeanette Nolan
9. "For Whom the Bell Tolls"	Vera Zorina	i. Vivian Blaine
10. "Greenwich Village"	Alice Faye	j. Rita Hayworth

_____points

(Answers on page 206)

10. PLAY BALL!

A number of films which focus on baseball have used actual major league teams as a part of the plot and the production. Below, in Column One, we list a number of such films, and ask you to name the major league team which was featured. Take 15 points for each correct answer.

1. "Angels in the Outfield" _____
2. "The Kid from Cleveland" _____
3. "Damn Yankees" _____
4. "The Stratton Story" _____
5. "Fear Strikes Out" _____
6. "Alibi Ike" _____
7. "Death on the Diamond" _____
8. "It Happened in Flatbush" _____
9. "Warming Up" _____
10. "The Jackie Robinson Story" _____

_____points

(Answers on page 206)

10. PLAY BALL!—DUFFERS' TEE

A number of films which focus on baseball have used actual league teams as a part of the plot and the production. Below, in Column One, we list a number of such films, and ask you to match them (from Column Two) with the major league teams used. Take 15 points for each correct pairing.

1. "Angels in the Outfield"		a.	Brooklyn Dodgers
2. "The Kid from Cleveland"		b.	New York Yankees
3. "Damn Yankees"		c.	Chicago Cubs
4. "The Stratton Story"		d.	Boston Red Sox
5. "Fear Strikes Out"		e.	Washington Senators
6. "Alibi Ike"		f.	Pittsburgh Pirates
7. "Death on the Diamond"		g.	Cleveland Indians
8. "It Happened in Flatbush"		h.	St. Louis Cardinals
9. "Warming Up"		i.	Brooklyn Dodgers
10. "The Jackie Robinson Story"		j.	Chicago White Sox

_____points

(*Answers on page 206*)

11. QUOTABLES

This is an uncomplicated quiz, relying solely on your movie memory—and maybe a little deduction and common sense. Below, we list ten excerpts of dialogue from ten well-known films. Your task is to come up with the title of the film in which the dialogue was included. Just fill in the blanks and you'll have the title. Simple? Take 15 points for each correct identification.

1. "The first law is that Harry does not hold."

   "_ _ _ _ _ _ _ _ _ _ _ _ _ _ _ _ _ _"

2. "I haven't the foggiest—"

   "_ _ _ _ _ _ _ _ _ _ _ _ _ _ _ _ _ _ _ _ _ _"

3. "It profiteth not a man to gain the whole world, and lose his soul . . . but for Wales?"

   "_ _ _ _ _ _ _ _ _ _ _ _ _ _ _ _"

4. "The first part of the party of the first part shall be known in this contract— Look, why should we quarrel about a thing like this? We'll take it right out!"

18

"_ _____ __ ___ _____"

5. If there is ever to be law and order in the West, the first thing we've got to do is take all the lawyers out and shoot 'em down like dogs."

"_____ _____"
6. "Oh, so?"

"_____ _____, __. _____"
7. "You can print it if you want to. Kurt Schneider was a monster who murdered two girls and got away with it. High time somebody put the fear of God into 'im. The law wouldn't, so I did!"

"_____ _____"
8. "You clittering, clattering collection of caliginous junk!"

"___ _____ __ ___"
9. "You're no more my mother than a toad!"

"___ _____ _____"
10. "It is widely held that too much wine will dull a man's desires. Indeed it will—in a dull man."

"___ _____"

_____points

(Answers on page 207)

11. QUOTABLES—DUFFERS' TEE

This is an uncomplicated quiz, relying solely on your movie memory—and maybe a little deduction and common sense. Below, we list ten excerpts of dialogue we've dredged up from as many well-known films. Your task is to match the dialogue with the title of the film in which it was included—and you'll find these, out of order, in Column Two. You may have 15 points for each correct pairing.

1. "The first law is that Harry does not hold."   a. "Think Fast, Mr. Moto"

2. "I haven't the foggiest—"   b. "A Man for All Seasons"

3. "It profiteth not a man to gain the whole world, and lose his soul . . . but for Wales?"

c. "The Shanghai Gesture"

4. "The first part of the party of the first part shall be known in this contract— Look, why should we quarrel about a thing like this? We'll take it right out!"

d. "Bridge on the River Kwai"

5. "If there is ever to be law and order in the West, the first thing we've got to do is take all the lawyers out and shoot 'em down like dogs."

e. "A Night at the Opera"

6. "Oh, so?"

f. "Tom Jones"

7. "You can print it if you want to. Kurt Schneider was a monster who murdered two girls and got away with it. High time somebody put the fear of God into 'im. The law wouldn't, so I did!"

g. "The Wizard of Oz"

8. "You clittering, clattering collection of caliginous junk!"

h. "Harry in Your Pocket"

9. "You're no more my mother than a toad!"

i. "Detective Story"

10. "It is widely held that too much wine will dull a man's desires. Indeed it will—in a dull man!"

j. "Jesse James"

_____points

(*Answers on page 207*)

12. POTSHOTS

Here are a number of random questions which don't particularly fit into any specific category. Enjoy them singly—and perhaps you might use a few of these the next time you're sitting around a warm glass of something playing "movie trivia." Take 10 points for each question you answer correctly.

1. The "Good Witch" in "The Wizard of Oz"—what was her name?
2. What was the name of the newspaper owned by Raymond Massey in "The Fountainhead"?

3. What was the name of the Japanese farmer Spencer Tracy was seeking in "Bad Day at Black Rock"?
4. What was the name of the college everyone was attending in "Good News"?
5. How about naming the school where the boys invited their girls for the big dance in "Best Foot Forward"?
6. What was the name of the auto sold by Douglas Fairbanks, Jr., in "The Young in Heart"?
7. What was the name of the boat in "Show Boat"?
8. Name the single film in which Humphrey Bogart appeared which was produced by Samuel Goldwyn.
9. What was the name of the song which was fully staged and photographed for "The Wizard of Oz" but which was removed before the film's release?
10. What was the name of the famed Parisian restaurant shown in "Gigi"?

_____points

(*Answers on page 207*)

12. POTSHOTS—DUFFERS' TEE

Here are a number of random questions which don't particularly fit into any specific category. Enjoy them singly—and perhaps you might use a few of these the next time you're engaged in a "fight-to-the-finish movie trivia shoot-out"! We've supplied a multiple choice for you, inasmuch as this is the Duffers' Tee, but each question answered is good for 15 points. Knock 'em dead!

1. The "Good Witch" in "The Wizard of Oz"—was her name: (a) Wanda, (b) Glinda, or (c) Melba?
2. What was the name of the newspaper owned by Raymond Massey in "The Fountainhead"? Was it: (a) the *Banner,* (b) the *Herald Tribune,* or (c) the *Courier?*
3. What was the name of the Japanese farmer Spencer Tracy was seeking in "Bad Day at Black Rock"? Was it: (a) Hiyashi, (b) Suzukida, or (c) Kimoto?
4. What was the name of the college everyone was attending in "Good News"? Was it: (a) Tait College, (b) Brewster College, or (c) Wupperman U.?
5. How about naming the school where the boys invited their girl friends for the big dance in "Best Foot Forward"? Was it: (a) Winslow, (b) Winsocki, or (c) Woonsocket?

6. What was the name of the auto sold by Douglas Fairbanks, Jr., in "The Young in Heart"? Was it: (a) "The Streaker," (b) "The Fordham Flash," or (c) "The Wombat"?

7. What was the name of the boat in "Show Boat"? Was it: (a) the *Southern Queen,* (b) the *Delta Queen,* or (c) the *Cotton Blossom?*

8. Name the single film in which Humphrey Bogart appeared which was produced by Samuel Goldwyn. Was it: (a) "The Real Glory," (b) "Glory for Me," or (c) "Dead End"?

9. What was the name of the song which was fully staged and photographed for "The Wizard of Oz" but which was removed from the film prior to its release? Was it: (a) "The Munchkin March," (b) "The Jitterbug," or (c) "Dorothy's Home"?

10. What was the name of the famed Parisian restaurant shown in "Gigi"? Was it: (a) Antoine's, (b) Maxim's, or (c) Le Tour d'Argent?

———————points

(*Answers on page 207*)

13. UNIQUE CHARACTERS

This quiz is just a bit different from those you've run across earlier. The characters didn't exactly have a character name in the usual sense—rather, more of a nickname. Below in Column One, we've listed some Unique Characters. And in Column Two we've listed—out of order—the players who portrayed these characters, and you must pair these correctly with the characters in Column One. Once the pairing has been done properly, you must complete the film title in which the portrayal was included. Just fill in the blanks of Column Three. For each correct pairing, take 10 points. And for each title completed correctly, you may have 15 more points. That's a possible 25 points per question, and a potential of 250 points on this quiz alone. Laws-a-mercy!

1. "Cherokee Jim"   a. Arnold Stang   "_ _ _ _ _ _ _ _ _ _ _ _ _ _ _ _ _"

2. "Mosquito"   b. Lynne Overman   "_ _ _ _ _ _ _ _ _ _ _ _ _ _ _ _ _ _"

3. "Pluto"   c. Chill Wills   "_ _ _ ' _ _ _ _ _ _ _ _ _ _ _"

4. "Pretty Boy"   d. Leo Carrillo   "_ _ _ _ _ _ _ _ _ _ _ _ _ _ _ _"

5. "Gold Dust"   e. Harold Sakata   "_ _ _ _ _ _ _ _ _"
6. "Moustache"   f. Skip Homeier   "_ _ _ _ _ _ _ _ _ _ _"
7. "Sparrow"   g. Charlie Ruggles   "_ _ _ _ _ _ _ _ _ _

                                       _ _ _ _ _ _ _ _ _ _ _ _"
8. "Regret"   h. Claire Trevor   "_ _ _ _ _ _ _ _ _ _

                                       _ _ _ _ _ _"
9. "Southeast"   i. Buddy Hackett   "_ _ _ _ _ _ _ _ _ _ _ _ _"
10. "Odd Job"   j. Lou Jacobi   "_ _ _ _ _ _ _ _ _ _"

_____points

(*Answers on page 208*)

13. UNIQUE CHARACTERS—DUFFERS' TEE

We're intrigued by names of characters in films, and those we've listed below in Column One are a bit out of the ordinary. You'll see what we mean. In Column Two, out of order, are the players who portrayed these characters. And in Column Three we have listed the films (also out of order) in which these portrayals were included. Match the player from Column Two correctly with the character in Column One, and that's 10 points. Then, match the correct film title to that correct combination, and you may add 10 more points. That's a possible 20 points per question, and a potential of 200 points for the quiz—not as much as the Buffs can amass, but what the hell, it's early yet—

1. "Cherokee Jim"	a. Arnold Stang	A. "The Halls of Montezuma"
2. "Mosquito"	b. Lynne Overman	B. "Goldfinger"
3. "Pluto"	c. Chill Wills	C. "Irma La Douce"
4. "Pretty Boy"	d. Leo Carrillo	D. "The Westerner"
5. "Gold Dust"	e. Harold Sakata	E. "God's Little Acre"
6. "Moustache"	f. Skip Homeier	F. "Incendiary Blonde"
7. "Sparrow"	g. Charlie Ruggles	G. "Little Miss Marker"
8. "Regret"	h. Claire Trevor	H. "Honky Tonk"
9. "Southeast"	i. Buddy Hackett	I. "The Man with the Golden Arm"
10. "Odd Job"	j. Lou Jacobi	J. "Girl of the Golden West"

_____points

(*Answers on page 208*)

23

14. CHICAGO, CHICAGO

Since Chicago is our home—and we love it—we are well aware of its importance in the cinema—as a background for many excellent films, and also for its place in cinema history. Some time back, we developed a quiz about Our Home Town for the Chicago *Daily News*. And we didn't think it too provincial to include portions of it here. See how well you do, and if you're lucky, you, too, can call Chicago "my kind of town." (Individual scores for each question on this one.)

1. The Chicago Cubs' famed triple-play combination, Tinkers-to-Evers-to-Chance, served as the inspiration for a cinematic counterpart: "O'Brien-to-Ryan-to-Goldberg." In what 1949 musical did this trio appear?
   (Score 10 points.)

2. Assuming you got that one, who played O'Brien, Ryan, and Goldberg?

_____   _____   _____

   (Score 15 points.)

3. A number of films have used "Chicago" in their title, some of which we have listed in Column One below. We ask you to complete the blanks in Column Two and thus name the star of each film listed. (Score 5 points for each star name completed.)

   a. "Chicago Calling"   D _ _ D _ _ _ _ _ _
   b. "Chicago Confidential" B _ _ _ _ _ K _ _ _ _ _
   c. "The Earl of Chicago"   R _ _ _ _ _ _ M _ _ _ _ _ _ _ _ _ _
   d. "Chicago Deadline"   A _ _ _ _ L _ _ _
   e. "The Chicago Kid"   D _ _ B _ _ _ _ _
   f. "Chicago Syndicate"   D _ _ _ _ _ _ O' _ _ _ _ _

4. In what Tyrone Power film of 1947 was the Sherman Hotel (now defunct) prominent and integral to the plot? (Score 15 points.)

5. Below, in Column One, we list five major events of Chicago's past. In Column Two, we provide some clues of the films in which these events were re-created. Complete the blanks, and take 10 points for each title you get correct.

   a. The Great Chicago Fire   "I _ O _ _ C _ _ _ _ _ _"
   b. The Columbian
      Exposition of 1894   "T _ _ G _ _ _ _ Z _ _ _ _ _ _ _ _"
   c. The St. Valentine's Day
      massacre   "S _ _ _ L _ _ _ I _ H _ _"
   d. The building of the Chicago
      Opera House   "C _ _ _ _ _ _ _ K _ _ _"
   e. The Loeb-Leopold trial   "C _ _ _ _ _ _ _ _ _"

6. Which of the following films did *not* include scenes set in Chicago (take 15 points, *only* if you get all answers correct): (a) "Robin and the Seven Hoods," (b) "The Joker Is Wild," (c) "North by Northwest," (d) "The Benny Goodman Story," (e) "Mickey One," (f) "Pal Joey"?

7. The first talking picture about baseball was "Fast Company" in 1929. The film was about a small-town boy who became a star slugger for the Chicago Cubs. The star was J _ _ _ O _ _ _ _ _. (Score 10 points.)

8. The film was remade six years later, in 1935. Though the Chicago Cubs were still prominent, the title had been changed to "Alibi Ike." Name the star—and this time, no hints! (Score 15 points.)

9. Every Hollywood hopeful remembers that Dorothy Lamour, at one time in her struggle to the top, operated an elevator in a Loop department store. But what screen heavyweight and Oscar-winning actor once worked as a floorwalker in the Ladies' Lingerie Department at Marshall Field's? (Score 10 points.)

10. Each of the following personalities had a place in Chicago history. In Column One below, we list the personality, and ask you to complete the blanks in Column Two to tell us the name of the performer who played the role. Take 10 points for coming up with the correct performer's name—and 10 additional points if you can name the film in which the portrayal was included.

   1. Eddie Foy   B _ _ H _ _ _
   2. John Dillinger   L _ _ _ _ _ _ _ T _ _ _ _ _ _ _
   3. Al Capone   R _ _ S _ _ _ _ _ _
   4. Grover Cleveland Alexander   R _ _ _ _ _ R _ _ _ _ _ _
   5. Baby Face Nelson   M _ _ _ _ _ _ R _ _ _ _ _
   6. Ruth Etting   D _ _ _ _ D _ _
   7. Stephen A. Douglas   M _ _ _ _ _ _ _ S _ _ _ _ _
   8. Benny Goodman   S _ _ _ _ A _ _ _ _ _
   9. Little Egypt   R _ _ _ _ _ F _ _ _ _ _ _ _
   10. Abraham Lincoln   H _ _ _ _ _ F _ _ _ _

_____points

(*Answers on page 208*)

14. CHICAGO, CHICAGO—DUFFERS' TEE

Since Chicago is our home—and we love it—we are well aware of its importance in the cinema—as a background for many excellent films, and also for its place in cinema history. Some time back, we developed a quiz about Our Home Town for the Chicago *Daily News*. And we didn't think it too provincial to include portions of it here. See how well you do in this Duffers' version, and if you're very lucky, you, too, can call Chicago "my kind of town." (There is individual scoring for each question on this one.)

1. The Chicago Cubs' famed triple-play combination, Tinkers-to-Evers-to-Chance, served as the inspiration for a cinematic counterpart: "O'Brien-to-Ryan-to-Goldberg." Was the 1949 film in which they appeared: (a) "Murder on the Diamond," (b) "Angels in the Outfield," or (c) "Take Me Out to the Ball Game"? (Score 10 points.)

2. Referring back to Question 1 above, who played O'Brien, Ryan, and Goldberg: (a) Dennis Morgan, Jack Carson, and Gil Lamb; (b) The Ritz Brothers; or (c) Gene Kelly, Frank Sinatra, and Jules Munshin? (Score 15 points.)

3. A number of films have used "Chicago" in their title, some of which we have listed in Column One below. We ask you to complete the answers by matching each title with its star, listed out of order in Column Two. (Score 5 points for each star properly paired with the title.)

   a. "Chicago Calling"   A. Don Barry
   b. "Chicago Confidential"   B. Alan Ladd
   c. "The Earl of Chicago"   C. Dennis O'Keefe
   d. "Chicago Deadline"   D. Dan Duryea
   e. "The Chicago Kid"   E. Robert Montgomery
   f. "Chicago Syndicate"   F. Brian Keith

4. In what Tyrone Power film of 1947 was the famed Sherman Hotel (now defunct) prominent and integral to the plot? Was it: (a) "Love Is News," (b) "That Wonderful Urge," or (c) "Nightmare Alley"? (Score 15 points.)

5. Below, in Column One, we list five major events of Chicago's past. In Column Two, we provide titles of films, out of order, in which these events were re-created. Match the title to the event, and take 10 points for each correct pairing.

   a. The Great Chicago Fire   A. "Some Like It Hot"
   b. The Columbian Exposition of 1894   B. "Citizen Kane"
   c. The St. Valentine's Day massacre   C. "Compulsion"
   d. The building of the Chicago
        Opera House   D. "The Great Ziegfeld"
   e. The Loeb-Leopold trial   E. "In Old Chicago"

6. Which of the following films did *not* include scenes set in Chicago (take 15 points, only if you get *all* answers correct): (a) "A Dream of Kings," (b) "Love Me or Leave Me," (c) "The Sting," (d) "My Name is Rocco Pappaleo," (e) "The Man with the Golden Arm," (f) "Pal Joey"?

7. The first talking picture about baseball was "Fast Company" in 1929. The film was about a small-town boy who became a star slugger for the Chicago Cubs. Was its star: (a) Richard Arlen, (b) Jack Oakie, or (c) Richard Barthelmess? (Score 15 points.)

8. The film was remade six years later, in 1935. Though the Chicago Cubs were still prominent, the title had been changed to "Alibi Ike." Was the star: (a) Buster Keaton, (b) Gary Cooper, or (c) Joe E. Brown? (Score 10 points.)

9. Every Hollywood hopeful remembers that Dorothy Lamour, at one time in her struggle to the top, operated an elevator in a Loop department store. But a screen heavyweight and an Oscar-winning actor once worked as a floorwalker in the Ladies' Lingerie Department at Marshall Field's. Was he (a) John Wayne, (b) Jack Lemmon, or (c) Burt Lancaster? (Score 15 points.)

10. Each of the personalities in Column One below had a place in Chicago history. In Column Two, we list out of order the performer who played that personality, and we ask you to match the player with the historical personality he or she portrayed. Take 10 points for pairing the personality with the player—plus an additional 10 points if you can name the film in which the portrayal was included.

1. Eddie Foy	a. Doris Day
2. John Dillinger	b. Henry Fonda
3. Al Capone	c. Mickey Rooney
4. Grover Cleveland Alexander	d. Rhonda Fleming
5. Baby Face Nelson	e. Steve Allen
6. Ruth Etting	f. Bob Hope
7. Stephen A. Douglas	g. Lawrence Tierney
8. Benny Goodman	h. Rod Steiger
9. Little Egypt	i. Milburn Stone
10. Abraham Lincoln	j. Ronald Reagan

_____points

(*Answers on page 208*)

15. ANYTHING YOU CAN DO, I CAN DO BETTER

Below, we provide two columns composed of the names of film players. Each of the players in Column One portrayed a historical character in a film. The same historical character was also portrayed (in another film, of course) by one of the players in Column Two. Your task is to pair the players who portrayed the same character at one time or another—and you may take 5 points for each correct pairing. In addition, you may have 10 points for identifying the historical character in question. And—because we're the generous souls we are, we're also allowing you to claim an additional 10 points for each title of the films in which the portrayals were included. That's a possible 35 points per question—or a possible increase to your score of 350 points! But one clue: though we're dealing in each question with the *same* character, remember the two characterizations may have focused on different periods of the character's life.

		CHARACTER	TITLE	TITLE
1. Tyrone Power	A. Hugh Sothern	_____	___	____
2. Robert Taylor	B. Walter Pidgeon	_____	___	____
3. James Mason	C. Victor Mature	_____	___	____
4. George Arliss	D. Kirk Douglas	_____	___	____
5. Charlton Heston	E. Ian Hunter	_____	___	____
6. William Powell	F. Erich von Stroheim	_____	___	____
7. George C. Scott	G. Alec Guinness	_____	___	____
8. Charles Laughton	H. Kris Kristofferson	_____	___	____
9. Henry Wilcoxon	I. Robert Shaw	_____	___	____
10. Howard Keel	J. Wendell Corey	_____	___	____

_____points

(*Answers on page 209*)

15. ANYTHING YOU CAN DO, I CAN DO BETTER— DUFFERS' TEE

Below, in Column One, we provide the name of a player as well as the name of a historical character he portrayed and the film in which the portrayal was included. In Column Two, we provide the name of another player who portrayed that same character (in another film, of course), though Column Two is out of order (now, *that's* no surprise!). Your task is to match each player from Column Two with the appropriate player in Column One. Do that, and you have earned 15 points per question. But that's not all! From the jumbled list of films in Column Three, select the film in which the portrayal was included, and match it to the correct pairing of Columns One and Two. Got that? Match Column Two to Column One (player to player), and Column Three to Column Two. For this latter pairing, you may also earn 15 points per question—so that's a total of 30 points per question, or a possible 300 points. Go get 'em!

1. Tyrone Power; Jesse James in "Jesse James"	A. Walter Pidgeon	a. "Five Graves to Cairo"
2. Robert Taylor; Billy the Kid in "Billy the Kid"	B. Robert Shaw	b. "Funny Girl"
3. James Mason; Field Marshall Rommel in "The Desert Fox"	C. Kirk Douglas	c. "Pat Garrett and Billy the Kid"
4. George Arliss: Benjamin Disraeli in "Disraeli"	D. Wendell Corey	d. "The Adventures of Robin Hood"
5. Charlton Heston; Andrew Jackson in "The President's Lady"	E. Ian Hunter	e. "A Man for All Seasons"
6. William Powell; Florenz Ziegfeld in "The Great Ziegfeld"	F. Hugh Sothern	f. "The Buccaneer"
7. George C. Scott; Gen. George Patton in "Patton"	G. Victor Mature	g. "Alias Jesse James"
8. Charles Laughton; Henry VIII in "The Private Life of Henry VIII"	H. Kris Kristofferson	h. "Is Paris Burning?"
9. Henry Wilcoxon; Richard the Lion-Hearted in "The Crusades"	I. Alec Guinness	i. "Hannibal"
10. Howard Keel; Hannibal in "Jupiter's Darling"	J. Erich von Stroheim	j. "The Mudlark"

———points

(*Answers on page 210*)

16. THE "THEY WENT THATAWAY" CRISSCROSS

Here's a CRISSCROSS for you—and it is completely devoted to the Western. If you'd like to step out for a plate of beans and a tin cup full of coffee, we'll wait for you. But you can enrich your score by 500 points simply by completing the seventy-six surnames below with the proper Western player—and then using them in the diagram which follows. Better proceed cautiously, and keep a big eraser in your saddlebag. There's only one lady in the group, and we've started you out with her. (You ready, Dale?) So head 'em up and move 'em out for 500 points.

THREE-LETTER NAME

M _ _ _, Tom

FOUR-LETTER NAMES

B _ _ _ _, Rex
B _ _ _ _, Monte
B _ _ _ _, William
C _ _ _ _, Edmund
C _ _ _ _, "Iron Eyes"
D _ _ _ _, Eddie
H _ _ _ _, William S.
H _ _ _ _, Jack
K _ _ _ _, Charlie
L _ _ _ _, "Rocky"

FIVE-LETTER NAMES

A _ _ _ _ _, Art
A _ _ _ _ _, Ernie
A _ _ _ _ _, Rex
A _ _ _ _ _, Gene
B _ _ _ _ _, Bob
B _ _ _ _ _, Donald "Red"
B _ _ _ _ _, Noah
B _ _ _ _ _, Johnny Mack
C _ _ _ _ _, Harry
  Evans, Dale
H _ _ _ _ _, "Gabby"
H _ _ _ _ _, Jack
J _ _ _ _ _, Si
J _ _ _ _ _, Buck
K _ _ _ _ _, Tom
L _ _ _ _ _, Lash
M _ _ _ _ _, Col. Tim

M _ _ _ _ _, Clayton
S _ _ _ _ _, Randolph
T _ _ _ _ _, Tom
W _ _ _ _ _, John
W _ _ _ _ _, Harry

SIX-LETTER NAMES

B _ _ _ _ _ _, Smith
B _ _ _ _ _ _, Jim
C _ _ _ _ _ _, Yakima
C _ _ _ _ _ _, "Sunset"
C _ _ _ _ _ _, Tris
C _ _ _ _ _ _, George
C _ _ _ _ _ _, Larry
D _ _ _ _ _ _, Kenne
G _ _ _ _ _ _, "Hoot"
H _ _ _ _ _ _, Raymond
H _ _ _ _ _ _, Russell
K _ _ _ _ _ _, "Fuzzy"
K _ _ _ _ _ _, Fred
L _ _ _ _ _ _, Tom
M _ _ _ _ _ _, Joel
M _ _ _ _ _ _, John
O' _ _ _ _ _ _, George
R _ _ _ _ _ _, Tex
R _ _ _ _ _ _, Roy
S _ _ _ _ _ _, Al "Fuzzy"
S _ _ _ _ _ _, Sid
S _ _ _ _ _ _, Bob
W _ _ _ _ _ _, Jimmy
W _ _ _ _ _ _, Whip

SEVEN-LETTER NAMES
B _ _ _ _ _ _, Pat
E _ _ _ _ _ _, Wild Bill
E _ _ _ _ _ _, James
K _ _ _ _ _ _, Bob
M _ _ _ _ _ _, Guy
M _ _ _ _ _ _, Ken
R _ _ _ _ _ _, Duncan
T _ _ _ _ _ _, Max

EIGHT-LETTER NAMES
A _ _ _ _ _ _ _, Bronco Billy
B _ _ _ _ _ _ _, Trevor
B _ _ _ _ _ _ _, Edgar
B _ _ _ _ _ _ _, Smiley

C _ _ _ _ _ _ _, Leo
L _ _ _ _ _ _ _, Frank
S _ _ _ _ _ _ _, Charles
W _ _ _ _ _ _ _, Guinn "Big Boy"

NINE-LETTER NAME
Y _ _ _ _ _ _ _ _, Chief

TEN-LETTER NAME
L _ _ _ _ _ _ _ _ _, Robert

ELEVEN-LETTER NAME
S _ _ _ _ _ _ _ _ _ _, Jay

_ _ _ _ _ _ _points

(*Answers on page 211*)

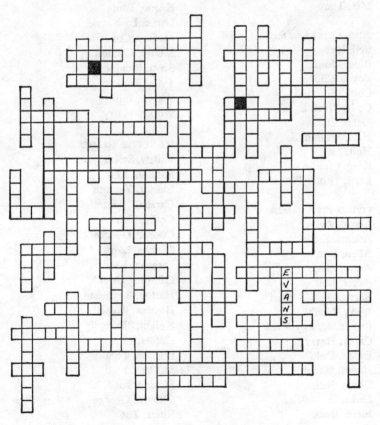

31

16. THE "THEY WENT THATAWAY" CRISSCROSS— DUFFERS' TEE

Welcome to CRISSCROSS—and in case you're wondering, this one has to do with the Western film. The diagram preceding will accommodate precisely 76 names, *if* you put them in the proper spaces. Each of the names is the surname of a player who has appeared in Western films many, many times. Count the spaces carefully, and plan ahead. Of course, if you wish to attack this one with a ballpoint, that's okay with us. So circle up them wagons, and keep a watch out fer the night. Them pesky savages're out there. But git this one right, and add 350 points to your score. We've started you off ladies first—in fact, the only lady in the quiz is in place for you.

THREE-LETTER NAME
Mix, Tom

FOUR-LETTER NAMES
Bell, Rex
Blue, Monte
Boyd, William
Cobb, Edmund
Cody, "Iron Eyes"
Dean, Eddie
Hart, William S.
Holt, Jack
King, Charlie
Lane, "Rocky"

FIVE-LETTER NAMES
Acord, Art
Adams, Ernie
Allen, Rex
Autry, Gene
Baker, Bob
Barry, Donald "Red"
Beery, Noah
Brown, Johnny Mack
Carey, Harry
Evans, Dale
Hayes, "Gabby"
Hoxie, Jack
Jenks, Si
Jones, Buck

Keene, Tom
Larue, Lash
McCoy, Col. Tim
Moore, Clayton
Scott, Randolph
Tyler, Tom
Wayne, John
Woods, Harry

SIX-LETTER NAMES
Ballew, Smith
Bannon, Jim
Canutt, Yakima
Carson, "Sunset"
Coffin, Tris
Cooper, George
Crabbe, Larry
Duncan, Kenne
Gibson, "Hoot"
Hatton, Raymond
Hayden, Russell
Knight, "Fuzzy"
Kohler, Fred
London, Tom
McCrea, Joel
Merton, John
O'Brien, George
Ritter, Tex

Rogers, Roy
St. John, Al "Fuzzy"
Saylor, Sid
Steele, Bob
Wakely, Jimmy
Wilson, Whip

SEVEN-LETTER NAMES
Buttram, Pat
Elliott, Wild Bill
Ellison, James
Kortman, Bob
Madison, Guy
Maynard, Ken
Renaldo, Duncan
Terhune, Max

EIGHT-LETTER NAMES
Anderson, Bronco Billy
Bardette, Trevor
Buchanan, Edgar
Burnette, Smiley
Carrillo, Leo
Lackteen, Frank
Starrett, Charles
Williams, Guinn "Big Boy"

NINE-LETTER NAME
Yowlachie, Chief

TEN-LETTER NAME
Livingston, Robert

ELEVEN-LETTER NAME
Silverheels, Jay

_____points

(Answers on page 211)

17. THE BIG BULB

We suppose it was inevitable that a book about feature films
should eventually get to television—but as Hollywood went, so goes
Son of The Compleat Motion Picture Quiz Book. As double bills
and Dish Night faded into fond memory, fewer films were being
done, but TV's voracious appetite prompted producers to dip into
the great Hollywood talent reservoir. This quiz is the first of several
which will examine the television activities of many of Hollywood's
excellent talents. Bear in mind, we're not talking about talents who
first made their name in television and *then* moved into features.
Rather, we're talking in these quizzes about well-known stars, feature
players, and even bit players who moved over from the large screen
to the small one. Below, in Column One, we list a number of these,
and ask you to name the TV series they appeared in by completing
the titles suggested in Column Two. Take 15 points for each series
title properly completed.

1. Bill Williams   "T __ __   A __ __ __ __ __ __ __ __ __   __ __   __ __ __
                                  __ __ __ __ __ __ "
2. Joel McCrea   "W __ __ __ __ __ __ __   T __ __ __ "
3. Ray Milland   "M __ __ __   __ __.   M __ __ __ __ __ __ __ __ "
4. Roscoe Karns   "R __ __ __ __ __   __ __ __ __ ,   D __ __ __ __ __ __ __ __
5. Robert Taylor   "T __ __   D __ __ __ __ __ __ __ __ __ "
6. Broderick
    Crawford   "H __ __ __ __ __ __   P __ __ __ __ __ __ "
7. J. Carroll Naish   "L __ __ __   w __ __ __   L __ __ __ __ "
8. Jeffrey Lynn   "M __   S __ __   J __ __ __ "
9. Stuart Erwin   "T __ __   T __ __ __ __ __ __   w __ __ __
                             F __ __ __ __ __ "
10. Peter Lawford   "D __ __ __   P __ __ __ __ __ __ "
11. Leon Ames   "L __ __ __   w __ __ __   F __ __ __ __ __ "
12. Jackie Cooper   "H __ __ __ __ __ __ __ __ "

_____points

(Answers on page 211)

17. THE BIG BULB—DUFFERS' TEE

We suppose it was inevitable that a book about feature films should eventually get into television—but as Hollywood went, so goes *Son of The Compleat Motion Picture Quiz Book.* As double bills, newsreels, bank nights, and Dish Night faded away, fewer films were being done. Nevertheless, TV's voracious appetite finally turned to Hollywood and Vine, and producers were prompted to dip into the great Hollywood talent reservoir. This quiz is the first of several which will examine the television activities of many of Hollywood's excellent talents. Before you cry "foul," we assert that to stay apart from television is a little like trying to escape the atmosphere—and the real movie fan is as aware of what a once favorite Hollywood star is doing on "the Big Bulb" as he was of even a minor studio's latest programmer. As we pointed out to the Buffs, these quizzes will *not* include those many talents who first made their mark in TV and then moved on into feature films. Rather, we're talking about well-known movie stars, feature players, and even bit players who moved over from the large screen to the small screen. Below, in Column One, we list a dozen of these Hollywood names. And in Column Two, out of order, we list the names of the TV series in which these names appeared as regular talents. Match the name with the series in which these names appeared as regular talents. Match the name with the series, and take 15 points for each correct pairing.

1. Bill Williams	a. "Highway Patrol"
2. Joel McCrea	b. "The Trouble with Father"
3. Ray Milland	c. "The Detectives"
4. Roscoe Karns	d. "The Adventures of Kit Carson"
5. Robert Taylor	e. "Meet Mr. McNutley"
6. Broderick Crawford	f. "Wichita Town"
7. J. Carroll Naish	g. "Hennessey"
8. Jeffrey Lynn	h. "Life with Father"
9. Stuart Erwin	i. "Rocky King, Detective"
10. Peter Lawford	j. "Dear Phoebe"
11. Leon Ames	k. "My Son Jeep"
12. Jackie Cooper	l. "Life with Luigi"

_____points

(*Answers on page 211*)

18. HAIL TO THE CHIEF

As this is being written, the country is alive with the celebration of our bicentennial, and history is "in"! Surprisingly, Hollywood has for many years turned to history for plots, and American history (though perhaps a bit distorted occasionally) has been handled in a number of films. The portrayal of American Presidents and Americans who *became* President has frequently been a part of the American film. Below, we list a number of U. S. Presidents who have been portrayed in films. We list the film in which the portrayal was included, and ask you to tell us who did the portraying. We've added a few clues to help you, and will generously award 10 points for each correct answer.

1. Chester Alan Arthur	"Cattle King"	L _ _ _ _ G _ _ _ _
2. William McKinley	"This Is My Affair"	F _ _ _ _ _ C _ _ _ _ _
3. Grover Cleveland	"Lillian Russell"	W _ _ _ _ _ _ D _ _ _ _ _ _ _

4. William Henry Harrison   "Ten Gentlemen from West Point"   D _ _ _ _ _ _
D _ _ _ _ _ _ _ _

5. Thomas Jefferson   "America"   F _ _ _ _ W _ _ _ _

6. U. S. Grant   "The Adventures of Mark Twain"   J _ _ _ _ _ C _ _ _ _ _ _

7. Martin Van Buren   "The Gorgeous Hussy"   C _ _ _ _ _ _
T _ _ _ _ _ _ _ _ _

8. Franklin Pierce   "The Great Moment"   P _ _ _ _ _ H _ _ _

9. Theodore Roosevelt   "The Wind and the Lion"   B _ _ _ _ K _ _ _ _

10. U. S. Grant   "How the West Was Won"   H _ _ _ _ M _ _ _ _ _

11. Thomas Jefferson   "The Remarkable Andrew"   G _ _ _ _ _ _ E _ _ _ _

12. Woodrow Wilson   "The Story of Will Rogers"   E _ _ _ L _ _

13. Theodore Roosevelt   "My Girl Tisa"   S _ _ _ _ _ _
B _ _ _ _ _ _ _ _

14. Andrew Johnson   "Tennessee Johnson"   V _ _ H _ _ _ _ _

15. Abraham Lincoln   "The Littlest Rebel"   F _ _ _ _ M _ _ _ _ _ _

_____points

(Answers on page 212)

18. HAIL TO THE CHIEF—DUFFERS' TEE

As this is being written, the country is alive with the celebration of our bicentennial, and history is "in"! Surprisingly, Hollywood has for many years turned to history for plots, and American history (though perhaps a bit distorted occasionally) has been handled in a number of films. We pointed out in the Buffs' version of this quiz that many films include the portrayal of U. S. Presidents, or Americans who *became* President. And because some of them are a bit obscure, we are varying this version of the quiz somewhat. (And no fair peeking back at the Buff's version.) In Column One below, we list the name of an actor who portrayed a President of the United States; and in Column Two, we give you the title of the film in which this presidential portrayal was included. Presuming you *know* something about films or history—or both—we don't think we're asking too much to have you select the President portrayed from the out-of-order list of Column Three and match it with the player and film title. Take 10 points for each correct matching.

1. Larry Gates	"Cattle King"	a. Theodore Roosevelt
2. Frank Conroy	"This Is My Affair"	b. Grover Cleveland
3. William Davidson	"Lillian Russell"	c. William Henry Harrison
4. Douglas Dumbrille	"Ten Gentlemen from West Point"	d. U. S. Grant
5. Frank Walsh	"America"	e. Andrew Johnson
6. Joseph Crehan	"The Adventures of Mark Twain"	f. Woodrow Wilson
7. Charles Trowbridge	"The Gorgeous Hussy"	g. Chester Alan Arthur
8. Porter Hall	"The Great Moment"	h. William McKinley
9. Brian Keith	"The Wind and the Lion"	i. Franklin Pierce
10. Henry Morgan	"How the West Was Won"	j. Theodore Roosevelt
11. Gilbert Emery	"The Remarkable Andrew"	k. Martin Van Buren
12. Earl Lee	"The Story of Will Rogers"	l. Thomas Jefferson

13.	Sidney Blackmer	"My Girl Tisa"	m.	U. S. Grant
14.	Van Heflin	"Tennessee Johnson"	n.	Abraham Lincoln
15.	Frank McGlynn (Sr.)	"The Littlest Rebel"	o.	Thomas Jefferson

_____points

(*Answers on page 212*)

19. SPOT THE BIO: SHOW BIZ

One of the mainstays of movie musicals has been the biographical role. A number of onetime show business luminaries have been portrayed in films. Below, in Column One, we list a number of players. In Column Two are the feature films in which each player portrayed a onetime show business great. Complete the blanks in Column Three and give us the show business personalities portrayed. Take 15 points for each correct answer.

1.	Dinah Shore	"Till the Clouds Roll By"	J _ _ _ _ _ S _ _ _ _ _ _ _ _ _
2.	Judy Guild	"Till the Clouds Roll By"	M _ _ _ _ _ _ _ M _ _ _ _ _ _
3.	Martin Noble	"Rhapsody in Blue"	J _ _ _ _ _ _ H _ _ _ _ _ _ _
4.	Eddie Kane	"The Jolson Story"	F _ _ _ _ _ _ _ Z _ _ _ _ _ _ _ _
5.	Betty Hutton	"Incendiary Blonde"	T _ _ _ _ _ G _ _ _ _ _ _
6.	Edwin Maxwell	"The Jolson Story"	O _ _ _ _ _ H _ _ _ _ _ _ _ _ _ _ _
7.	Bing Crosby	"Dixie"	D _ _ E _ _ _ _ _ _
8.	John Alexander	"Lillian Russell"	L _ _ D _ _ _ _ _ _ _ _ _
9.	Ray Daley	"The Five Pennies"	G _ _ _ _ _ M _ _ _ _ _ _
10.	Eduard Franz	"The Great Caruso"	G _ _ _ _ _ _ G _ _ _ _ _- C _ _ _ _ _ _

_____points

(*Answers on page 213*)

19. SPOT THE BIO: SHOWBIZ—DUFFERS' TEE

One of the mainstays of movie musicals has been the biographical role. A number of onetime show business luminaries have been portrayed in films, sometimes as the star, sometimes in lesser roles as onetime acquaintances of the show business personality on whom the film focuses. Below, in Column One, we list a number of players, and follow in Column Two with a film in which that player portrayed a major show business personality. These personalities are listed in Column Three—out of order, of course—and you are to pair the real person with the player who portrayed that person and the film in which the portrayal was included. Take 15 points for each correct combination.

1. Dinah Shore	"Till the Clouds Roll By"	a. "Texas" Guinan
2. Judy Guild	"Till the Clouds Roll By"	b. Glenn Miller
3. Martin Noble	"Rhapsody in Blue"	c. Florenz Ziegfeld
4. Eddie Kane	"The Jolson Story"	d. Giulio Gatti-Casazza
5. Betty Hutton	"Incendiary Blonde"	e. Lew Dockstader
6. Edwin Maxwell	"The Jolson Story"	f. Julia Sanderson
7. Bing Crosby	"Dixie"	g. Jascha Heifetz
8. John Alexander	"Lillian Russell"	h. Marilyn Miller
9. Ray Daley	"The Five Pennies"	i. Oscar Hammerstein
10. Eduard Franz	"The Great Caruso"	j. Dan Emmett

_____points

(*Answers on page 213*)

20. TYPE-CASTING?

The motion picture is a global art, and the screenplay has spanned the planet for locales and incidents. The Hollywood player then has been called upon to portray a vast array of different international types—and it is surprising how a number of major stars have met this need. Below, we list in each question four different types played by the same actor. Your task is to identify the actor—for which you receive 10 points, *if* the identification is correct. In addition, if you name the film suggested by each clue, we'll award an additional 10 points for each correct film title you come up with. That's a possible 50 points on each question—or a total potential of 500 points on this quiz alone.

1. Greek general; Oriental detective; Seneca Indian; Chinese war lord.
2. Norwegian fisherman; Canadian Mountie; French criminal; Afghan horse dealer.
3. German juggler; Norwegian scientist; French army colonel; Greek warrior.
4. French army lieutenant; Italian artist; Russian prince; Czechoslovakian circus owner.
5. Polish composer; Mexican hotel clerk; British knight; French trapeze artist.
6. Chinese peasant; French trapper; Russian soldier; Mexican president.
7. French pirate; Oriental villain; Russian bureaucrat; Spanish soldier.
8. Siamese king; Mongolian warrior; Mexican revolutionary; Yugoslavian guerrilla.
9. French bell ringer; Italo-American farmer; Roman senator; Dutch artist.
10. Mexican revolutionary; Italian strong man; Eskimo hunter; Arab leader.

_____points

(Answers on page 214)

20. TYPE-CASTING?—DUFFERS' TEE

The versatility required of an actor is not extraordinary, but as Hollywood becomes more global in its appeal, the portrayal of a personality of a different ethnic background has come to require more than a little makeup and a well-adjusted rear-projection screen. The Hollywood player has been called upon to portray a wide range of international types—and we find it a bit surprising how a number of major stars have met this need. Below, we list in each question four different roles portrayed by the same actor. In Column Two, we list the actors—out of order—and ask you to match the actor with the groupings of Column One. We'll give you 10 points for each correct pairing—and if you can name *at least three* of the films suggested in the grouping, you may add *40 bonus points* for that question. That's ten questions, with a possible score of 50 points per question. Five hundred points! Lord-eee!

1. Greek general; Oriental detective; Seneca Indian; Chinese war lord.
2. Norwegian fisherman; Canadian Mountie; French criminal; Afghan horse dealer.
3. German juggler; Norwegian scientist; French army colonel; Greek warrior.
4. French army lieutenant; Italian artist; Russian prince; Czechoslovakian circus owner.
5. Polish composer; Mexican hotel clerk; British knight; French trapeze artist.
6. Chinese peasant; French trapper; Russian soldier; Mexican president.
7. French pirate; Oriental villain; Russian bureaucrat; Spanish soldier.
8. Siamese king; Mongolian warrior; Mexican revolutionary; Yugoslavian guerrilla.
9. French bell ringer; Italo-American farmer; Roman senator; Dutch artist.
10. Mexican revolutionary; Italian strong man; Eskimo hunter; Arab leader.

a. Yul Brynner
b. Kirk Douglas
c. Anthony Quinn
d. Errol Flynn
e. Charles Laughton
f. Fredric March
g. Boris Karloff
h. Basil Rathbone
i. Cornel Wilde
j. Paul Muni

_____points

(*Answers on page 214*)

21. DURABLE, AND DARLING

In case you're wondering about the title of this quiz, the female side of this writing team has taken over the typewriter for the moment, and the quiz is all hers (mine!). As you may have guessed, we're looking for a star who is Durable, and Darling! Below, in Column One, I've listed female stars whom our star romanced in films over nearly a third of a century. If you know films at all, spotting him should be no problem, and you can pick up 50 points for naming him. Give us the titles of the films in which these romances occurred, and you may have 5 points for each correct answer—or 150 *more* points! Pay attention, and there's a possible 200 points waiting for you.

1. Thelma Todd (1932)   "T _ _ _ I _ t _ _ N _ _ _ _"
2. Marlene Dietrich
   (1932)   "B _ _ _ _ _ V _ _ _ _"

3. Nancy Carroll (1932)   "H__ S_____"
 4. Sylvia Sidney (1933)   "T_____ D__ P_____"
 5. Mae West (1933)   "I_ N_ A____"
 6. Loretta Young (1934)   "B___ t_ B_ B__"
 7. Frances Drake (1934)   "L_____ S_____
                              L____"
 8. Jean Harlow (1936)   "S___"
 9. Constance Bennett
      (1937)   "T_____"
10. Katharine Hepburn
      (1938)   "H_____"
11. Jean Arthur (1939)   "O____ A_____ H____
                              W____"
12. Carole Lombard (1939)   "I_ N____ O____"
13. Irene Dunne (1940)   "M_ F_____ W___"
14. Rosalind Russell (1940) "H__ G___ F_____"
15. Joan Fontaine (1941)   "S_____"
16. Ginger Rogers (1942)   "O____ U___ a
                              H_____"
17. Laraine Day (1943)   "M_. L_____"
18. Janet Blair (1944)   "O____ U___ a T____"
19. Priscilla Lane (1944)   "A_____ and O__ L____"
20. Alexis Smith (1946)   "N_____ a__ D__"
21. Ingrid Bergman (1946)   "N_____"
22. Betsy Drake (1948)   "E_____ G___ S_____
                              B_ M_____"
23. Ann Sheridan (1949)   "I W__ a M___ W__
                              B____"
24. Jeanne Crain (1951)   "P_____ W___ T___"
25. Deborah Kerr (1953)   "D_____ W___"
26. Grace Kelly (1955)   "T_ C_____ a T_____"
27. Sophia Loren (1957)   "H_____"
28. Suzy Parker (1957)   "K___ T___ f__ M_"
29. Doris Day (1962)   "T___ T_____ o_ M___"
30. Audrey Hepburn (1962)   "C_____"

And the name of the star is ____ ____

                                        _____points

                                        _____title points
                                        _____
                                        _____total points

(*Answers on page 215*)

21. DURABLE, AND DARLING—DUFFERS' TEE

As I warned the Buffs, this is the female side of this here writing team, speaking to you from the captain's chair in front of the typewriter. And I've taken over for my own special quiz entitled DURABLE, AND DARLING. In this quiz, my assistant and I are looking for a star (male, of course) who is Durable, and Darling! Below, in Column One, you'll find listed female stars whom our star has romanced in feature films for nearly a third of a century. If you know your films, naming him should be no problem, and you can add fifty points (5-0 . . . 50!) by merely naming him. You can pick up another 150 points (nothing to sneeze at) by matching our he-man's co-stars with the proper title from Column Two. Match them correctly, and you may have 5 points for each correct pairing! ¡Buena suerte!

1. Thelma Todd (1932)		a.	"I'm No Angel"
2. Marlene Dietrich (1932)		b.	"Topper"
3. Nancy Carroll (1932)		c.	"Suspicion"
4. Sylvia Sidney (1933)		d.	"Night and Day"
5. Mae West (1933)		e.	"Dream Wife"
6. Loretta Young (1934)		f.	"Charade"
7. Frances Drake (1934)		g.	"Kiss Them for Me"
8. Jean Harlow (1936)		h.	"Ladies Should Listen"
9. Constance Bennett (1937)		i.	"Once Upon a Honeymoon"
10. Katharine Hepburn (1938)		j.	"People Will Talk"
11. Jean Arthur (1939)		k.	"Holiday"
12. Carole Lombard (1939)		l.	"Thirty Day Princess"
13. Irene Dunne (1940)		m.	"Only Angels Have Wings"
14. Rosalind Russell (1940)		n.	"Hot Saturday"
15. Joan Fontaine (1941)		o.	"Born to Be Bad"
16. Ginger Rogers (1942)		p.	"My Favorite Wife"
17. Laraine Day (1943)		q.	"Suzy"
18. Janet Blair (1944)		r.	"This Is the Night"
19. Priscilla Lane (1944)		s.	"His Girl Friday"
20. Alexis Smith (1946)		t.	"Blonde Venus"
21. Ingrid Bergman (1946)		u.	"In Name Only"
22. Betsy Drake (1948)		v.	"Arsenic and Old Lace"
23. Ann Sheridan (1949)		w.	"Notorious"
24. Jeanne Crain (1951)		x.	"Every Girl Should Be Married"
25. Deborah Kerr (1953)		y.	"Houseboat"
26. Grace Kelly (1955)		z.	"I Was a Male War Bride"

27. Sophia Loren (1957)   A. "That Touch of Mink"
28. Suzy Parker (1957)   B. "Mr. Lucky"
29. Doris Day (1962)   C. "Once Upon a Time"
30. Audrey Hepburn (1962)   D. "To Catch a Thief"

And the name of the star is _____ _____

_____points

_____title points

_____total points

(*Answers on page 215*)

22. ALMOST A LEGEND

One can look at various Hollywood careers and find that their scope can almost demonstrate why a career can develop into a legend. One undeniable luminary of the Hollywood galaxy spanned a relatively short number of years—but the films she made, her box office popularity, and the stature of the casts in which she appeared make it easy to see why such a career is not easily duplicated. The star, whose identity we are seeking in this quiz, appeared in films with all of the male stars we've listed in Column One below. For naming this star, we'll award 50 points—but if you can give the titles of the films in which she appeared with the stars named in Column One, you can have 5 more points for each such title. We have added some clues to help you, but you should do well, anyway. Just fill out the blanks in Column Two, and you'll have no trouble naming the star who is "almost a legend."

1. Warner Oland (1934)   "M _ _ _ _ _ _ _ _"
2. Warner Baxter (1934)   "S _ _ _ _ _ U _ a _ _ C _ _ _ _ _"
3. Spencer Tracy (1934)   "N _ _ I' _ _ T _ _ _ _"
4. Charles Farrell (1934)   "C _ _ _ _ _ _ o _ H _ _ _ _ _"
5. Gary Cooper (1934)   "N _ _ a _ _ F _ _ _ _ _ _ _"
6. Lionel Barrymore
   (1934)   "C _ _ _ _ _ _ _ _"
7. Joel McCrea (1935)   "O _ _ L _ _ _ _ _ _ G _ _ _"
8. John Boles (1935)   "C _ _ _ _ _ T _ _"
9. Jack Haley (1936)   "P _ _ _ L _ _ _ _ _ _ R _ _ _
   G _ _ _"
10. Robert Young (1936)   "S _ _ _ _ _ _ _ _"

11. Victor McLaglen
    (1937)   "W _ _ W _ _ _ _ _ W _ _ _ _ _"
12. George Murphy (1938)   "L _ _ _ _ _ M _ _ _
                               B _ _ _ _ _ _ _"
13. Randolph Scott (1939)   "R _ _ _ _ _ _ _ o _
                               S _ _ _ _ _ _ _ _ F _ _ _"
14. Richard Greene (1939)   "T _ _ L _ _ _ _ _ P _ _ _ _ _ _ _"
15. George Montgomery
    (1940)   "Y _ _ _ _ P _ _ _ _ _"
16. Herbert Marshall
    (1941)   "K _ _ _ _ _ _ _ _"
17. Joseph Cotten (1944)   "S _ _ _ _ _ Y _ _ W _ _ _ A _ _ _"
18. Robert Benchley
    (1945)   "K _ _ _ _ a _ _ T _ _ _"
19. Franchot Tone (1945)   "H _ _ _ _ _ _ _ _ _"
20. Cary Grant (1947)   "T _ _ B _ _ _ _ _ _ _ _ a _ _ t _ _
                               B _ _ _ _ _ _ _ _ _"

               And the name of the star is _____ _____

                                            _____points

                                            _____title points

                                            _____total points

                              (*Answers on page 215*)

22. ALMOST A LEGEND—DUFFERS' TEE

One can look at various Hollywood careers and find that their scope can almost demonstrate why a career can develop into a legend. One undeniable luminary of the Hollywood galaxy spanned a relatively short number of years—but the films she made, her box office popularity, and the stature of the casts in which she appeared make it easy to see why such a career is not easily duplicated. The star, whose identity we are seeking in this quiz, appeared in films with all of the male stars we've listed in Column One below. For naming this star, we'll award 50 points. But if you can match each male performer with the appropriate title from the out-of-order list in Column Two—a film in which he appeared with our star—you may have an additional 5 points for each such pairing. So, here's a possible 150 points for your score. Get them all, and in *our* book, you're "almost a legend."

45

1. Warner Oland (1934)	a. "Poor Little Rich Girl"
2. Warner Baxter (1934)	b. "Rebecca of Sunnybrook Farm"
3. Spencer Tracy (1934)	c. "Change of Heart"
4. Charles Farrell (1934)	d. "Carolina"
5. Gary Cooper (1934)	e. "Mandalay"
6. Lionel Barrymore (1934)	f. "Young People"
7. Joel McCrea (1935)	g. "Since You Went Away"
8. John Boles (1935)	h. "Kathleen"
9. Jack Haley (1936)	i. "Now I'll Tell"
10. Robert Young (1936)	j. "Our Little Girl"
11. Victor McLaglen (1937)	k. "Kiss and Tell"
12. George Murphy (1938)	l. "Honeymoon"
13. Randolph Scott (1939)	m. "The Bachelor and the Bobbysoxer"
14. Richard Greene (1939)	n. "Stowaway"
15. George Montgomery (1940)	o. "The Little Princess"
16. Herbert Marshall (1941)	p. "Wee Willie Winkie"
17. Joseph Cotten (1944)	q. "Little Miss Broadway"
18. Robert Benchley (1945)	r. "Now and Forever"
19. Franchot Tone (1945)	s. "Stand Up and Cheer"
20. Cary Grant (1947)	t. "Curly Top"

And the name of the star is _____ _____

_____points

_____title points
_____

_____total points

(*Answers on page 215*)

23. WHO WAS THAT LADY?

There have been a number of films bearing a one-word title which was a feminine name. We didn't realize just how many there were until one afternoon around the patio when we were playing games with a few hard-nosed movie buffs. Of course, the list could be several times longer if we included titles such as "Little Annie Rooney" or "My Friend Irma"—or even "Irma La Douce"—but we didn't. Column One below is composed entirely of bona fide *one-word* movie titles. And here's your chance for a 625-point addition to your score, since we're offering 25 points for each correct answer. Just tell us who played these fabled ladies by filling in the blanks in Column Two.

1. "Anna"   S_____ M_____
2. "Ada"   S_____ H_____
3. "Billie"   P_____ D___
4. "Emma"   M_____ D_____
5. "Fanny"   L_____ C_____
6. "Gidget"   S_____ D__
7. "Gigi"   L_____ C_____
8. "Gypsy"   N_____ W___
9. "Heidi"   S_____ T_____
10. "Irene"   A____ N_____
11. "Jennie"   V_____ G_____
12. "Jennifer"   I__ L_____
13. "Jessica"   A_____ D_____
14. "Josette"   S_____ S_____
15. "Judith"   S_____ L_____
16. "Julie"   D_____ D__
17. "Kathleen"   S_____ T_____
18. "Kitty"   P_____ G_____
19. "Laura"   G____ T_____
20. "Lili"   L_____ C_____
21. "Lilith"   J____ S_____
22. "Maisie"   A__ S_____
23. "Mickey"   L___ B_____
24. "Nana"   A___ S___
25. "Zaza"   C_____ C_____

_____points

(*Answers on page 216*)

23. WHO WAS THAT LADY?—DUFFERS' TEE

There have been a number of films bearing a one-word title which was a feminine name. As we told the Buffs, we didn't realize just how many there were until one afternoon around the patio when we were playing games with a few hard-nosed movie buffs. We grant the list could've been several times longer if we included titles such as "Little Annie Rooney," "My Friend Irma," "Irma La Douce"—or "The Strange Love of Martha Ivers"—but we didn't. Column One below is composed entirely of bona fide *one-word* movie titles. And this quiz is an opportunity to increase your score by 600 points (more than we gave the Buffs), since we're allowing 24 points for each correct pairing of the title from Column One with the actress in Column Two who played the part. And just to give the lady a rest, we did not include "Cleopatra"!

1. "Anna"	a.	Anna Sten
2. "Ada"	b.	Ann Sothern
3. "Billie"	c.	Anna Neagle
4. "Emma"	d.	Claudette Colbert
5. "Fanny"	e.	Natalie Wood
6. "Gidget"	f.	Patty Duke
7. "Gigi"	g.	Simone Simon
8. "Gypsy"	h.	Marie Dressler
9. "Heidi"	i.	Silvana Mangano
10. "Irene"	j.	Virginia Gilmore
11. "Jennie"	k.	Shirley Temple
12. "Jennifer"	l.	Leslie Caron
13. "Jessica"	m.	Lois Butler
14. "Josette"	n.	Gene Tierney
15. "Judith"	o.	Susan Hayward
16. "Julie"	p.	Leslie Caron
17. "Kathleen"	q.	Jean Seberg
18. "Kitty"	r.	Sandra Dee
19. "Laura"	s.	Leslie Caron
20. "Lili"	t.	Paulette Goddard
21. "Lilith"	u.	Ida Lupino
22. "Maisie"	v.	Shirley Temple
23. "Mickey"	w.	Doris Day
24. "Nana"	x.	Sophia Loren
25. "Zaza"	y.	Angie Dickinson

_____points

(*Answers on page 216*)

24. FILMS IN COMMON

With thirty-six basic dramatic situations and literally thousands of films produced, it is inescapable that some films bear some similarity to others, or have some bond of commonality. But this frequently goes beyond plot, we find—and if you know your films, you'll be able to detect the characteristic one film may have in common with another. In each question below, we list two films which have a common characteristic. And in the list of titles we've provided in Column Two there is a *third* film which possesses the same commonality with the two titles of Column One. Select the film from Column Two which has something in common with the pair of films in Column One. You may have 15 points for each film properly grouped with the two titles of Column One.

1. "Forbidden Planet" "West Side Story"
   a. "The Lady Vanishes"

2. "We Were Strangers" "Suddenly"
   b. "A Place in the Sun"

3. "Day for Night" "The Barefoot Contessa"
   c. "Call Northside 777"

4. "Bullitt" "Experiment in Terror"
   d. "We're No Angels"

5. "I'll Cry Tomorrow" "Love Me or Leave Me"
   e. "The Robe"

6. "Heaven Can Wait" "All That Money Can Buy"
   f. "Trial"

7. "Strange Cargo" "Papillon"
   g. "Lost Horizon"

8. "Executive Suite" "The Solid Gold Cadillac"
   h. "Barbary Coast"

9. "The Rogue Song" "Mr. Imperium"
   i. "Cabin in the Sky"

10. "Billy the Kid" (1930) "This Is Cinerama"
    j. "Joe Macbeth"

11. "Anatomy of a Murder" "Witness for the Prosecution"
    k. "With a Song in My Heart"

12. "Reap the Wild Wind" "Leave Her to Heaven"
    l. "Executive Action"

13. "All the President's Men" "30"
    m. "Two Weeks in Another Town"

14. "Murder on the Orient Express" "The Narrow Margin"
    n. "How to Succeed in Business Without Really Trying"

15. "She" "The Picture of Dorian Gray"
    o. "Aaron Slick from Punkin Crick"

————points

(*Answers on page 217*)

24. FILMS IN COMMON—DUFFERS' TEE

There have been in excess of twenty thousand American sound films produced, and with only thirty-six basic dramatic situations, there are bound to be some instances of similarity. We have dredged up some films which have some characteristic in common with other feature films and present them to you for this quiz we call FILMS IN COMMON. The two films in Column One have some factor in common. In Column Two, we present you with three *more* titles. Only one of these films possesses the same trait or characteristic in common with the films of Column One—the remaining films do not. Your task is to select the film title from Column Two which has some common characteristic with the two films of Column One. You may add 15 points to your score for eich title you select correctly. Think before you leap!

1. "Forbidden Planet"
   "West Side Story"

   a. "I Wanted Wings"
   b. "Joe Macbeth"
   c. "Rollerball"

2. "We Were Strangers"
   "Suddenly"

   a. "Executive Action"
   b. "Damn the Defiant"
   c. "The Bells Are Ringing"

3. "Day for Night"

   "The Barefoot Contessa"

   a. "Two Weeks in Another Town"
   b. "Swamp Water"
   c. "The Enforcer"

4. "Bullitt"
   "Experiment in Terror"

   a. "The Citadel"
   b. "Barbary Coast"
   c. "Bulldog Drummond"

5. "I'll Cry Tomorrow"
   "Love Me or Leave Me"

   a. "I Want to Live"
   b. "Be My Love"
   c. "With a Song in My Heart"

6. "Heaven Can Wait"
   "All That Money Can Buy"

   a. "East Side of Heaven"
   b. "Cabin in the Sky"
   c. "Between Heaven and Hell"

7. "Strange Cargo"
   "Papillon"

   a. "We're No Angels"
   b. "Butterflies are Free"
   c. "From Here to Eternity"

8. "Executive Suite"
   "The Solid Gold Cadillac"

   a. "How to Succeed in Business Without Really Trying"
   b. "The Longest Yard"
   c. "Adam's Rib"

9. "The Rogue Song"
   "Mr. Imperium"

   a. "Roques' Regiment"
   b. "Aaron Slick from Punkin Crick"
   c. "Destry Rides Again"

10. "Billy the Kid" (1930)

    "This Is Cinerama"

    a. "Demetrius and the Gladiators"
    b. "The 300 Spartans"
    c. "The Robe"

11. "Anatomy of a Murder"
    "Witness for the Prosecution"

    a. "Murder by Death"
    b. "Trial"
    c. "Reunion in France"

12. "Reap the Wild Wind"
    "Leave Her to Heaven"

    a. "East Side, West Side"
    b. "Any Number Can Play"
    c. "A Place in the Sun"

13. "All the President's Men"
    "30"

    a. "Call Northside 777"
    b. "The Fountainhead"
    c. "The Human Comedy"

14. "Murder on the Orient Express"
    "The Narrow Margin"

    a. "Murder, He Says"
    b. "The Last Time I Saw Paris"
    c. "The Lady Vanishes"

15. "She"

    "The Picture of Dorian Gray"

    a. "None but the Lonely Heart"
    b. "Trail of the Lonesome Pine"
    c. "Lost Horizon"

_____points

(*Answers on page 218*)

25. ALL WE NEED IS A TITLE

Frequently, a feature film can have one title all through its gestation period, through production, and suddenly, right before its release, a new title is added—which may or may not have some relationship to the original title and the plot. Below, we list a number of working titles, and ask you to supply—through deduction and memory—the title of the film as it finally ended up. We're giving 15 points for each correct title you supply, so think hard!

1. "The Townsend Harris Story"   "T__ B_____ a__ t__ G_____"
2. "The Silence of Helen McCord"   "T__ S_____ S_____"
3. "Where Men Are Men"   "F_____ P_____"
4. "Man on a Train"   "T__ T_____ T_____"
5. "The Californian"   "T__ M_____ o __ Z_____"
6. "Tribute to a Bad Man"   "T__ B __ a__ t__ B_____"
7. "Nearer My God to Thee"   "T_____"
8. "The Dr. Praetorious Story"   "P_____ W_____ T_____"
9. "Chuck-a-Luck"   "R_____ N_____"
10. "The House of Dr. Edwardes"   "S_____"
11. "Pylon"   "T__ T_____ A_____"
12. "The Fragile Fox"   "A_____"

_____points

(*Answers on page 219*)

25. ALL WE NEED IS A TITLE—DUFFERS' TEE

Frequently, a feature film can have one title all through its gestation period, through production, and suddenly, right before its release, a new title is added—which may or may not have some relationship to the original title and the plot. Below, in Column One, we list a number of such working titles, and ask you to select from Column Two the title which was finally used in general release. We're giving you 15 points for each correct match you make—or you may prefer to look at it as 180 possible points.

1. "The Townsend Harris Story"	a. "Attack"
2. "The Silence of Helen McCord"	b. "Titanic"
3. "Where Men Are Men"	c. "People Will Talk"
4. "Man on a Train"	d. "The Spiral Staircase"
5. "The Californian"	e. "The Bad and the Beautiful"
6. "Tribute to a Bad Man"	f. "The Barbarian and the Geisha"
7. "Nearer My God to Thee"	g. "Fancy Pants"
8. "The Dr. Praetorious Story"	h. "The Mark of Zorro"
9. "Chuck-a-Luck"	i. "The Tarnished Angels"
10. "The House of Dr. Edwardes"	j. "The Tall Target"
11. "Pylon"	k. "Rancho Notorious"
12. "The Fragile Fox"	l. "Spellbound"

_____points

(Answers on page 219)

26. THE BIG BULB PART II

Once again, we're looking at well-known Hollywood talents who, with fewer feature films being made, turned their talents to television, and became stars of their own TV series. In Column One below, we list a number of such Hollywood names, and ask you to tell us the TV series in which they found greater prominence by completing the blanks in Column Two. As before, we're allowing 15 points for each title correctly completed.

1. Walter Brennan "_ _ _ T_ _ _ _ _ _"
2. Reed Hadley "_ _ _ _ _ _ _ D_ _ _ _ _ _ _"
3. Wendell Corey "H_ _ _ _ _ _ C_ _ _ _ _ _ _"
4. Victor Jory "M_ _ _ _ _ _ _"
5. Charles Bickford "T_ _ M_ _ B_ _ _ _ _ _ t_ _ B_ _ _ _"
6. Ralph Bellamy "M_ _ A_ _ _ _ _ _ _ C_ _ _ _"
7. Boris Karloff "C_ _ _ _ _ _ _ _ M_ _ _ _ _ _ _ S_ _ _ _ _ _ _ _ Y_ _ _"
8. Rod Cameron "_ _ _ _ _ _ _ _ 9"
9. Kent Taylor "B_ _ _ _ _ _ B_ _ _ _ _ _"
10. Dennis Morgan "21 B_ _ _ _ _ _ S_ _ _ _ _"
11. Louis Jourdan "P_ _ _ _ _ P_ _ _ _ _ _ _ _"
12. Stephen McNally "T_ _ _ _ _ _: _ _ _ C_ _ _ _ _ _ _ _ _ _"

13. Macdonald Carey   "L_ _ _ _   _ _"
14. George Raft   "_'_ _ _ _   _ _ _"
15. Everett Sloane   "O_ _ _ _ _ _ _ D_ _ _ _ _ _ _ _"

_____points

(Answers on page 220)

26. THE BIG BULB PART II—DUFFERS' TEE

Once again, we're looking at well-known Hollywood talents who, with fewer feature films being made, turned their talents to television, and became stars of their own TV series. In Column One below, we list a number of such Hollywood names, and ask you to tell us the TV series in which they found greater prominence. Select the series from Column Two and match it with the star of Column One. As before, we're allowing 15 points for each title correctly matched.

1. Walter Brennan	a. "Paris Precinct"
2. Reed Hadley	b. "Man Against Crime"
3. Wendell Corey	c. "Target: The Corrupters"
4. Victor Jory	d. "Colonel March of Scotland Yard"
5. Charles Bickford	e. "Official Detective"
6. Ralph Bellamy	f. "21 Beacon Street"
7. Boris Karloff	g. "Manhunt"
8. Rod Cameron	h. "The Tycoon"
9. Kent Taylor	i. "Public Defender"
10. Dennis Morgan	j. "Harbor Command"
11. Louis Jourdan	k. "I'm the Law"
12. Stephen McNally	l. "Boston Blackie"
13. Macdonald Carey	m. "The Man Behind the Badge"
14. George Raft	n. "Coronado 9"
15. Everett Sloane	o. "Lock Up"

_____points

(Answers on page 220)

27. TELL US WHO

Below, in each question, we list two incidents or plot points from two films in which the same player—male or female—appeared.

From your memory, tell us the name of the performer we're seeking. Take 15 points for each correct identification. But if you can also correctly name the titles of the two films from which the incidents are taken, you may add another 10 points. But remember—you must name *both* films in order to claim the possible 25 points for each question. Do it—and you're 250 points ahead.

1. As a medieval monk, he summoned Henry Wilcoxon to his wedding date with Loretta Young, and he amused Carole Lombard with his imitation of an ape.
2. He visited his lifelong friend Clark Gable in the penitentiary's Death Row, and assisted Jack Lemmon in the manufacture of ersatz scotch.
3. He scampered all over the theater in his duel with Mel Ferrer, and was accompanied on a long safari by Deborah Kerr and Richard Carlson.
4. She had a tryst with Fred MacMurray in a grocery supermarket, and was involved in a train wreck with Joel McCrea.
5. He lost his stake in a poker game as he was outwitted by Paul Newman, and—aboard a royal barge—he came to visit Paul Scofield.
6. Though his head had turned into that of a donkey, he enchanted Anita Louise, and later he danced on a table top with Bob Hope.
7. He was a collaborator with the Nazis by acting as a stool pigeon against his comrades in a prison camp, and—along with his colleagues—he participated in the fatal beating of Walter Slezak.
8. She danced with Kay Kendall and Taina Elg, and later bathed in a jerry-rigged shower on an island during World War II.
9. As a blind pianist, he was loved by Joan Crawford, and he attempted to slip a glass slipper on Leslie Caron's foot.
10. She peddled apples on the streets of New York, and took dictation for Monty Woolley.

_____points

(*Answers on page 220*)

27. TELL US WHO—DUFFERS' TEE

Below we list in each question two incidents or plot points from two films in which the same player appeared. From your memory, tell us the name of the player we're seeking. We've provided the names, out of order, in Column Two, so for each star you can match with these incidents from his or her cinematic career, you may have 15 points. If you can also tell us *both* film titles represented, you may add another 10 points per question. So good luck for a possible 250-point addition to your score.

1. As a medieval monk, he summoned Henry Wilcoxon to his wedding date with Loretta Young, and he amused Carole Lombard with his imitation of an ape.

    a. Barbara Stanwyck

2. He visited his lifelong friend Clark Gable in the penitentiary's Death Row, and assisted Jack Lemmon in the manufacture of ersatz scotch.

    b. Stewart Granger

3. He scampered all over the theater in his duel with Mel Ferrer, and was accompanied on a long safari by Deborah Kerr and Richard Carlson.

    c. James Cagney

4. She had a tryst with Fred MacMurray in a grocery supermarket, and was involved in a train wreck with Joel McCrea.

    d. Mitzi Gaynor

5. He lost his stake in a poker game as he was outwitted by Paul Newman, and —aboard a royal barge—he came to visit Paul Scofield.

    e. Mischa Auer

6. Though his head had turned into that of a donkey, he enchanted Anita Louise, and later he danced on a table top with Bob Hope.

    f. Bette Davis

7. He was a collaborator with the Nazis by acting as a stool pigeon against his comrades in a prison camp, and —along with his colleagues—he participated in the fatal beating of Walter Slezak.

    g. Michael Wilding

8. She danced with Kay Kendall and Taina Elg, and later bathed in a jerry-rigged shower on an island in World War II.

    h. Robert Shaw

9. As a blind pianist, he was loved by Joan Crawford, and he attempted to slip a glass slipper on Leslie Caron's foot.

    i. Hume Cronyn

10. She peddled apples on the streets of New York, and took dictation for Monty Woolley.

    j. William Powell

_____points

(*Answers on page 220*)

56

28. CASTING DIRECTOR

Let's take a moment and see how good you'd be as a casting director. The producer has given you a script and isolated the various "types" of roles included in the script—which you'll find in Column One below. From Column Two below, select the player you'd cast for each part in Column One. Of course, you might go for some offbeat casting, but that's not what the producer wants—he's got a lot of money tied up in his production, and he's going for sure things. So select the well-known type for the part, and increase your score by 20 points for each correct pairing.

1. The evil and cunning Mohammed Khan	a. Paul Guilfoyle
2. The wisecracking, "stop-the-presses" reporter	b. Edward Arnold
3. The small-town constable	c. Thurston Hall
4. The top-hatted, white-tied happy drunk	d. Byron Foulger
5. The head thug's right-hand man	e. Chick Chandler
6. The dignified Mittel-European professor	f. Spencer Charters
7. The pompous, blustering politician	g. C. Henry Gordon
8. The big-business tycoon	h. Jack Norton
9. The cowardly stool pigeon	i. Joe Sawyer
10. The weak, unctuous assistant	j. Victor Francen

_____points

(*Answers on page 221*)

28. CASTING DIRECTOR—DUFFERS' TEE

Let's take a moment and see how good you'd be as a casting director. The producer has given you a script and isolated the various "types" of roles included in the script—which you'll find in Column One below. Opposite, in Column Two, you are given three choices, and you are to select the performer best suited for the role on the basis of past performance. As we told the Buffs, we're not looking for offbeat casting, because the producer has a lot of money tied up in the production and wants to play it as a sure thing. Select from the multiple choice in Column Two the performer best suited for the role, and increase your score by 20 points for each correct selection.

1. The evil and cunning Mohammed Khan

   a. Frank Ferguson
   b. C. Henry Gordon
   c. Christian Rub

2. The wisecracking, "stop-the-presses" reporter

   a. Henry Armetta
   b. Chick Chandler
   c. Chester Clute

3. The small-town constable

   a. Douglas Dumbrille
   b. Kurt Katch
   c. Spencer Charters

4. The top-hatted, white-tied happy drunk

   a. Harry Davenport
   b. Johnny "Skins" Miller
   c. Jack Norton

5. The head thug's right-hand man

   a. Joe Sawyer
   b. Irving Bacon
   c. Grady Sutton

6. The dignified Mittel-European professor

   a. Charles Winninger
   b. Herb Vigran
   c. Victor Francen

7. The pompous, blustering politician

   a. Thurston Hall
   b. "Slim" Summerville
   c. Hans Schumm

8. The big-business tycoon

   a. Leonid Kinsky
   b. Edward Arnold
   c. Felix Bressart

9. The cowardly stool pigeon

   a. Ernest Cossart
   b. George Bancroft
   c. Paul Guilfoyle

10. The weak, unctuous assistant

   a. Robert Warwick
   b. Samuel S. Hinds
   c. Byron Foulger

_____points

(*Answers on page 221*)

58

29. RIGHT AFTER THIS MESSAGE

The inclusion of a television reference in a book about movies is as inevitable as it has been in the careers of many movie stars. With fewer pictures being produced, and fewer roles being cast, many well-known personalities have turned to becoming television spokesmen or spokeswomen for commercial products. Let's see how good your eye has been in identifying stars who have turned up hawking products on the tube. Below, in Column One, we list some well-known talents; and in Column Two, out of order, we list these products with which they have been connected in television commercials. Match the talent with the product, and take 20 points for each correct pairing.

1. Virginia Christine	a.	Telegraph florists
2. Jonathan Winters	b.	Toothpaste
3. Gary Merrill	c.	Cream substitute
4. Joey Heatherton	d.	Canned vegetables
5. Andy Griffith	e.	Garbage bags
6. Arthur O'Connell	f.	Coffee
7. Louis Jourdan	g.	Beer
8. John Williams	h.	Steak sauce
9. Burgess Meredith	i.	Mattresses
10. Jim Davis	j.	Recordings

_____points

(*Answers on page 221*)

29. RIGHT AFTER THIS MESSAGE—DUFFERS' TEE

The inclusion of a television reference in a book about movies is as inevitable as it has been in the careers of many stars. With fewer pictures being produced, and fewer films being cast, many well-known personalities have turned to becoming spokesmen or spokeswomen for commercial products. Let's see how good your eye has been in identifying stars who have turned up hawking products on the tube. Below, in Column One, we list some fairly well-known personalities; and in Column Two, out of order, we list those products with which they have been connected in television commercials. Match the talent with the product, and take 20 points for each correct pairing.

1. Jane Withers	a. Instant coffee
2. Edie Adams	b. Instant cameras
3. Bing Crosby	c. Salad dressing
4. Henry Fonda	d. Auto repairs
5. Jane Russell	e. Airline travel
6. Orson Welles	f. Orange juice
7. Sir Laurence Olivier	g. Cigars
8. Anna Maria Alberghetti	h. Brassieres
9. Zsa Zsa Gabor	i. Cameras and floor tile
10. Patricia Neal	j. Drain solvent

_____points

(*Answers on page 222*)

30. LA RONDE

As we pointed out so brilliantly in *The Compleat Motion Picture Quiz Book,* it is possible to trace a connecting chain between a star and almost any other star by films in which they have appeared. For example, should you want to link Marjorie Main with Gertrude Lawrence—now *that's* far out—you might trace the linkage via this route:

Marjorie Main appeared with Percy Kilbride ("The Egg and I"—plus any number of "Ma and Pa Kettle" films) who played with Jack Benny ("George Washington Slept Here") who played with Carole Lombard ("To Be or Not to Be") who co-starred with Charles Laughton ("They Knew What They Wanted") who played opposite Gertrude Lawrence ("Rembrandt").

That's bouncing it around a bit, we admit, but if you know your films, you can connect virtually anybody. In fact, many times you can lead yourself back to the starting point—a complete circle—as we have done in the diagram on the page following.

To complete the wheel, supply the appropriate titles in the spaces we've designated with the symbols A. through L. Do this completely and correctly—and score 400 points.

1. Gary Cooper and Lilli Palmer   A. _____
2. Lilli Palmer and John Garfield   B. _____
3. John Garfield and Shelley Winters   C. _____

4. Shelley Winters and Ronald   D. _____
    Colman

60

5. Ronald Colman and Madeleine Carroll E. _____

6. Madeleine Carroll and Bob Hope F. _____

7. Bob Hope and Betty Hutton G. _____,__ ____ ____

8. Betty Hutton and Fred Astaire H. _____,__ _____

9. Fred Astaire and Leslie Caron I. _____

10. Leslie Caron and Cary Grant J. _____ ____

11. Cary Grant and Ingrid Bergman K. _____

12. Ingrid Bergman and Gary Cooper L. __ ____ ____ ____ ____ ____

_____points

(*Answers on page 222*)

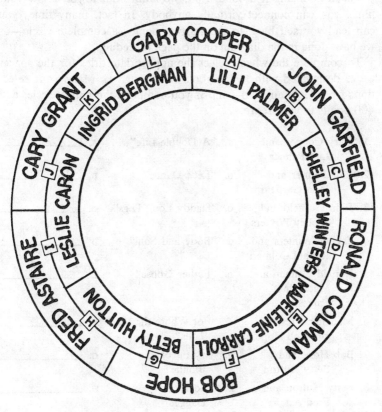

30. LA RONDE—DUFFERS' TEE

As we pointed out so brilliantly in *The Compleat Motion Picture Quiz Book,* it is possible to trace a connecting chain between a star and almost any other star by films in which they have appeared. For example, should you want to link Marjorie Main and Gertrude Lawrence—now *that's* far out—you might trace the linkage via this route:

Marjorie Main appeared with Percy Kilbride ("The Egg and I"—plus any number of "Ma and Pa Kettle" films) who played with Jack Benny ("George Washington Slept Here") who played with Carole Lombard ("To Be or Not to Be") who co-starred with Charles Laughton ("They Knew What They Wanted") who played opposite Gertrude Lawrence ("Rembrandt").

That's bouncing it around a bit, we admit, but if you know your films, you can connect virtually anybody. In fact, many times you can lead yourself back to the starting point—a complete circle—as we have done in the diagram on the page preceding.

To complete the wheel, select the appropriate titles for the spaces we've designated with the symbols A. through L. Make your selections from Column Two—and if you complete the entire circle, add 400 points to your score.

1. Gary Cooper and Lilli Palmer	a. "A Double Life"	A. _____
2. Lilli Palmer and John Garfield	b. "Let's Dance"	B. _____
3. John Garfield and Shelley Winters	c. "Daddy Long Legs"	C. _____
4. Shelley Winters and Ronald Colman	d. "Body and Soul"	D. _____
5. Ronald Colman and Madeleine Carroll	e. "Father Goose"	E. _____
6. Madeleine Carroll and Bob Hope	f. "For Whom the Bell Tolls"	F. _____
7. Bob Hope and Betty Hutton	g. "My Favorite Blonde"	G. _____
8. Betty Hutton and Fred Astaire	h. "Cloak and Dagger"	H. _____

9. Fred Astaire and Leslie Caron	i. "He Ran All the Way"	I. _____
10. Leslie Caron and Cary Grant	j. "Let's Face It"	J. _____
11. Cary Grant and Ingrid Bergman	k. "The Prisoner of Zenda"	K. _____
12. Ingrid Bergman and Gary Cooper	l. "Notorious"	L. _____

_____points

(*Answers on page 222*)

31. SATURDAY NIGHT AT THE FLICKS PART II

Earlier we asked you to match American film titles with the export title by which the films were known for their British exposure. In Column One, we list the export title, and ask you to complete the film titles in Column Two—which were the titles by which the American audiences came to know these features. As before, take 20 points for each title you complete correctly.

1. "Spirit of the People"   "A _ _   L _ _ _ _ _ _ _   i_
                                I _ _ _ _ _ _ _ _"

2. "I Shall Return"   "A _   A _ _ _ _ _ _ _ _
                            G _ _ _ _ _ _ _ _   i_   t_ _
                            P _ _ _ _ _ _ _ _ _ _ _"

3. "Polly Fulton"   "B. _.'_   D _ _ _ _ _ _ _ _ _"

4. "The Flaming Torch"   "T _ _ _   B _ _   M _ _ _ _ _ _
                            S _ _ _ _"

5. "The Curse of the Allenbys"   "S _ _-W _ _ _   o_   L _ _ _ _ _"

6. "Get Off My Back"   "S _ _ _ _ _ _"

7. "The Gay Mrs. Trexel"   "S _ _ _ _   a _ _   G _ _"

8. "Chicago, Chicago"   "G _ _ _ _ ,   G _ _ _ _"

9. "Chicago Masquerade"   "L _ _ _ _ _ _   E _ _ _ _"

10. "Southwest to Sonora"   "T _ _ _   A _ _ _ _ _ _ _ _ _"

_____points

(*Answers on page 223*)

31. SATURDAY NIGHT AT THE FLICKS PART II—DUFFERS' TEE

Earlier we asked you to match American film titles with the export title by which the films were known for their British exposure. In Column One, we list the original American titles, while in Column Two, we list (out of order, naturally) their British export titles. Match the original American title with its British counterpart and pick off 20 points for each correct pairing.

1. "Abe Lincoln in Illinois"
2. "The Appaloosa"
3. "Susan and God"

4. "An American Guerilla in the Philippines"
5. "Little Egypt"
6. "She-Wolf of London"
7. "Synanon"
8. "The Bob Mathias Story"
9. "B.F.'s Daughter"
10. "Gaily, Gaily"

a. "Get Off My Back"
b. "I Shall Return"
c. "The Curse of the Allenbys"

d. "Polly Fulton"
e. "Chicago, Chicago"
f. "The Flaming Torch"
g. "Spirit of the People"
h. "The Gay Mrs. Trexel"
i. "Southwest to Sonora"
j. "Chicago Masquerade"

_____points

(*Answers on page 223*)

32. PENCILED IN: MALES

In an earlier exercise, we listed a number of female players who originally had been penciled in for roles in a motion picture but who, for one reason or another, had been replaced by another player in the final film. This is essentially the same type of quiz, but here we are dealing with male performers. In Column One below, we list the male players who had *originally* been cast in a role in the films listed in Column Two. Since these players did not appear in the films, we ask you to supply in Column Three the name of the actors who finally did play the roles. Take 15 points for each name you can supply correctly.

1. George Raft   "High Sierra"   _____
2. Frank Sinatra   "The Only Game in Town"   _____

3.	Montgomery Clift	"Moby Dick"	_____
4.	Sammy Davis, Jr.	"Never So Few"	_____
5.	George Raft	"The Maltese Falcon"	_____
6.	Robert Alda	"Somebody Loves Me"	_____
7.	Burt Lancaster	"Les Miserables"	_____
8.	Tony Randall	"The Young Lions"	_____
9.	Marlon Brando	"The Egyptian"	_____
10.	Scott Brady	"Come Back, Little Sheba"	_____

_____points

(Answers on page 224)

32. PENCILED IN: MALES—DUFFERS' TEE

As before, we're concerned with the cases where a player *originally* announced for a role in a film was replaced, for one reason or another, by another player in the final version of the film as it was released. You may remember some of the original press hoop-la, or your good sense of casting might tip you off. In this one we're dealing with male players only. As before, we list in Column One features which had casting changes from the original conception to the final release version. In Column Two, we list the personalities originally announced for roles in the films of Column One. Finally, in Column Three, out of order, we provide a list of the players who ultimately played the roles referred to in Columns One and Two. Your task is to match the player from Column Three with the correct film title (Column One) and the player originally announced for that role (Column Two). Take 10 points for each correct match you make.

1.	"High Sierra"	George Raft	a.	Michael Rennie
2.	"The Only Game in Town"	Frank Sinatra	b.	Ralph Meeker
3.	"Moby Dick"	Montgomery Clift	c.	Edmund Purdom
4.	"Never So Few"	Sammy Davis, Jr.	d.	Richard Basehart
5.	"The Maltese Falcon"	George Raft	e.	Richard Jaeckel
6.	"Somebody Loves Me."	Robert Alda	f.	Humphrey Bogart
7.	"Les Miserables"	Burt Lancaster	g.	Humphrey Bogart

8. "The Young Lions"	Tony Randall	h. Steve McQueen
9. "The Egyptian"	Marlon Brando	i. Warren Beatty
10. "Come Back, Little Sheba"	Scott Brady	j. Dean Martin

_____points

(Answers on page 224)

33. SPOT THE RINGER

Each question below has to do with a single director. In the question, we list three films which were directed by the same director and one which was not. Your task is to isolate the feature which was *not* directed by the director responsible for the other three. For naming the director, you get 10 points—and for throwing out the film *not* directed by him, you get 10 points more. That's 20 points a question, or a possible 300 points if you can spot the ringer!

1. "The Winslow Boy"; "The Yellow Rolls-Royce"; "Glory Alley"; "The Browning Version."
2. "The Wagons Roll at Night"; "Gung Ho"; "Paint Your Wagon"; "The Spoilers."
3. "Walk East on Beacon"; "I Love Melvin"; "Critic's Choice"; "A Slight Case of Larceny."
4. "The Adventures of Sherlock Holmes"; "Kidnapped"; "The Stranger"; "The House of Rothschild."
5. "Robin and the Seven Hoods"; "Harlow"; "Come Fill the Cup"; "The Last Time I Saw Archie."
6. "The King's Pirate"; "The D.I."; "Pete Kelly's Blues"; "Dragnet."
7. "The Petrified Forest"; "The Spirit of St. Louis"; "The Adventures of Marco Polo"; "A Night in Casablanca."
8. "The Little Minister"; "Sinbad the Sailor"; "A Kiss for Corliss"; "Bordertown."
9. "Walk East on Beacon"; "Mysterious Island"; "Sands of the Kalahari"; "Zulu."
10. "The Hound of the Baskervilles" (1939); "Swanee River"; "The Lemon Drop Kid"; "Operation Petticoat."
11. "The Indian Fighter"; "Flaming Feather"; "Slattery's Hurricane"; "House of Wax."
12. "Call Me Madam"; "The Mighty Barnum"; "Mother Wore Tights"; "The Great Impersonation."

13. "D.O.A."; "Tales of Manhattan"; "Lydia"; "Flesh and Fantasy."
14. "Great Expectations"; "Zaza"; "Suez"; "Brewster's Millions."
15. "Blonde Venus"; "The Great Gabbo"; "Shanghai Express"; "Jet Pilot."

_____points

(*Answers on page 224*)

33. SPOT THE RINGER—DUFFERS' TEE

Each question below has to do with a single director. And we should tell you (in case you're feeling picked on) the directors we're dealing with here are far better-known than the directors we worked over in the Buffs' version of this quiz. In each of the fifteen questions below, we list three films which were directed by the same director and one which was not. Your task is to isolate the feature which was *not* directed by the director responsible for the other three. For naming the director, you get 10 points—and for isolating the film within the four which that director did *not* direct, you get 10 points more. That's 20 points a question, or a possible 300 points if you can spot the ringer.

1. "The Hunchback of Notre Dame"; "Love Letters"; "Indiscreet"; "Portrait of Jennie."
2. "Tender Comrade"; "The Caine Mutiny"; "Trapeze"; "Crossfire."
3. "East of Eden"; "Man on a Tightrope"; "Sea of Grass"; "The High and the Mighty."
4. "Once More with Feeling"; "Charade"; "The Pajama Game"; "The War Lord."
5. "Captain Horatio Hornblower"; "Objective Burma"; "White Heat"; "The Professionals."
6. "Chimes at Midnight"; "The Trial"; "Lady from Shanghai"; "The Spirit of St. Louis."
7. "Darling Lili"; "A Shot in the Dark"; "Days of Wine and Roses"; "Crack in the World."
8. "Cool Hand Luke"; "Beau Geste"; "The Ox-Bow Incident"; "Battleground."
9. "The Day the Earth Stood Still"; "Executive Suite"; "Underworld U.S.A."; "West Side Story."
10. "Elmer Gantry"; "Sweet Bird of Youth"; "Lord Jim"; "Weekend at the Waldorf."
11. "Hondo"; "Wee Willie Winkie"; "Blaze of Noon"; "Alias Nick Beal."

12. "Patton"; "The Best Man"; "Planet of the Apes"; "A Night at the Opera."
13. "Kiss Me, Stupid"; "The Fortune Cookie"; "Sunset Boulevard"; "The Eve of St. Mark."
14. "Mr. Deeds Goes to Town"; "Dirigible"; "You Can't Take It with You"; "Craig's Wife."
15. "Fanny"; "Bus Stop"; "Panic in the Streets"; "Sayonara."

_____points

(Answers on page 225)

34. WHO SANG . . . ?

Below, in Column One, we list a number of song titles. Now, at the outset, we warn you that not all of these were big, full-blown Busby Berkeley-type production numbers. As a matter of fact, some of their presentations were rather modest. In Column Two (out of order, of course) you'll find listed the player or players who performed the songs, while in Column Three (also out of order) you'll find clues relating to the titles of the films in which the songs were included. So match the song to the performer and then to the film in which it was included, and take five points for each part completed correctly. With two parts per question, you can get 100 more points added to your score. Ready? Play, Don—

1. "I'm Writing a   A. Irving Berlin   a. "R_____ w__ B_____"
   Letter to
   Daddy"

2. "Night and   B. The Andrews   b. "T__ O_____ K__"
   Day"   Sisters

3. "Gettin' Corns c. Betty Hutton   c. "W__ E__ H_____
   for My   t__ B_____
   Country"   J_____?"

4. "I Don't Want   D. Frank Sinatra   d. "B_____ P_____"
   to Play in
   Your
   Yard"

68

5. "Oh, How I Hate to Get Up in the Morning"	E. Vivian Blaine	e. "T_____ I__ t__ A_____"
6. "You're a Lucky Fellow, Mr. Smith"	F. The Andrews Sisters	f. "S_____ F__"
7. "Isn't It Kinda Fun?"	G. Connie Gilchrist Judy Garland	g. "R_____ H__"
8. "Arthur Murray Taught Me Dancing in a Hurry"	H. Cass Daley	h. "T__ F_____'s I__"
9. "Ev'ry Little Movement Has a Meaning All Its Own"	I. James Cagney	i. "P_____ L__ M__"
10. "Willy, the Wolf of the West"	J. Bette Davis	j. "H_____ C_____"

_____points

(*Answers on page 225*)

34. WHO SANG . . . ?—DUFFERS' TEE

Below, in Column One, we list a number of song titles. Now, at the outset, we warn you that not all of these were big, full-blown Busby Berkeley-type production numbers. As a matter of fact, some of their presentations were rather modest. In Column Two, out of order, you'll find listed the player or players who performed the songs, while in Column Three, we have provided the titles of the films in which the songs were included. By the way, this Column Three is also listed out of order (what else?). We're giving 5 points for each part you complete correctly—so with two parts per question, you can get 100 more points for your ever growing score. Think about it, but don't move your lips while working on this quiz.

1. "I'm Writing a Letter to Daddy"   A. Irving Berlin   a. "Reveille with Beverly"

2. "Night and Day"   B. The Andrews Sisters   b. "The Oklahoma Kid"

3. "Gettin' Corns for My Country"   C. Betty Hutton   c. "What Ever Happened to Baby Jane?"

4. "I Don't Want to Play in Your Yard"   D. Frank Sinatra   d. "Buck Privates"

5. "Oh, How I Hate to Get Up in the Morning"   E. Vivian Blaine   e. "This Is the Army"

6. "You're a Lucky Fellow, Mr. Smith"   F. The Andrews Sisters   f. "State Fair"

7. "Isn't It Kinda Fun?"   G. Connie Gilchrist Judy Garland   g. "Riding High"

8. "Arthur Murray Taught Me Dancing in a Hurry"   H. Cass Daley   h. "The Fleet's In"

9. "Ev'ry Little Movement Has a Meaning All Its Own"   I. James Cagney   i. "Presenting Lily Mars"

10. "Willy, the Wolf of the West"   J. Bette Davis   j. "Hollywood Canteen"

_____points

(*Answers on page 225*)

35. THE LITTLE WOMAN

Below, we list a dozen triplets of film players. One of the things those in each triplet had in common—and on which we focus in this quiz—is that they all appeared as husbands to the same cinematic wife. In this exercise—THE LITTLE WOMAN—we'll give you 15 points for your correct deduction of the actress who played the wife. In addition, we'll allow you double score (!)—or 30 points—if you can come up with the film titles in which the marital relationship was included. So here's your chance for a fast 360 points. Grab it!

1. Charles Boyer, Henry Fonda, Fred MacMurray.
2. Brian Aherne, Paul Lukas, Errol Flynn.
3. Paul Henreid, Charles Boyer, Joseph Cotten.
4. Jeffrey Lynn, William Holden, Farley Granger.
5. Robert Young, Joel McCrea, Jackie Gleason.
6. John Lund, Cary Grant, Laurence Olivier.
7. Clark Gable, Glenn Ford, Macdonald Carey.
8. Fredric March, Don Ameche, John Forsythe.
9. Dana Andrews, Richard Conte, Ray Milland.
10. Rex Harrison, Paul Douglas, Dana Andrews.
11. Ralph Richardson, Peter O'Toole, Paul Henreid.
12. Philip Dorn, Alexander Knox, William Powell.

_____points

(*Answers on page 226*)

35. THE LITTLE WOMAN—DUFFERS' TEE

Below, we list a dozen triplets of film players. Listed with each player is a film in which he appeared. Each triplet in these films had one thing in common—the same cinematic wife. From these triplets of actors, and the related films, tell us the name of the actress we're seeking who played THE LITTLE WOMAN. Take 25 points for each correct answer!

1. Charles Boyer	"Tovarich"	
Henry Fonda	"Drums Along the Mohawk"	
Fred MacMurray	"The Egg and I"	_____
2. Brian Aherne	"Juarez"	
Paul Lukas	"Watch on the Rhine"	
Errol Flynn	"The Sisters"	_____
3. Paul Henreid	"Casablanca"	
Charles Boyer	"Gaslight"	
Joseph Cotten	"Under Capricorn"	_____

4. Jeffrey Lynn   "A Letter to Three Wives"

   William Holden   "Apartment for Peggy"

   Farley Granger   "O. Henry's Full House" _____

5. Robert Young   "Sitting Pretty"

   Joel McCrea   "Buffalo Bill"

   Jackie Gleason   "How Do I Love Thee" _____

6. John Lund   "Darling, How Could You!"

   Cary Grant   "Suspicion"

   Laurence Olivier   "Rebecca" _____

7. Clark Gable   "Homecoming"

   Glenn Ford   "Follow the Sun"

   Macdonald Carey   "My Wife's Best Friend" _____

8. Fredric March   "Bedtime Story"

   Don Ameche   "The Story of Alexander Graham Bell"

   John Forsythe   "It Happens Every Thursday" _____

9. Dana Andrews   "The Iron Curtain"

   Richard Conte   "Whirlpool"

   Ray Milland   "Close to My Heart" _____

10. Rex Harrison   "Unfaithfully Yours"

   Paul Douglas   "A Letter to Three Wives"

   Dana Andrews   "Zero Hour" _____

11. Ralph Richardson   "A Long Day's Journey into Night"

   Peter O'Toole   "The Lion in Winter"

   Paul Henreid   "Song of Love" _____

12. Philip Dorn   "I Remember Mama"

   Alexander Knox   "Over Twenty-one"

   William Powell   "Life with Father" _____

_____points

(*Answers on page 226*)

36. CONTINUED NEXT WEEK

We consider any cinematic basic training incomplete without a number of hours spent on Saturday afternoons waiting for the next installment of a breath-taking serial. It would seem impossible that the heroes could get out of the certain-death predicaments they found themselves in. But sure enough, they always managed—even though by the end of the installment, they'd face a fate even more horrendous. We've selected a number of serial titles and ask you to tell us who played the title role. These are toughies, so we're allowing 15 points for each correct answer—or a possible 225 points for the quiz.

1. "Nyoka and the Tigermen"   K _ _ A _ _ _ _ _ _ _
2. "The Mysterious Dr. Satan"   E _ _ _ _ _ _ C _ _ _ _ _ _ _ _
3. "Don Daredevil"   K _ _ C _ _ _ _ _
4. "Commando Cody, Sky Marshal of the Universe"   J _ _ _ _ H _ _ _ _ _ _
5. "Federal Operator 99"   M _ _ _ _ _ _ L _ _ _ _ _
6. "King of the Carnival"   H _ _ _ _ _ L _ _ _ _ _
7. "Man with the Steel Whip"   R _ _ _ _ _ _ _ S _ _ _ _ _ _ _
8. "King of Jungleland"   C _ _ _ _ _ B _ _ _ _ _
9. "Panther Girl of the Kongo"   P _ _ _ _ _ _ _ C _ _ _ _ _
10. "King of the Texas Rangers"   S _ _ _ _ _ B _ _ _ _ _
11. "Zorro's Fighting Legion"   R _ _ _ H _ _ _ _ _ _
12. "King of the Rocket Men"   T _ _ _ _ _ _ _ _ C _ _ _ _ _ _
13. "The Purple Monster Strikes"   R _ _ B _ _ _ _ _ _ _ _
14. "Burn 'Em Up Barnes"   J _ _ _ M _ _ _ _ _ _ _
15. "Zorro Rides Again"   J _ _ _ C _ _ _ _ _ _ _

_____points

(*Answers on page 227*)

36. CONTINUED NEXT WEEK—DUFFERS' TEE

As we told the Buffs, it is expected that a fan of the movies be conversant with the talents of Peckinpah, Milos Forman, Ingmar Bergman, and Antonioni . . . but the real movie fan can't claim all his stripes unless he spent a number of youthful hours huddled in for a double feature and the week's installment of a hair-raising serial. Each week our dauntless hero faced certain death, only to be rescued or saved at the last minute so that he could find himself in another certain-death situation minutes later, to be followed by that hateful phrase: "Continued Next Week." Below, in Column One, we have listed a number of favorite old serials. In Column Two, out of order, we have listed those players who limned the title role of the serials in Column One. Your job is to match up the proper player from Column Two with the correct serial title from Column One. Take 15 points for each correct matching you make. And good luck!

1. "Nyoka and the Tigermen"	a.	Judd Holden
2. "The Mysterious Dr. Satan"	b.	Sammy Baugh
3. "Don Daredevil"	c.	Roy Barcroft
4. "Commando Cody, Sky Marshal of the Universe"	d.	Kay Aldridge
5. "Federal Operator 99"	e.	Eduardo Ciannelli
6. "King of the Carnival"	f.	Richard Simmons
7. "Man with the Steel Whip"	g.	Jack Mulhall
8. "King of Jungleland"	h.	Reed Hadley
9. "Panther Girl of the Kongo"	i.	John Carroll
10. "King of the Texas Rangers"	j.	Harry Lauter
11. "Zorro's Fighting Legion"	k.	Ken Curtis
12. "King of the Rocket Men"	l.	Phyllis Coates
13. "The Purple Monster Strikes"	m.	Tristram Coffin
14. "Burn 'Em Up Barnes"	n.	Clyde Beatty
15. "Zorro Rides Again"	o.	Marten Lamont

_____points

(*Answers on page 227*)

37. MORE "NAME THE STAR"

Once again, we ask you to NAME THE STAR—and we warn you, things are getting tougher. If you want to go out for popcorn and skip this one, we'll understand. But if you want to pile up points, here's a way to grab a fast 400 points. As we said, these are a little bit tougher, so we're awarding 10 points for each star you name correctly that is represented by the characters in the two columns below. If you can also name the *films* in which our elusive star played each role you make an additional 15 points for each such title. That's a possible 10 points on naming the star, plus 30 more points for naming the two features involved. Good luck!

1. Ted Barrie	Jamiel
2. Helen Bartlett	Irene Bullock
3. Sorrowful Jones	Jim O'Connor
4. Asher Gomer	Jean Lafitte
5. Lionel Durand	Jacques De Lisle
6. Harriet Putnam	Edna Philby
7. Mayor Orden	Horace P. Bogardus
8. The Missouri Kid	Judge Purcell
9. Hjalmar Poelzig	Baron Ledrantz
10. Icarus Xenophon	E. K. Hornbeck

_____points

(*Answers on page 227*)

37. MORE "NAME THE STAR"—DUFFERS' TEE

It's time to NAME THE STAR again—and let us warn you, things are getting tougher. The Buffs' version of MORE "NAME THE STAR" was a rough road, and this Duffers' version is little better. But if you stick to it and wrack your memory, you might escape unscathed. Again, from the two characters in Columns One and Two below, you must name the star who played both those characters. Come up with the name of the star, and you get 10 points. Come up also with the titles of the two films represented, and take 15 points for each correct title. That's a possible 40 points per question. Why, it's a veritable bonanza!

1. Lao Er	Aesop
2. Maria Tura	Hazel Flagg
3. Nikolai Nicoleff	General Broulard
4. Rameses II	Taras Bulba
5. King Louis XVI	Capt. Pierre Matard
6. Shannon Prentiss	Rose of Cimarron
7. The Angel Clarence	Eugene Curie
8. Herbert Gelman	Father Ned Halley
9. Chief Guyasuta	General Pherides
10. Harry Palmer	Don Lockwood

_____points

(*Answers on page 228*)

38. WHAT SEEMS TO BE THE PROBLEM?

Though Hollywood itself has put great emphasis on physical perfection, a number of Hollywood plots have leaned heavily on physical (and mental) *im*perfections. Below, we provide two columns of clues. Column One lists a player and a film in which that player suffered some affliction. In Column Two, we list (out of order) an equal number of *different* players. Each of those listed in Column Two (in one of his or her films) suffered the same affliction as the victims in Column One. Your task is to (a) recall the affliction suffered by the players in Column One, and (b) match the proper player from Column Two with the appropriate victim of Column One. We'll award 20 points for each proper pairing. Moreover, if you can provide the *title* of the film in which the Column Two player portrayed the sufferer of the affliction in question, we'll let you have an additional 30 points. That's a possible 50 points per question—or a potential score of 600 points! Don't worry, nurse—it only hurts when we laugh!

1. Charles Laughton "The Hunchback of Notre Dame"	a. Sam Jaffe	_____
2. Peter Ustinov "The Egyptian"	b. Ronald Colman	_____
3. Edward Arnold "The Night Has a Thousand Eyes"	c. Gene Kelly	_____
4. Lionel Atwill "Son of Frankenstein"	d. Boris Karloff	_____
5. Wallace Beery "Treasure Island"	e. James Cagney	_____
6. Gregory Peck "Mirage"	f. Marty Feldman	_____
7. Joan Leslie "High Sierra"	g. Tyrone Power	_____
8. Audrey Hepburn "Wait Until Dark"	h. John Wayne	_____
9. Marlon Brando "One-Eyed Jacks"	i. Wallace Beery	_____

76

10. Karl Malden   j. Jane Wyman   _____
"Operation Secret"

11. Ray Milland   k. Richard   _____
"The Lost Weekend"   Widmark

12. Dorothy McGuire   l. Gene   _____
"The Spiral Staircase"   Hackman

_____points

(Answers on page 229)

38. WHAT SEEMS TO BE THE PROBLEM?—DUFFERS' TEE

Though Hollywood itself has put great emphasis on physical perfection, a number of Hollywood plots have leaned heavily on physical (and mental) *im*perfections. Below, we provide two columns of clues. Column One lists a player and a film in which that player suffered some affliction. In Column Two, we list (out of order) an equal numbers of players, and the films in which each suffered the *same* affliction. Your task is to pair the victims, with the particular affliction being the common characteristic for the pairing. We'll award 25 points for each correct pairing. And if you can identify the common affliction correctly, we'll award an additional 25 points. So with a possible 50 points per question, you can fatten your score by 600 points! Your son will never play the violin again—but he'll play a helluva bass drum!

1. Charles Laughton   a. Sam Jaffe
"The Hunchback of Notre   "Lost
Dame"   Horizon"   _____

2. Peter Ustinov   b. Ronald
"The Egyptian"   Colman
     "Random
     Harvest"   _____

3. Edward Arnold   c. Gene Kelly
"The Night Has a Thousand   "For Me and
Eyes"   My Gal"   _____

4. Lionel Atwill   d. Boris Karloff
"Son of Frankenstein"   "Tower of
     London"   _____

5. Wallace Beery "Treasure Island"	e. James Cagney "City for Conquest"	_____
6. Gregory Peck "Mirage"	f. Marty Feldman "Young Frankenstein"	_____
7. Joan Leslie "High Sierra"	g. Tyrone Power "Nightmare Alley"	_____
8. Audrey Hepburn "Wait Until Dark"	h. John Wayne "True Grit"	_____
9. Marlon Brando "One-Eyed Jacks"	i. Wallace Beery "O'Shaughnessy's Boy"	_____
10. Karl Malden "Operation Secret"	j. Jane Wyman "Johnny Belinda"	_____
11. Ray Milland "The Lost Weekend"	k. Richard Widmark "Alvarez Kelly"	_____
12. Dorothy McGuire "The Spiral Staircase"	l. Gene Hackman "Young Frankenstein"	_____

_____points

(*Answers on page 229*)

39. THE BIG BULB PART III

We are again looking at THE BIG BULB and those Hollywood names who moved their talents over from the large screen to the small screen. Below, in Column One, we list sixteen such names that were well-established in feature films. In Column Two, we provide a suggestion of those series in which our stars gained new-found fame. Complete the titles suggested in Column Two by filling in the blanks correctly, and you may add 15 points to your score for each one you get correct. Don't touch that dial!

1. Fred MacMurray   "M _ T _ _ _ _ _ S _ _ _"
2. Charlie Ruggles   "T _ _ W _ _ _ _ o _ M _.
           S _ _ _ _ _ _"

3.	Eddie Albert	"G _ _ _ _ _ A _ _ _ _ _"
4.	Brandon de Wilde	"J _ _ _ _ _"
5.	Marshall Thompson	"A _ _ _ _ _"
6.	William Demarest	"L _ _ _ a _ _ M _ _ _ _ _ _ _ _"
7.	Jackie Cooper	"T _ _ P _ _ _ _ _ _ ' C _ _ _ _ _ _"
8.	Pat O'Brien	"H _ _ _ _ _ _ _ _ a _ _ S _ _"
9.	Robert Young	"F _ _ _ _ _ K _ _ _ _ _ B _ _ _"
10.	William Bendix	"T _ _ L _ _ _ o _ R _ _ _ _"
11.	William Lundigan	"M _ _ i _ _ _ S _ _ _ _"
12.	Richard Greene	"R _ _ _ _ _ H _ _ _"
13.	Robert Stack	"T _ _ U _ _ _ _ _ _ _ _ _ _"
14.	Edmund Lowe	"F _ _ _ _ _ P _ _ _ D _ _ _ _ _ _ _ _"
15.	Barry Sullivan	"T _ _ _ _ _ _ _ _ _ _ _ _ 'X' "
16.	Richard Basehart	"V _ _ _ _ _ _ t _ t _ _ B _ _ _ _ _ _ o _ t _ _ S _ _"

_____points

(Answers on page 230)

39. THE BIG BULB PART III—DUFFERS' TEE

We are again looking at THE BIG BULB and those Hollywood names who moved their talents over from the large screen to the small screen. Below, in Column One, we list a number of such names that were well-established in feature films. In Column Two, out of order, we list the series in which the same names gained new-found fame on television. Your task is to match the talent from Column One with the appropriate TV series in Column Two. You may add 15 points to your score for each correct pairing. Don't touch that dial!

1. Fred MacMurray	a. "Love and Marriage"
2. Charlie Ruggles	b. "The People's Choice"
3. Eddie Albert	c. "Robin Hood"
4. Brandon de Wilde	d. "Men into Space"
5. Marshall Thompson	e. "Voyage to the Bottom of the Sea"
6. William Demarest	f. "Front Page Detective"
7. Jackie Cooper	g. "My Three Sons"
8. Pat O'Brien	h. "The Man Called 'X' "
9. Robert Young	i. "The World of Mr. Sweeney"

79

10. William Bendix	j. "The Untouchables"
11. William Lundigan	k. "Green Acres"
12. Richard Greene	l. "Harrigan and Son"
13. Robert Stack	m. "Angel"
14. Edmund Lowe	n. "Jamie"
15. Barry Sullivan	o. "Father Knows Best"
16. Richard Basehart	p. "The Life of Riley"

_____points

(*Answers on page 230*)

40. WILD CARD—BUFFS AND DUFFERS

Here's one both Buffs and Duffers can work on—and the only difference is that we're awarding different point values. Read the letter printed below, and keep track of the many movie titles you detect. You may have 10 points for each title you uncover if you've been playing the Duffers' Tee. But take only 5 points per title if you've been playing as a Buff. Now, you're on your honor . . . !

HOTEL PARADISO
13 Rue Madeleine

The night of January 16th

Dear Ruth:

So this is Paris! Having wonderful time. My room at the top of the small hotel is great. Room 43. From the window, I can see the Cafe Metropole and there's a great view of the city across the river. My room has a canopied bed, and I sleep in the four poster like a baby. There are the table and the twelve chairs, and room for one more—though I don't know why I'd need the thirteenth chair.

I bumped into David and Lisa, and we were asked to attend a royal wedding. It was very nice, except the bride wore red, and with the blue veil yet! The father of the bride—H. M. Pulham, Esq.—sent an invitation to a gunfighter named Mr. Buddwing, and the reception was a place for lovers. They say that any number can play, but actually, only two can play. I asked Marnie if she was a bride by mistake or whether the bride came C.O.D.—the lady said "no"! There was splendor in the grass in the red tent, but the wild party was inside. Daisy Clover was there with B.F.'s daughter, and Mildred Pierce was with Alice Adams. She needs help!

Mongo's back in town. I met him in Paris, and he couldn't say "no"! Dynamite! We're a twosome in name only, but I'll get by. Do you remember last night? We had a rendezvous at midnight, and it was a night

80

to remember. There's something about Paris after dark. I'll never forget what's 'is name! Oh, boy!

Marty had a date with Judy—but the girl can't help it. Mother didn't tell me it's a man's world, but Pop always pays. Oh well—play it as it lays! I'm from Missouri! I'll be seeing you . . .

Sincerely yours,
Julie

_____points

(*Answers on page 230*)

41. THE MEN FROM THE BOYS

The story line of a number of films spans many years, and frequently we watch the aging process as it transforms our hero from stripling to senior citizen. This quiz is concerned with those instances where we meet the hero as a lad, and after a reel or so—and perhaps a slow dissolve—he is magically transformed into our favorite movie hero. Below, in Column One, we list a number of titles in which this phenomenon is included. In Column Two, we list the young actor who portrayed the character as a boy. In Column Four, we ask you to tell us the name of the actor who portrayed the grown-up version of the character. As an added clue, we've added the character name involved, and you'll find these aids in Column Three. Take 15 points for each grown-up actor you can identify.

1. "Young Man with a Horn"	Orley Lindgren	Rick	K_____	D_____
2. "Blood and Sand"	Rex Downing	Juan	T_____	P_____
3. "Lloyds of London"	Freddie Bartholomew	Jonathan	T_____	P_____
4. "The Egyptian"	Peter Reynolds	Sinuhe	E_____	P_____
5. "Manhattan Melodrama"	Mickey Rooney	Blackie	C_____	G_____
6. "The Adventures of Mark Twain"	Jackie Brown	Sam	F_____	M_____
7. "The Light That Failed"	Ronald Sinclair	Dick	R_____	C_____
8. "Heaven Can Wait"	Scotty Beckett	Henry	D_____	A_____

9.	"The Great Caruso"	Peter Price	Enrico	M_____ L_____
10.	"Follow the Sun"	Harold Blade	Ben	G_____ F_____
11.	"There's No Business Like Show Business"	Billy Chapin	Steve	J_____ R_____
12.	"Angels with Dirty Faces"	William Tracy	Jerry	P_____ O'_____
13.	"Public Enemy"	Frankie Darro	Matt	E_____ W_____
14.	"Beau Geste"	Billy Cook	John	R_____ M_____
15.	"Beau Geste"	Martin Spellman	Digby	R_____ P_____

_____points

(*Answers on page 231*)

41. THE MEN FROM THE BOYS—DUFFERS' TEE

The story line of a number of films spans many years, and frequently we watch the aging process as it transforms our hero from stripling to senior citizen. This quiz is concerned with those instances where we meet the hero as a lad, and after a reel or so—and perhaps a slow dissolve—he is magically transformed into our favorite movie hero! Below, in Column One, we list a number of films in which this phenomenon is included. In Column Two, we list the young actor who played the character as a boy—and as an added clue we have listed the *name* of the character in Column Three. From the out-of-order list in Column Four, select the adult actor who portrayed the character as an adult. For every correct matching of the grownup to the boy, you may claim 15 points for your score.

1.	"Young Man with a Horn"	Orley Lindgren	Rick	a. Glenn Ford
2.	"Blood and Sand"	Rex Downing	Juan	b. Johnnie Ray
3.	"Lloyds of London"	Freddie Bartholomew	Jonathan	c. Ray Milland
4.	"The Egyptian"	Peter Reynolds	Sinuhe	d. Kirk Douglas
5.	"Manhattan Melodrama"	Mickey Rooney	Blackie	e. Mario Lanza

82

6. "The Adventures of Mark Twain"	Jackie Brown	Sam	f. Robert Preston
7. "The Light That Failed"	Ronald Sinclair	Dick	g. Tyrone Power
8. "Heaven Can Wait"	Scotty Beckett	Henry	h. Edmund Purdom
9. "The Great Caruso"	Peter Price	Enrico	i. Edward Woods
10. "Follow the Sun"	Harold Blade	Ben	j. Don Ameche
11. "There's No Business Like Show Business"	Billy Chapin	Steve	k. Clark Gable
12. "Angels with Dirty Faces"	William Tracy	Jerry	l. Ronald Colman
13. "Public Enemy"	Frankie Darro	Matt	m. Tyrone Power
14. "Beau Geste"	Billy Cook	John	n. Fredric March
15. "Beau Geste"	Martin Spellman	Digby	o. Pat O'Brien

_____points

(*Answers on page 231*)

42. HOW MANY CAN YOU GET?

Here's a game we play with other movie buffs, and we're passing it on to you. Basically, one player names a movie and challenges his opponent to come up with as many recognizable player names who appeared in the picture as he can. Stars, of course, are a starting point, but the expert gets into supporting roles, and even bit players *who received billing.* No fair coming up with Aunt Effie or Cousin Ernie, who, as extras, stood at the rear of a crowd scene murmuring, "Rhubarb, rhubarb." In this version of HOW MANY CAN YOU GET?, we'll name a feature and expect you to fill in the blanks with the names we're seeking. You get 5 points for each name you fill in correctly.

1. "It Happened One Night"
   (2 players)

        ___r_ __b__

        _____d_____ ___b___

2. "Mr. Blandings Builds His
   Dream House" (3
   players)

        __r_ _____

        __r__ ___

        ___v__ ____l__

3. "Singin' in the Rain" (4
   players)

        ____ __l__

        _____ _e_____

        _____d _'__n___

        ____ ____n

4. "Beau Geste" (5 players)

        __r_ ___p__

        ___ _____nd

        _o____ _r____n

        ___a_ __n____

        ___a_ _____r_

5. "The Last Angry Man" (6
   players)

        ____ __n_

        __v__ _____

        ____y _____

        _____ _d___

        _____ __n___

        __b_ __k__

6. "Edge of Darkness" (7
   players)

        _____ __y__

        ___ _____d__

        _____ ___t__

        ____y _____

        _____ ___t___

        _____ __d_____

        ____ ___d__

7. "Anatomy of a Murder" (8
   players)

        _____ ___w___

        ___ _____c_

        ___ ____r_

        _____ _'_____

        _v_ _____

        _____y_ __n_

        _____ C. _____

        _____ _____t__

8. "Lawrence of Arabia" (9
   players)

        _____ _'_____

        ____ ____n___

        _____ ___n_

        ____ _____n_

        ____ ___r__

        ____ ____r

        _____ ___n_

9. "From Here to Eternity" (10 players)

```
_ _ _ _ _ _ _ _   _ _ _ _ l _
_ _ _ h _ _   _ _ _ _ _ _ _
_ _ _ _ _   _ _ n _ _ _ _ _ _
_ _ _ _ g _ _ _ _ _   _ _ _ _ _
_ e _ _ _ _ h   _ _ _ _
_ _ _ n _ _   _ _ n _ _ _ _
_ _ n _ _   _ _ _ _
_ _ _ _ _ _ _   _ b _ _
_ _ _ _ _ _
_ h _ _ _ _ _ _ _ _ _
```

10. "Citizen Kane" (11 players)

```
_ _ _ _ _   _ _ _ _ _ v _ _
_ _ n _ _ _   _ _ _ _ _ _ _ n _
_ _ _ _   _ _ _ _ _ n
_ _ _ _ _   _ _ l _ _ _
_ _ _ _ _ _   _ _ _ _ _ _ n
_ _ _ _   _ _ _ _ _ _ k
_ _ _ _ _ _ _ _   _ _ _ _ _ _ _ r _
_ v _ _ _ _ _   _ _ _ _ n _
_ _ _   _ _ _ _ _ n _
_ _ _ r _ _   _ _ _ _ _ _ _ r _ _
_ _ n _ _   _ _ _ r _ _ _ _ d
```

11. "Casablanca" (12 players)

```
_ _ _ _   _ _ _ w _ _ _
_ _ r r _   _ _ _ n _ _ n
_ _ _ _ _ _ n _ _   _ _ _ _ _ _ _ v _
_ _ _ _ _ _ _ _ _   _ _ _ _ r _
_ _ _ r _ _   _ _ _ _ _ _ n
_ _ _ _   _ _ _ _ _ _ d
_ _ _ _ _ _   _ _ _ n _
_ _ _ _ _ _   _ _ _ d _
_ _ _ n _ _
_ _ _ _ _ _ _ _ _ _ t
_ _ _ _ _   _ _ _ r _
_ . _ .   _ _ _ _ _ l
_ _ _ _ _ _   _ _ _ _ _ n
_ _ _   _ _ _ _ _ n
_ _ _ n _ _   _ _ _ _ k _ _
_ _ _ _ _ _   _ _ _ _ _ n _
```

_____points

(*Answers on page 232*)

42. HOW MANY CAN YOU GET?—DUFFERS' TEE

Here is a version of a game we play with other movie buffs, and we're passing it on to you, albeit in a somewhat simplified version—because, after all, this *is* the Duffers' Tee (no pun intended). Basically, one player names a movie and challenges his opponent to come up with as many recognizable player names who appeared in the movie as he can. Stars, of course, are a starting point, but the true expert gets into supporting roles, and even bit players *who received billing*. No fair coming up with Aunt Effie or Cousin Ernie, who, as extras, stood at the rear of a crowd murmuring, "Rhubarb, rhubarb." In this version of HOW MANY CAN YOU GET?, we'll name a feature and tell you how many player names we expect you to come up with. We asked the Buffs to fill in blanks, but this version is slightly different. We name eleven features, as you'll see (in Column One), and ask you to supply in Column Two *precisely* the number of player names we request. You must take the names from those we have provided in Column Three, at the right of the page. There are seventy-seven cast blanks to be assigned, and precisely seventy-five names for you to draw from. (Trust us!) So move carefully, and we'll give you one tip—two names, and only two names, are repeated. You may have 5 points for each proper assignment of a player name to the correct feature. That's a possible score of 385 points on this quiz. Go get 'em!

1. "It Happened One Night" (2 players)   ____ ____
   ____ ____

2. "Mr. Blandings Builds His Dream House" (3 players)   ____ ____
   ____ ____

3. "Singin' in the Rain" (4 players)   ____ ____
   ____ ____
   ____ ____

4. "Beau Geste" (5 players)   ____ ____
   ____ ____

a. Luther Adler
b. Judith Anderson
c. Eve Arden
d. Joby Baker
e. Harry Bellaver
f. Ingrid Bergman
g. Humphrey Bogart
h. Fortunio Bonanova
i. Ernest Borgnine
j. Montgomery Clift
k. Claudette Colbert

	＿＿＿ ＿＿＿	l.	Nancy Coleman
	＿＿＿ ＿＿＿	m.	Ray Collins
	＿＿＿ ＿＿＿	n.	Dorothy Comingore
5. "The Last Angry Man" (6 players)	＿＿＿ ＿＿＿	o.	Gary Cooper
	＿＿＿ ＿＿＿	p.	Joseph Cotten
	＿＿＿ ＿＿＿	q.	George Coulouris
	＿＿＿ ＿＿＿	r.	Helmut Dantine
	＿＿＿ ＿＿＿	s.	Brian Donlevy
	＿＿＿ ＿＿＿	t.	Melvyn Douglas
6. "Edge of Darkness" (7 players)	＿＿＿ ＿＿＿	u.	Jose Ferrer
	＿＿＿ ＿＿＿	v.	Errol Flynn
	＿＿＿ ＿＿＿	w.	Clark Gable
	＿＿＿ ＿＿＿	x.	Ben Gazzara
	＿＿＿ ＿＿＿	y.	Ruth Gordon
	＿＿＿ ＿＿＿	z.	Cary Grant
	＿＿＿ ＿＿＿	A.	Kathryn Grant
7. "Anatomy of a Murder" (8 players)	＿＿＿ ＿＿＿	B.	Sydney Greenstreet
	＿＿＿ ＿＿＿	C.	Alec Guinness
	＿＿＿ ＿＿＿	D.	Jean Hagen
	＿＿＿ ＿＿＿	E.	Murray Hamilton
	＿＿＿ ＿＿＿	F.	Jack Hawkins
	＿＿＿ ＿＿＿	G.	Susan Hayward
	＿＿＿ ＿＿＿	H.	Paul Henreid
	＿＿＿ ＿＿＿	I.	Walter Huston
8. "Lawrence of Arabia" (9 players)	＿＿＿ ＿＿＿	J.	Gene Kelly
	＿＿＿ ＿＿＿	K.	Arthur Kennedy
	＿＿＿ ＿＿＿	L.	Deborah Kerr
	＿＿＿ ＿＿＿	M.	Leonid Kinskey
	＿＿＿ ＿＿＿	N.	Burt Lancaster
	＿＿＿ ＿＿＿	O.	Peter Lorre
	＿＿＿ ＿＿＿	P.	Myrna Loy
	＿＿＿ ＿＿＿	Q.	Claudia McNeil
	＿＿＿ ＿＿＿	R.	Ray Milland
9. "From Here to Eternity" (10 players)	＿＿＿ ＿＿＿	S.	Agnes Moorehead
	＿＿＿ ＿＿＿	T.	Paul Muni
	＿＿＿ ＿＿＿	U.	Philip Ober
	＿＿＿ ＿＿＿	V.	Arthur O'Connell

87

		w. Donald O'Connor
		x. Peter O'Toole
___ ___		Y. Betsy Palmer
___ ___		z. Robert Preston
___ ___		aa. John Qualen
___ ___		bb. Anthony Quayle

10. "Citizen Kane"
    (11 players)

cc. Anthony Quinn
dd. Claude Rains
ee. Donna Reed
ff. Lee Remick
gg. Debbie Reynolds
hh. S. Z. Sakall
ii. George C. Scott
jj. Harry Shannon
kk. Omar Sharif
ll. Mickey Shaughnessy
mm. Ann Sheridan

11. "Casablanca"
    (12 players)

nn. Frank Sinatra
oo. Everett Sloane
pp. James Stewart
qq. Paul Stewart
rr. Conrad Veidt
ss. Jack Warden
tt. Ruth Warrick
uu. David Wayne
vv. Dooley Wilson
ww. Orson Welles

_____points

(*Answers on page 232*)

43. THE MAN

No, we're not speaking of the screen adaptation of Irving Wallace's novel, starring James Earl Jones. But there were a number of other films which centered on "The Man" or "A Man"—and your task in this quiz is to tell us the name of the star we're seeking. One clue: the star did not necessarily portray the title role; i.e., he was not necessarily "The Man"—though he is closely identified with the film itself. You may have 15 points for each correct answer.

 1. "The Man in the Net"   A_____   L_____
 2. "The Man on the Eiffel Tower"   F_____   T_____
 3. "The Man Who Came to Dinner"   M_____   W_____
 4. "The Man Who Could Work
         Miracles"   R_____   Y_____
 5. "Little Big Man"   D_____   H_____
 6. "The Man in the Gray Flannel Suit" G_____   P_____
 7. "Man in the Attic"   J_____   P_____
 8. "Man of Conquest"   R_____   D_____
 9. "The Man Who Never Was"   C_____   W_____
10. "The Sheepman"   G_____   F_____
11. "The Man from Down Under"   C_____   L_____
12. "The Third Man"   O_____   W_____
13. "The Best Man"   C_____   R_____
14. "The Man in the Iron Mask"   L_____   H_____
15. "The Man in Half Moon Street"   N_____   A_____
16. "The Illustrated Man"   R_____   S_____
17. "The Wrong Man"   H_____   F_____
18. "The Man Who Knew Too Much"   J_____   S_____
19. "The Man from the Diners' Club"   D_____   K_____
20. "The Quiet Man"   J_____   W_____

                                       _____points

(*Answers on page 234*)

43. THE MAN—DUFFERS' TEE

In this quiz, we're not speaking only of the screen adaptation of Irving Wallace's novel, starring James Earl Jones. But there were a number of other films which centered on "The Man" or "A Man"— and your task in this quiz is to match the title of the film (from Column One) with the appropriate star of that film (from Column Two). We warn you now that the crux of the quiz is *which* star. If you select a star other than the one which we're seeking (even though *your* choice may have appeared in the film), you may have used a name which should be used for another title. There are twenty questions and twenty possible answers—and each star name may be used only once. So tread slowly, and carry a big eraser. Take 20 points for each correct pairing *after* you've finished with the whole bloomin' mess!

1.	"The Man in the Net"	a.	Clifton Webb
2.	"The Man on the Eiffel Tower"	b.	Jack Palance
3.	"The Man Who Came to Dinner"	c.	Glenn Ford
4.	"The Man Who Could Work Miracles"	d.	Henry Fonda
5.	"Little Big Man"	e.	Nils Asther
6.	"The Man in the Gray Flannel Suit"	f.	Louis Hayward
7.	"Man in the Attic"	g.	John Wayne
8.	"Man of Conquest"	h.	Roland Young
9.	"The Man Who Never Was"	i.	Franchot Tone
10.	"The Sheepman"	j.	Monty Woolley
11.	"The Man from Down Under"	k.	James Stewart
12.	"The Third Man"	l.	Danny Kaye
13.	"The Best Man"	m.	Rod Steiger
14.	"The Man in the Iron Mask"	n.	Dustin Hoffman
15.	"The Man in Half Moon Street"	o.	Richard Dix
16.	"The Illustrated Man"	p.	Gregory Peck
17.	"The Wrong Man"	q.	Orson Welles
18.	"The Man Who Knew Too Much"	r.	Alan Ladd
19.	"The Man from the Diners' Club"	s.	Charles Laughton
20.	"The Quiet Man"	t.	Cliff Robertson

_____points

(*Answers on page 234*)

44. ANYTHING YOU CAN DO, I CAN DO BETTER PART II

Again, we're zeroing in on instances where two different players have portrayed the same real-life character, though in different films (what else?). A list of players is provided for you in Column One, while Column Two is a list of players all of whom also portrayed these same characters. Your task is to pair the two players who portrayed the same character—and win 5 points for each correct pairing. You may have 10 additional points for identifying the historical character in question. And again, you can have 10 more *points* for identifying each film in which these portrayals were included. You can fatten up your tally (presuming you *want* a fattened-up tally) by 350 points on this quiz alone! Honest!!

	CHARACTER	TITLE	TITLE
1. Charles Laughton	A. Robert Shaw	_____	___ ___
2. Sidney Blackmer	B. John Derek	_____	___ ___
3. Thomas Mitchell	C. Richard Todd	_____	___ ___
4. Louis Calhern	D. Simon Ward	_____	___ ___
5. Bobby Watson	E. James Ellison	_____	___ ___
6. Francis McDonald	F. Burt Lancaster	_____	___ ___
7. Vincent Price	G. Peter Ustinov	_____	___ ___
8. Henry Wilcoxon	H. Brian Keith	_____	___ ___
9. Ronald Reagan	I. Richard Basehart	_____	___ ___
10. Dudley Field Malone	J. Marlon Brando	_____	___ ___

_____points

(*Answers on page 235*)

44. ANYTHING YOU CAN DO, I CAN DO BETTER PART II—DUFFERS' TEE

As before, we have provided in Column One below the name of a player, as well as the name of a historical character he portrayed—plus the film in which the portrayal was included. In Column Two, out of order, there is a list of players who also portrayed these same characters. Your task is to match the correct player from Column Two with the appropriate player in Column One. A correct pairing will give you 15 points. But from the (also) out-of-order list of film titles in Column Three, you are to select the film in which the portrayal indicated in Column Two was included—and you must match it with the correct pairing from Columns One and Two in order to receive 15 *more* points. Okay, Gracie—once again from the top. Match Column Two to Column One (player to player) and Column Three to Column Two. So there you have it—a possible 300 points! Good night, George!

1. Charles Laughton; Nero in "Sign of the Cross"	A. Robert Shaw	a. "Young Winston"
2. Sidney Blackmer; Theodore Roosevelt in "My Girl Tisa"	B. John Derek	b. "Julius Caesar"

3. Thomas Mitchell; Ned Buntline in "Buffalo Bill"

C. Richard Todd

c. "The Wind and the Lion"

4. Louis Calhern; Buffalo Bill in "Annie Get Your Gun"

D. Simon Ward

d. "Prince of Players"

5. Bobby Watson; Adolf Hitler in "The Hitler Gang"

E. James Ellison

e. "Custer of the West"

6. Francis McDonald; John Wilkes Booth in "The Prisoner of Shark Island"

F. Burt Lancaster

f. "Hitler"

7. Vincent Price; Sir Walter Raleigh in "The Private Lives of Elizabeth and Essex"

G. Peter Ustinov

g. "The Plainsman"

8. Henry Wilcoxon; Marc Antony in "Cleopatra"

H. Brian Keith

h. "The Virgin Queen"

9. Ronald Reagan; Gen. George A. Custer in "Santa Fe Trail"

I. Richard Basehart

i. "Quo Vadis"

10. Dudley Field Malone; Winston Churchill in "Mission to Moscow"

J. Marlon Brando

j. "Buffalo Bill and the Indians, or Sitting Bull's History Lesson"

_____points

(*Answers on page 235*)

45. BUCKLE MY SWASH!

The adventure has always been a staple of many Hollywood plots —and the inclusion of the word "Adventures" in a number of titles promised thrills and excitement. Below, we list a number of such films—all of which had "Adventures" in the title. In Column One, we provide you with the star who experienced these adventures, and ask you to complete the title by filling out the blanks in Column Two. You may have 15 points for each title correctly completed.

1. Richard Beymer   "Adventures of _ _ _ _ _ _ _ _ _ _"
2. Jean Collins   "The Adventures of _ _ _ _ _"
3. Gary Cooper   "The Adventures of _ _ _ _ _ _ _ _ _"
4. Arturo de Cordova   "The Adventures of _ _ _ _ _ _ _ _"
5. John Derek   "The Adventures of _ _ _ _ _ _ _ _ _"
6. Robert Donat   "The Adventures of _ _ _ _ _"
7. Errol Flynn   "The Adventures of _ _ _ _ _ _ _ _ _"
8. Errol Flynn   "The Adventures of _ _ _ _ _ _ _"
9. Errol Flynn   "The Adventures of _ _ _ _ . _ _ _ _ _ _ _"
10. Eddie Hodges   "The Adventures of _ _ _ _ _ _ _ _ _ _ _ _ _ _ _"
11. Tommy Kelly   "The Adventures of _ _ _ _ _ _ _ _ _"
12. Fredric March   "The Adventures of _ _ _ _ _ _ _ _ _"
13. Kim Novak   "The Amorous Adventures of _ _ _ _ _ _ _ _ _ _ _ _"
14. Jean Parker   "The Adventures of _ _ _ _ _ _ _ _ _ _"
15. Basil Rathbone   "The Adventures of _ _ _ _ _ _ _ _ _ _ _ _ _ _"

_____points

(*Answers on page 236*)

45. BUCKLE MY SWASH!—DUFFERS' TEE

The adventure has long been a staple of many Hollywood plots—and the inclusion of the word "Adventures" in a number of titles promised thrills and excitement. Below, we list a number of such films—all of which had "Adventures" in the title. Match the player from Column One who starred in the adventurous title of Column Two, and you may have 15 points for each correct pairing.

1. Richard Beymer   a. "The Adventures of Tartu"
2. Joan Collins   b. "The Adventures of Mark Twain"
3. Gary Cooper   c. "The Adventures of Capt. Fabian"
4. Arturo de Cordova   d. "The Adventures of Huckleberry Finn"
5. John Derek   e. "The Adventures of Sherlock Holmes"
6. Robert Donat   f. "The Adventures of Tom Sawyer"

7. Errol Flynn	g. "The Adventures of Hajji Baba"
8. Errol Flynn	h. "The Adventures of Sadie"
9. Errol Flynn	i. "The Adventures of Casanova"
10. Eddie Hodges	j. "The Adventures of Robin Hood"
11. Tommy Kelly	k. "The Adventures of Don Juan"
12. Fredric March	l. "The Adventures of Marco Polo"
13. Kim Novak	m. "The Adventures of Kitty O'Day"
14. Jean Parker	n. "Adventures of a Young Man"
15. Basil Rathbone	o. "The Amorous Adventures of Moll Flanders"

_____points

(*Answers on page 236*)

46. WHAT'S THE TITLE?

Below, we list three players who appeared in a film. From this meager clue, you are to name the motion picture we're seeking. In some instances we omit the obvious stars, just to make it more difficult. In some instances the stars are included but may have made more than one picture together, in which case the third member of the trio is the deciding factor. At any rate, if you know your films and can remember some of the casts, you should be in good shape. You may take 15 points for each title you correctly deduce.

1. Wallace Beery, Lionel Barrymore, "Chic" Sale _____

2. Humphrey Bogart, Zasu Pitts, Jeffrey Lynn _____

3. Raymond Massey, Priscilla Lane, Jack Carson _____

4. Jean Simmons, Robert Keith, Johnny Silver _____

5. Edmond O'Brien, Rossano Brazzi, Ava Gardner _____

6. Agnes Moorehead, Harvey Lembeck, Jeffrey Hunter _____

7. Thomas Mitchell, Richard Barthelmess, Noah Beery, Jr. _____

8. Marlene Dietrich, Ruta Lee, Elsa Lanchester _____

94

9. Barbara Stanwyck, Richard Haydn,
   Oscar Homolka   _____

10. Brian Aherne, Allyn Joslyn, Debra
    Paget   _____

_____points

(*Answers on page 237*)

46. WHAT'S THE TITLE?—DUFFERS' TEE

Below, we list three players who appeared in a film, and it is the film title we are seeking. In some instances we have omitted the obvious stars, just to make it more difficult. In some instances the stars are included but may have made more than one picture together, in which case the third member of the trio is the deciding factor. If you still haven't tumbled, then fill in the blanks at the right (which should give you some clue). But wrack your brain, remember the cast credits, and tell us WHAT'S THE TITLE? Take 20 points for each correct answer.

1. Wallace Beery, Lionel Barrymore,
   "Chic" Sale   "T _ _ _ _ _ _ _
        I _ _ _ _ _ _"

2. Humphrey Bogart, Zasu Pitts,
   Jeffrey Lynn   "I _ A _ _ C _ _ _
        T _ _ _"

3. Raymond Massey, Priscilla Lane,
   Jack Carson   "A _ _ _ _ _ _ _ a _ _
        O _ _ L _ _ _"

4. Jean Simmons, Robert Keith,
   Johnny Silver   "G _ _ _ _ a _ _ D _ _ _ _ _"

5. Edmond O'Brien, Rossano Brazzi,
   Ava Gardner   "T _ _ B _ _ _ _ _ _ _
        C _ _ _ _ _ _ _ _"

6. Agnes Moorehead, Harvey Lembeck,
   Jeffrey Hunter   "F _ _ _ _ _ _ _
        H _ _ _ _ _"

7. Thomas Mitchell, Richard
   Barthelmess, Noah Beery, Jr.   "O _ _ _ _ A _ _ _ _ _ _
        H _ _ _ W _ _ _ _"

8. Marlene Dietrich, Ruta Lee, Elsa
   Lanchester   "W _ _ _ _ _ _ _ f _ _ t _ _
        P _ _ _ _ _ _ _ _ _ _"

9. Barbara Stanwyck, Richard Haydn,
   Oscar Homolka   "B _ _ _ _ o _ F _ _ _"

10. Brian Aherne, Allyn Joslyn, Debra
    Paget   "T _ _ _ _ _ _"

_____points

(*Answers on page 237*)

95

47. MIX-UP IN THE TITLING DEPARTMENT—BUFFS AND DUFFERS

We have to interrupt things for a moment here in order to take care of a little accident in the Titling Department. On the way to that department, Clarence Klutz—the apprentice—dropped some cards he was carrying, and is having a terrible time getting them back in order. If you have been playing the Buffs' version, help Clarence by sorting out the various credits and take 10 points for each credit you straighten out. However, if you've been playing the Duffers' version, you may up the count to 15 points a credit. Merely sort out the credits by assigning the title in Column One to the person with the most renowned expertise in that field who appears in Column Two. Clarence thanks you, Howard thanks you, and we thank you!

1. Produced by . . .	a. Lee Garmes
2. Directed by . . .	b. Farciot Edouart
3. Written by . . .	c. Anne Bauchens
4. Cinematographer	d. Howard Christie
5. Score composed by . . .	e. Saul Bass
6. Art Director	f. H. Bruce Humberstone
7. Edited by . . .	g. Seymour Felix
8. Special Effects by . . .	h. Yakima Canutt
9. Costumes by . . .	i. Slavko Vorkapich
10. Stuntwork Supervised by . . .	j. Robert Riskin
11. Montages by . . .	k. Edith Head
12. Dance Director	l. Bernard Herrmann
13. Second Unit Director	m. Hans Dreier
14. Title Design by . . .	n. Andrew Marton

_____points

(*Answers on page 237*)

48. THE WOMAN

As we looked at THE MAN earlier, it is only fair that we also look at THE WOMAN. Below, we list twenty-five titles, and we are seeking the *female* star of the film. A word of warning: the star we're seeking may or may not have played the "Woman" referred to in the title, so don't be misled. Merely fill in each set of blanks with the female star most closely related to the film, and take 15 points for each correct answer. *Cherchez la femme!*

1. "The Other Woman"	C_____	M_____
2. "Woman Chases Man"	M_____	H_____
3. "The Woman on Pier 13"	L_____	D_____
4. "Wicked Woman"	B_____	M_____
5. "I Take This Woman"	H_____	L_____
6. "Woman of the Town"	C_____	T_____
7. "The Tiger Woman"	A_____	M_____
8. "This Woman Is Mine"	C_____	B_____
9. "Woman Doctor"	F_____	I_____
10. "A Woman Alone"	A_____	S_____
11. "That Certain Woman"	B_____	D_____
12. "This Woman Is Dangerous"	J_____	C_____
13. "That Forsyte Woman"	G_____	G_____
14. "The Woman Accused"	N_____	C_____
15. "That Kind of Woman"	S_____	L_____
16. "Woman in the Window"	J_____	B_____
17. "Woman of the Year"	K_____	H_____
18. "A Woman of Affairs"	G_____	G_____
19. "Woman in Hiding"	I_____	L_____
20. "The Woman and the Hunter"	A_____	S_____
21. "That Hamilton Woman"	V_____	L_____
22. "Woman Obsessed"	S_____	H_____
23. "A Woman of Straw"	G_____	L_____
24. "Woman Wanted"	M_____	O'_____
25. "Woman Times Seven"	S_____	M_____

_____points

(*Answers on page 238*)

48. THE WOMAN—DUFFERS' TEE

Looking at THE MAN and ignoring THE WOMAN is just not done—what's more, it makes for incomplete movie quizzes. We've come up with twenty-five movie titles involving a "Woman," and ask you to identify the female star most closely associated with those films. We've provided you with the names (out of order) in Column Two, and you're to match the appropriate female to each title. Bear in mind, the actress we've proposed did not necessarily portray the "Woman" of the title. But take 20 points for each pairing you get correct.

1. "The Other Woman"	a. Greta Garbo
2. "Woman Chases Man"	b. Greer Garson
3. "The Woman on Pier 13"	c. Gina Lollobrigida
4. "Wicked Woman"	d. Joan Bennett
5. "I Take This Woman"	e. Nancy Carroll
6. "Woman of the Town"	f. Laraine Day
7. "The Tiger Woman"	g. Shirley MacLaine
8. "This Woman Is Mine"	h. Frieda Inescort
9. "Woman Doctor"	i. Cleo Moore
10. "A Woman Alone"	j. Ann Sheridan
11. "That Certain Woman"	k. Miriam Hopkins
12. "This Woman Is Dangerous"	l. Susan Hayward
13. "That Forsyte Woman"	m. Vivien Leigh
14. "The Woman Accused"	n. Maureen O'Sullivan
15. "That Kind of Woman"	o. Sophia Loren
16. "Woman in the Window"	p. Beverly Michaels
17. "Woman of the Year"	q. Joan Crawford
18. "A Woman of Affairs"	r. Anna Sten
19. "Woman in Hiding"	s. Bette Davis
20. "The Woman and the Hunter"	t. Ida Lupino
21. "That Hamilton Woman"	u. Carol Bruce
22. "Woman Obsessed"	v. Hedy Lamarr
23. "A Woman of Straw"	w. Katharine Hepburn
24. "Woman Wanted"	x. Adele Mara
25. "Woman Times Seven"	y. Claire Trevor

_____points

(*Answers on page 238*)

49. FIND THE TITLE

In the diagram following, we have tucked away titles of fifty films, and the unique thing about these titles is that they all consist of only one word. Once you locate them all you'll find that even though *some* of the letters are used more than once, there will be twenty letters which have not been used at all. Search out the titles (which you'll have to deduce from the clues below) and end up with twenty unused letters. You may have seven points for each title you ferret out—so you can increase your score by 350 points. But if you can put the remaining letters together and find the one remaining title we're looking for, you may claim a bonus of 150 *more* points. So here's your chance to increase your score by a whopping 500 points. One more flash: the titles in the diagram following may run vertically, horizontally, or diagonally. Go get that big 500!

1. Clark Gable and Greer Garson in   "A _ _ _ _ _ _ _ _ _"
2. Sophia Loren and Lois Maxwell in   "A _ _ _"
3. Carol Dempster and Neil
    Hamilton in   "A _ _ _ _ _ _"
4. Marlene Dietrich and Melvyn
    Douglas in   "A _ _ _ _"
5. Silvana Mangano and Raf Vallone
    in   "A _ _ _"
6. Robert Mitchum and Peter Falk in   "A _ _ _ _"
7. Burt Lancaster and Jean Peters
    in   "A _ _ _ _ _"
8. Michael Forest and Frank Wolff
    in   "A _ _ _ _"
9. Jack Palance and Eddie Albert in   "A _ _ _ _ _"
10. Warner Baxter and Alice Faye in   "B _ _ _ _ _ _ _ _"
11. Lee Harcourt Montgomery and
    Joseph Campanella in   "B _ _"
12. Elizabeth Taylor and Richard
    Burton in   "B _ _ _!"
13. Richard Todd and Richard
    Attenborough in   "B _ _ _ _ _ _ _"
14. David Brian and Frank Lovejoy
    in   "B _ _ _ _ _ _ _ _ _ _ _"
15. Marlon Brando and Richard
    Burton in   "C _ _ _ _"
16. A documentary of 1927 by
    Merian Cooper and Ernest
    Schoedsack   "C _ _ _ _"
17. Rod Taylor and Ernest
    Borgnine in   "C _ _ _ _"
18. Greta Garbo and Charles Boyer in   "C _ _ _ _ _ _ _"
19. Groucho Marx and Carmen
    Miranda in   "C _ _ _ _ _ _ _ _"
20. William Bendix and Gene Evans
    in   "C _ _ _ _ _ _ _"
21. Cary Grant and Jose Ferrer in   "C _ _ _ _ _"
22. Marie Dressler and Jean
    Hersholt in   "E _ _ _"
23. Spencer Tracy and Sylvia Sidney
    in   "F _ _ _"
24. Gibson Gowland and Jean Hersholt
    in   "G _ _ _ _"
25. Joan Fontaine and Patric Knowles
    in   "I _ _"

26. Roy Scheider and Richard
    Dreyfuss in   "J _ _ _"
27. Peter Boyle and Dennis Patrick in   "J _ _"
28. Glenn Ford and Ernest Borgnine
    in   "J _ _ _ _"
29. Peter Lawford and Richard
    Boone in   "K _ _ _ _ _ _ _"
30. Michael Gough and Margo
    Johns in   "K _ _ _ _"
31. Dustin Hoffman and Valerie
    Perrine in   "L _ _ _ _"
32. Dolores Hart and Stephen
    Boyd in   "L _ _ _"
33. Marilyn Monroe and Joseph
    Cotten in   "N _ _ _ _ _ _"
34. Glenn Ford and Donna Reed in   "R _ _ _ _ _"
35. Joan Fontaine and Laurence
    Olivier in   "R _ _ _ _ _ _"
36. Alan Ladd and Shelley
    Winters in   "S _ _ _ _ _ _ _ _ _ _"
37. Lew Ayres and Joan Perry in   "S _ _ _ _ _ _ _ _"
38. Alan Ladd and Van Heflin in   "S _ _ _ _"
39. Ursula Andress and John
    Richardson in   "S _ _"
40. Kirk Douglas and Jean Simmons
    in   "S _ _ _ _ _ _ _"
41. Julie Andrews and Richard
    Crenna in   "S _ _ _!"
42. Janet Gaynor and George
    O'Brien in   "S _ _ _ _ _ _"
43. Carroll Baker and George
    Maharis in   "S _ _ _ _ _"
44. Glenn Ford and William
    Holden in   "T _ _ _ _"
45. Glenn Ford and Dorothy
    McGuire in   "T _ _ _ _"
46. Joan Crawford and Michael
    Gough in   "T _ _ _"
47. Jeanne Crain and Jean Peters in   "V _ _ _ _"
48. Jane Russell and Howard Keel in   "W _ _ _"
49. Paul Newman and Joanne
    Woodward in   "W _ _ _"
50. Victor Mature and Anita
    Ekberg in   "Z _ _ _ _"

_____points

And the remaining title, from the unused letters, is:

A _ _ _ _ _ _ _ _ _ _ _ _ _ _ _ _ _ _ "

_____bonus points

TOTAL:_____points

(Answers on page 238)

```
C R I S I S W F U R Y J U B A L
C R J B E N A W R R E B E C C A
S P A R T A C U S T A R B O O M
Y A W E C E O S H A N E S P N E
L I S A S H X A E P I A H A Q R
V I C K I A A A A A A K A C U I
I A H O A T S N S C G T K A E C
A D U U M T R O G H A H E B S A
I V K T A A C R R E R R D A T C
D E A R J C T H E E A O O N S R
A N Z I O K A E E E N U W A U A
N T A A E O I N D W N G N T N S
G U R L E N N Y D D A H E L R H
E R A E E G N I V Y D N M A I O
L E K T K A N G A R O O M S S U
R A N S O M B A R R I C A D E T
```

49. FIND THE TITLE—DUFFERS' TEE

In the diagram above, we have tucked away titles of fifty films, and the unique thing about these titles is that they all consist of only one word. Once you locate them all, you'll find that even though *some* letters are used more than once, there will be twenty letters remaining which have not been used at all. Search out the titles, which are listed below, and end up with twenty unused letters which you can soon put to work. You may have seven points for each title you ferret out— and thereby increase your score by 350 points. But if you can put the remaining letters together and find the one remaining title we're looking for, you may claim a bonus of 150 *more* points. Of course you know that the titles in the diagram may run horizontal, vertical, and even diagonal—and some letters may do "double-duty." Go get the big 500!

1. "Adventure"	18. "Conquest"	35. "Rebecca"
2. "Aida"	19. "Copacabana"	36. "Saskatchewan"
3. "America"	20. "Crashout"	37. "Shakedown"
4. "Angel"	21. "Crisis"	38. "Shane"
5. "Anna"	22. "Emma"	39. "She"
6. "Anzio"	23. "Fury"	40. "Spartacus"
7. "Apache"	24. "Greed"	41. "Star!"
8. "Atlas"	25. "Ivy"	42. "Sunrise"
9. "Attack"	26. "Jaws"	43. "Sylvia"
10. "Barricade"	27. "Joe"	44. "Texas"
11. "Ben"	28. "Jubal"	45. "Trial"
12. "Boom!"	29. "Kangaroo"	46. "Trog"
13. "Breakout"	30. "Konga"	47. "Vicki"
14. "Breakthrough"	31. "Lenny"	48. "Waco"
15. "Candy"	32. "Lisa"	49. "WUSA"
16. "Chang"	33. "Niagara"	50. "Zarak"
17. "Chuka"	34. "Ransom"	

_____points

And the remaining title, from the unused letters, is:

A _ _ _ _ _ _ _ _ _ _ _ _ _ _ _ _ _ _ _ _ _"

_____bonus points

TOTAL:_____points

(*Answers on page 238*)

50. Y'ALL REMEMBER WORLD WAR II?

For some reason, the films about World War II remain vivid in the memory of the real movie freak—and we wanted to recall a few of them for you. Some of this recalling will depend on you, but below, we are "suggesting" fifteen titles which should tickle your memory. It's a simple quiz. We supply you with several members of the cast of each film *and* the year the film was released. Your task is to come up with the title. For each one you can put your finger on, we'll let you add 15 points to your score.

1. Don Ameche, Dana Andrews, William Eythe (1943)
2. Humphrey Bogart, Bruce Bennett, Lloyd Bridges (1943)
3. Errol Flynn, William Prince, George Tobias (1945)

4. Gregory Peck, Dean Jagger, Hugh Marlowe (1950)
5. John Garfield, Gig Young, George Tobias (1943)
6. Claudette Colbert, Paulette Goddard, Veronica Lake (1943)
7. Clark Gable, John Hodiak, Walter Pidgeon (1949)
8. Tyrone Power, Tom Ewell, Micheline Presle (1950)
9. Gary Cooper, Signe Hasso, Dennis O'Keefe (1944)
10. Sir Cedric Hardwicke, William Eythe, Lee J. Cobb (1943)

_____points

(*Answers on page 239*)

50. Y'ALL REMEMBER WORLD WAR II?—DUFFERS' TEE

For some reason, it seems, the films about World War II remain vivid in the memory of the real movie freak—and we wanted to recall a few of them for you. Some of this recalling will depend on you, but below, we are "suggesting" fifteen titles which should tickle your memory. We supply you with several of the cast members of a film about World War II—plus the year of its release, if that's any help. Your task is to come up with the title merely by filling in the blanks of Column Two. For each title you correct completely, we'll let you add 15 points to your score.

1. Don Ameche, Dana Andrews, William Eythe (1943)
   "_ ____ ___ _ _____"

2. Humphrey Bogart, Bruce Bennett, Lloyd Bridges (1943)
   "_____"

3. Errol Flynn, William Prince, George Tobias (1945)
   "_____ _____"

4. Gregory Peck, Dean Jagger, Hugh Marlowe (1950)
   "_____ , _____ ____"

5. John Garfield, Gig Young, George Tobias (1943)
   "___ _____"

6. Claudette Colbert, Paulette Goddard, Veronica Lake (1943)
   "__ _____ __ ____"

7. Clark Gable, John Hodiak, Walter Pidgeon (1949)
   "_____ _____"

8. Tyrone Power, Tom Ewell, Micheline Presle (1950)
   "__ _____ _____ __ ___ _____"

103

9. Gary Cooper, Signe Hasso,   "___ _____ __
       Dennis O'Keefe (1944)   __. _____"
10. Sir Cedric Hardwicke, William   "___ _____ __
       Eythe, Lee J. Cobb (1943)   ____"

_____points

(*Answers on page 239*)

51. THE BIG BULB: LADIES

As the actors of Hollywood found new employment in television, so did the ladies! A number of actresses who theretofore had been supporting players or even stars of secondary features made the move to television, and many soon emerged as major stars in the new medium. Below, we list a dozen actresses who moved into television, and ask you to tell us the series in which they found even more widespread fame by filling in the blanks of Column Two. You may have 15 points for each series title correctly completed.

1. Barbara Hale   "P_____ M_____"
2. Minerva Urecal   "T_____ A_____"
3. Joan Caulfield   "S_____"
4. Ann Sothern   "P_____ S_____"
5. Lucille Ball   "_ L____ ____"
6. Joanne Dru   "G_____ H_!"
7. Spring Byington   "D_____ B_____"
8. Eve Arden   "___ M___ _____"
9. Joan Caulfield   "__ F_____ H_____"
10. Joan Davis   "_ M_____ J____"
11. June Lockhart   "____ __ S____"
12. Ellen Corby   "___. W_____"

_____points

(*Answers on page 240*)

51. THE BIG BULB: LADIES—DUFFERS' TEE

As the actors of Hollywood found new employment opportunities in television, so did many actresses. A number of actresses who theretofore had been supporting players or even the leads of secondary features made the move to television, and many soon emerged as major stars of the new medium. Below, in Column One, we list a dozen actresses who moved into television, and in Column Two, we list (out of order) the series in which they enjoyed even greater fame. Match the actresses of Column One with the proper TV series title of Column Two, and take 15 points for each correct pairing.

1. Barbara Hale		a.	"December Bride"
2. Minerva Urecal		b.	"The Waltons"
3. Joan Caulfield		c.	"Guestward Ho!"
4. Ann Sothern		d.	"I Love Lucy"
5. Lucille Ball		e.	"Tugboat Annie"
6. Joanne Dru		f.	"My Favorite Husband"
7. Spring Byington		g.	"Lost in Space"
8. Eve Arden		h.	"Private Secretary"
9. Joan Caulfield		i.	"I Married Joan"
10. Joan Davis		j.	"Our Miss Brooks"
11. June Lockhart		k.	"Perry Mason"
12. Ellen Corby		l.	"Sally"

_____points

(Answers on page 240)

52. HERE'S LOOKIN' AT YOU, BOGIE!

There probably has never been such a posthumous surge of popularity for any actor as there has been for Humphrey Bogart. Films he made which were little more than insignificant programmers at the time have become screen classics, and Bogart has taken his rightful place among screen immortals. Indeed, the names of the characters he portrayed have become almost as well-known among film fans as the titles of the films themselves. Below, we list some of the characters portrayed by Bogart, and ask you to place them in the films from which they came. Match the character to the film by completing the blanks of the title, and take 15 points for each title properly completed. Here's lookin' at *you*, kid!

1. Nick "Bugs"
    Fenner   "B _ _ _ _ _ _ _ _ _ _ _ _ _ _ _ _ _ _"
2. Frank Taylor   "B _ _ _ _ _ L _ _ _ _ _ _"
3. "Hap" Stuart   "C _ _ _ _ _ C _ _ _ _ _ _ _ _"
4. Richard Mason   "C _ _ _ _ _ _ _ _"

105

5.	Joe Barrett	"T _ _ _ _ _ J _ _"
6.	Maj. Jed Webbe	"B _ _ _ _ _ _ C _ _ _ _ _ _"
7.	Nick Coster	"T _ _ _ _ _ _ _ _ _ R _ _ _ _ _ N _ _ _ _ _"
8.	Ed Hutchinson	"D _ _ _ _ _ _ _ _, _ _ _-_"
9.	Harry Smith	"S _ _ _ _ _ _ _"
10.	Geoffrey Carroll	" _ _ _ _ _ _ _ _ _ _. C _ _ _ _ _ _ _ _"
11.	Frank Wilson	"Y _ _ _ _ _ ' _"
12.	Jack Buck	"B _ _ _ _ _ _ _ O _ _ _ _ _ _"
13.	Marshall Quesne	" _ _ _ _ _ _ _ _ _ _ _ _ _ _ _. X"
14.	Duke Berne	" _ _ _ B _ _ S _ _ _ _"

_____points

(*Answers on page 240*)

52. HERE'S LOOKIN' AT YOU, BOGIE!—DUFFERS' TEE

There probably has never been such a surge of posthumous popularity for any actor as there has been for Humphrey Bogart. Films he made which were little more than insignificant programmers at the time have grown to be screen classics, and Bogart has taken his rightful place among screen immortals. Indeed, the names of the characters he played have become almost as well-known among film fans as the titles of the films themselves—and we have a hunch that even Duffers can hold their own in this quiz. Below, we list some well-known characters portrayed by Bogie (the characters listed in the Buffs' version were a trifle more obscure), and ask you to place them in the films which gave them birth by completing the titles in Column Two. Fill in the blanks and complete the Bogart titles, and take 15 points for each title you get right. Here's lookin' at *you*, kid!

1.	Roy "Mad Dog" Earle	" _ _ _ _ _ S _ _ _ _ _ _ _"
2.	Charlie Allnut	" _ _ _ _ _ _ _ _ _ _ _ _ Q _ _ _ _"
3.	Capt. Philip Francis Queeg	" _ _ _ C _ _ _ _ _ M _ _ _ _ _ _"
4.	Fred C. Dobbs	" _ S _ _ _ _ _ _ M _ _ _ _"
5.	Sam Spade	" _ _ _ M _ _ _ _ _ _ _ _ F _ _ _ _ _ _"
6.	Philip Marlowe	" _ _ _ B _ _ _ _ _ _ _ _"
7.	Harry Dawes	" _ _ _ B _ _ _ _ _ _ _ _ C _ _ _ _ _ _ _ _"

8. Paul Fabrini   "_ _ _ _ _ D _ _ _ _ _ b _ N _ _ _ _ _"
9. Michael O'Leary   "D _ _ _ _ V _ _ _ _ _ _ _"
10. "Turkey" Morgan   "K _ _ G _ _ _ _ _ _ _"
11. Matrac   "P _ _ _ _ _ _ _ _ _
        M _ _ _ _ _ _ _ _ _ _"
12. Joe Rossi   "A _ _ _ _ _ _ _ _ _ _ _ _ _ _ _ _
         _ _ _ _ _ _ _ _"
13. Harry Morgan   "_ _ _ _ _ _ _ _ _ _ _ _ _ _ _ _ _ _"
14. "Rip" Murdock   "C _ _ _ _ L _ _ _ _ _ _ _ _ _"

_____points

(*Answers on page 240*)

53. THAT OL' GANG OF MINE

Here's a new quiz we haven't shown you before, but you should enjoy it. ("You *will* enjoy!") And your success with it will depend on how well you paid attention when you were watching films, or when the credits rolled by. In this one, each question lists the names of four or five characters from a film. From these character names, you are to tell us the title of the film we're seeking. Now, obviously, we're not going to make it a piece of cake with characters like Shane or David Copperfield or Cat Ballou. You're going to have to earn the 10 points we're allowing for each correct answer. We'll start slowly, but look out for the homestretch!!!

1. Margaret Gautier; Armand Duval; General Duval; Baron de Varville.
2. Lieut. Harry Brubaker (USNR); Nancy Brubaker; Rear Adm. George Tarrant; Mike Forney.
3. Holly Golightly; Paul Varjak; 2-E; O. J. Berman; Mr. Yunioshi.
4. Billie Dawn; Harry Brock; Paul Verrall; Jim Devery.
5. John Morgan; Butch Schmidt; Warden James Adams; Kent Marlowe.
6. Hillary Fairfield; Sydney Fairfield; Margaret Fairfield; Kit Humphrey.
7. Shepherd Henderson; Gillian Holroyd; Nicky Holroyd; Sidney Redlitch; Bianca De Pass.
8. Harry Dawes; Maria Vargas; Oscar Muldoon; Kirk Edwards; Vincenzo Torlato-Favrini.
9. Georgia Lorrison; Jonathan Shields; Harry Pebbel; James Lee Bartlow; Fred Amiel.
10. John J. MacReedy; Reno Smith; Liz Wirth; Tim Horn; Coley Trimble; Hector David.

11. Milly Stephenson; Al Stephenson; Fred Derry; Homer Parrish.
12. Walter Neff; Phyllis Dietrichson; Barton Keyes; Nino Zachetti.
13. Lonesome Rhodes; Marcia Jeffries; Joey Kiely; Betty Lou Fleckum.
14. Jerry Plunkett; Father Duffy; Wild Bill Donovan; Joyce Kilmer; "Crepe Hanger" Burke.
15. Grusinskaya; Baron Felix von Geigern; Flaemmchen; Preysing; Otto Kringelein.
16. Marianne Patourel; Timothy Haslam; Marguerite Patourel; William Ozanne.
17. Leslie Gallant III; Professor Fate; Maggie DuBois; Maximillian Meen.
18. Victor Albee Norman; Kay Dorrance; Evan Llewellyn Evans; Jean Ogilvie.
19. Judge Dan Haywood; Ernst Janning; Col. Tad Lawson; Mme. Bertholt; Irene Hoffman.
20. Frank Skeffington; Adam Caulfield; Maeve Caulfield; John Gorman; Norman Cass, Sr.
21. Diego Vega; Lolita Quintero; Capt. Esteban Pasquale; Don Luis Quintero.
22. Otis B. Driftwood; Rosa Castaldi; Fiorello; Riccardo Baroni; Tomasso; Rodolfo Lassparri.
23. Terry Malloy; Father Barry; Johnny Friendly; Edie Doyle.
24. Stephen Tolliver; Cap. Jack Stuart; Loxi Claiborne; King Cutler.
25. Laura Reynolds; Dr. Edward Hewitt; Claire Hewitt; Cos Erickson.

———————points

(*Answers on page 241*)

53. THAT OL' GANG OF MINE—DUFFERS' TEE

Here's a quiz that was new to the Buffs, and it'll be new for you. And your success with it will depend on how well you paid attention when you were watching films, or when the credits rolled by. In this one, each question lists the names of several of the main characters from a film. There are twenty-five such groups of characters, and in Column Two, you'll find all twenty-five films listed—but wouldn't you know it, they're out of order. Select the title that goes with the appropriate group of characters—and if your matching is correct, don't hesitate to grab the 20 points we're allowing. And don't look for characters' names like Shane or David Copperfield, or Cat Ballou. You're Duffers, we know—but if it's too easy, it's no fun for anybody. Check?

1. Margaret Gautier; Armand Duval; General Duval; Baron de Varville.

2. Lieut. Harry Brubaker (USNR); Nancy Brubaker; Rear Adm. George Tarrant; Mike Forney.

3. Holly Golightly; Paul Varjak; 2-E; O. J. Berman; Mr. Yunioshi.

4. Billie Dawn; Harry Brock; Paul Verrall; Jim Devery.

5. John Morgan; Butch Schmidt; Warden James Adams; Kent Marlowe.

6. Hillary Fairfield; Sydney Fairfield; Margaret Fairfield; Kit Humphrey.

7. Shepherd Henderson; Gillian Holroyd; Nicky Holroyd; Sidney Redlitch; Bianca De Pass.

8. Harry Dawes; Maria Vargas; Oscar Muldoon; Kirk Edwards; Vincenzo Torlato-Favrini.

9. Georgia Lorrison; Jonathan Shields; Harry Pebbel; James Lee Bartlow; Fred Amiel.

10. John J. MacReedy; Reno Smith; Liz Wirth; Tim Horn; Coley Trimble; Hector David.

11. Milly Stephenson; Al Stephenson; Fred Derry; Homer Parrish.

12. Walter Neff; Phyllis Dietrichson; Barton Keyes; Nino Zachetti.

13. Lonesome Rhodes; Marcia Jeffries; Joey Kiely; Betty Lou Fleckum.

14. Jerry Plunkett; Father Duffy; Wild Bill Donovan; Joyce Kilmer; "Crepe Hanger" Burke.

15. Grusinskaya; Baron Felix von Geigern; Flaemmchen; Preysing; Otto Kringelein.

a. "The Fighting 69th"

b. "The Great Race"

c. "The Last Hurrah"

d. "On the Waterfront"

e. "The Sandpiper"

f. "Camille"

g. "Reap the Wild Wind"

h. "Born Yesterday"

i. "The Bridges at Toko-Ri"

j. "The Mark of Zorro"

k. "Breakfast at Tiffany's"

l. "The Big House"

m. "A Night at the Opera"

n. "Grand Hotel"

o. "Double Indemnity"

16. Marianne Patourel; Timothy Haslam; Marguerite Patourel; William Ozanne.

    p. "The Barefoot Contessa"

17. Leslie Gallant III; Professor Fate; Maggie DuBois; Maximillian Meen.

    q. "Bell, Book, and Candle"

18. Victor Albee Norman; Kay Dorrance; Evan Llewellyn Evans; Jean Ogilvie.

    r. "A Bill of Divorcement"

19. Judge Dan Haywood; Ernst Janning; Col. Tad Lawson; Mme. Bertholt; Irene Hoffman.

    s. "Bad Day at Black Rock"

20. Frank Skeffington; Adam Caulfield; Maeve Caulfield; John Gorman; Norman Cass, Sr.

    t. "Judgment at Nuremberg"

21. Diego Vega; Lolita Quintero; Capt. Esteban Pasquale; Don Luis Quintero.

    u. "The Hucksters"

22. Otis B. Driftwood; Rosa Castaldi; Fiorello; Riccardo Baroni; Tomasso; Rodolfo Lassparri.

    v. "Green Dolphin Street"

23. Terry Malloy; Father Barry; Johnny Friendly; Edie Doyle.

    w. "A Face in the Crowd"

24. Stephen Tolliver; Capt. Jack Stuart; Loxi Claiborne; King Cutler.

    x. "The Best Years of Our Lives"

25. Laura Reynolds; Dr. Edward Hewitt; Claire Hewitt; Cos Erickson.

    y. "The Bad and the Beautiful"

_____points

(*Answers on page 241*)

54. THAT OL' GANG OF MINE: FOLLOW-UP!

Quick!! Want to grab a fast 250 points? Just turn back to the quiz you just completed. Tell us quickly who played the *first character* listed in the group casts of each question, and you may add 10 points to your score for each player correctly identified.

_____points

(*Answers on page 242*)

54. THAT OL' GANG OF MINE: FOLLOW-UP!—DUFFERS' TEE

We offered it to the Buffs, and we offer it to you—and if you move quickly, you can increase your score by 250 points. To get theirs, the Buffs had to identify the player who portrayed the first character in each of the group cast lists in the quiz just completed. If you can identify the player who portrayed that character, you may add 10 points for each correct answer. But since you're playing the Duffers' version, we're offering some assistance, and have provided some clues. Just fill in the blanks with letters—the right ones!—and sweeten up your score too.

1. Margaret Gautier   G _ _ _ _ G _ _ _ _
2. Lieut. Harry Brubaker
      (USNR)   W _ _ _ _ _ _ H _ _ _ _ _
3. Holly Golightly   A _ _ _ _ _ _ H _ _ _ _ _ _
4. Billie Dawn   J _ _ _ _ H _ _ _ _ _ _ _
5. John Morgan   C _ _ _ _ _ _ M _ _ _ _ _ _
6. Hillary Fairfield   J _ _ _ B _ _ _ _ _ _ _ _
7. Shepherd Henderson   J _ _ _ _ _ S _ _ _ _ _ _ _
8. Harry Dawes   H _ _ _ _ _ _ _ _ B _ _ _ _ _
9. Georgia Lorrison   L _ _ _ T _ _ _ _ _
10. John J. MacReedy   S _ _ _ _ _ _ T _ _ _ _
11. Milly Stephenson   M _ _ _ _ L _ _
12. Walter Neff   F _ _ _ M _ _ _ _ _ _ _ _
13. Lonesome Rhodes   A _ _ _ G _ _ _ _ _ _ _ _
14. Jerry Plunkett   J _ _ _ _ _ C _ _ _ _ _ _
15. Grusinskaya   G _ _ _ _ G _ _ _ _
16. Marianne Patourel   L _ _ _ T _ _ _ _ _ _
17. Leslie Gallant III   T _ _ _ C _ _ _ _ _ _
18. Victor Albee Norman   C _ _ _ _ _ G _ _ _ _
19. Judge Dan Haywood   S _ _ _ _ _ _ _ T _ _ _ _
20. Frank Skeffington   S _ _ _ _ _ _ _ T _ _ _ _
21. Diego Vega   T _ _ _ _ _ _ P _ _ _ _

22. Otis B. Driftwood   G _ _ _ _ _ _ _ M _ _ _
23. Terry Malloy   M _ _ _ _ _ _ B _ _ _ _ _ _
24. Stephen Tolliver   R _ _ M _ _ _ _ _ _ _
25. Laura Reynolds   E _ _ _ _ _ _ _ _ T _ _ _ _ _

_____points

(*Answers on page 242*)

55. ELEMENTARY, MY DEAR WATSON

As we're sure you're aware, Sir Arthur Conan Doyle's great detective Sherlock Holmes has been portrayed in a number of different productions of the Doyle thrillers, and by several different actors. Below, in Column One, we've listed a number of Sherlock Holmes films, and in Columns Two and Three, we have listed (out of order) those actors who played Holmes (Column Two) and those who played Watson. Your task is to match the correct Holmes and Watson with the correct film title. Take 15 points for each correct matching.

1. "Sherlock Holmes" (1922)	A. Raymond Massey	a. Fred Lloyd
2. "The Sign of the Four" (1923)	B. Clive Brook	b. Ian Hunter
3. "The Return of Sherlock Holmes" (1929)	C. Robert Rendel	c. Roland Young
4. "Sherlock Holmes' Fatal Hour" (1930)	D. John Barrymore	d. Colin Blakely
5. "The Speckled Band" (1931)	E. Clive Brook	e. Andre Morell
6. "The Sign of the Four" (1932)	F. Peter Cushing	f. Nigel Bruce
7. "The Hound of the Baskervilles" (1932)	G. Basil Rathbone	g. Ian Fleming
8. "Sherlock Holmes" (1932)	H. Arthur Wontner	h. H. Reeves-Smith
9. "A Study in Scarlet" (1933)	I. Reginald Owen	i. Reginald Owen
10. "The Adventures of Sherlock Holmes" (1939)	J. Arthur Wontner	j. Warburton Gamble

11. "The Hound of the   K. Robert   k. Athole Stewart
    Baskervilles"   Stephens
    (1959)
12. "The Private Life of   L. Eille Norwood   l. Hubert Willis
    Sherlock Holmes"
    (1969)

_____points

(Answers on page 243)

55. ELEMENTARY, MY DEAR WATSON—DUFFERS' TEE

This quiz might have been "elementary" for the Buffs, but we admit it's more difficult than the usual quiz, so we'll go easy on you. As you obviously are aware, movie-makers for years have turned to Arthur Conan Doyle's great detective Sherlock Holmes for cinematic thrills. Below, to the left, we list a number of such films. Being the nice chaps that we are, we're also telling you the year of the film as well as the actor who portrayed Holmes. Naturally, we want to know who played Watson—and to assist you, we list, below to the right, the twelve actors to whom Holmes was speaking when he said: "Elementary, my dear Watson!" From this out-of-order list, merely match the proper Watson with the correct film title and the correct Holmes. Go to it, and you may have 15 points for each correct match!

1. "Sherlock Holmes" (1922), starring John   a. Fred Lloyd
   Barrymore
2. "The Sign of the Four" (1923), starring   b. Ian Hunter
   Eille Norwood
3. "The Return of Sherlock Holmes" (1929),   c. Roland Young
   starring Clive Brook
4. "Sherlock Holmes' Fatal Hour" (1930),   d. Colin Blakely
   starring Arthur Wontner
5. "The Speckled Band" (1931), starring   e. Andre Morell
   Raymond Massey
6. "The Sign of the Four" (1932), starring   f. Nigel Bruce
   Arthur Wontner
7. "The Hound of the Baskervilles" (1932),   g. Ian Fleming
   starring Robert Rendel
8. "Sherlock Holmes" (1932), starring   h. H. Reeves-Smith
   Clive Brook

9. "A Study in Scarlet" (1933), starring Reginald Owen

    i. Reginald Owen

10. "The Adventures of Sherlock Holmes" (1939), starring Basil Rathbone

    j. Warburton Gamble

11. "The Hound of the Baskervilles" (1959), starring Peter Cushing

    k. Athole Stewart

12. "The Private Life of Sherlock Holmes" (1969), starring Robert Stephens

    l. Hubert Willis

_____points

(*Answers on page 243*)

56. FROM "A" TO "Z"—BUFFS AND DUFFERS

Twenty-five movie titles are involved here—and we'd have gone the entire alphabetical route if some producer had obliged us by having a title including a proper name beginning with "X." At any rate, your task is to complete the titles in Column One, and match the correct player from Column Two who appeared in each film of Column One. With 4 points for each completed title, and 4 more points for each player properly matched, you can win 8 points for each question, or a total of 200 points for this quiz. And if you've been playing the Duffers' Tees right along (and you're on your honor), we'll allow a double score for a possible 400 points! Go get 'em—from "A" to "Z"!

1. "A _ _"
2. "B _ _ _ _ Budd"
3. "C _ _ _ _ _ _"
4. "D _ _ _ _ _ and Bathsheba"
5. "E _ _ _ _ _ Gantry"
6. "F _ _ _ _"
7. "G _ _ _ _ _ _ Girl"
8. "H _ _ _ _ _ _ Lee"
9. "I _ _ _ _ _"
10. "A Date with J _ _ _"
11. "Kiss Me, K _ _ _ _"
12. "L _ _ _ _ _"
13. "M _ _ _ _ _ _ _ Pierce"
14. "N _ _ _ Carter, Master Detective"
15. "O _ _ _ _ _ _ Twist"

a. Jane Powell
b. Kirk Douglas
c. Susan Hayward
d. Anthony Quinn
e. Walter Pidgeon
f. June Haver
g. Lilli Palmer
h. Anita Ekberg
i. Rita Hayworth
j. Sue Lyon
k. Lucille Bremer
l. Anna Neagle
m. Joanne Dru
n. Richard Todd
o. Burt Lancaster

16. "A Man Called P _ _ _ _"
17. "Q _ _ _ _ _ _ Durward"
18. "The Daughter of R _ _ _ _ _ O'Grady"
19. "S _ _ _ _ _ _"

20. "My Girl T _ _ _"
21. "U _ _ _ _ _ _"
22. "V _ _ _ _ _ _"
23. "Wee W _ _ _ _ _ _ Winkie"
24. "Y _ _ _ _ _ _ _ and the Thief"
25. "Z _ _ _ _ _ the Greek"

p. Gregory Peck
q. Terence Stamp
r. Shirley Temple
s. John Howard
   Davies
t. Lynn Redgrave
u. Leslie Caron
v. Dorothy McGuire
w. Kathryn Grayson
y. Joan Crawford
z. Robert Taylor

_____points

(*Answers on page 243*)

57. MORE QUOTABLES

Again, we are having some fond memories with dialogue we've enjoyed from a number of well-known films. And once again, we're asking you to identify the films from which the dialogue is taken. You may have 15 points for each correct identification. This, of course, is in addition to the thrill of a cherished recollection . . . though in the case of the first question below, we're not so sure about that . . .

1. "Speak! You have a civil tongue in your head! I ought to know—I sewed it there!"

"_ _"

2. "You handle a sword like a devil from hell!"

"_ _ _ _ _ _ _ _ _ _ _ _ _ _"

3. "Remember what Johnny Dillinger said about guys like you and him . . . he said you're just rushin' toward death. That's it— you're just rushin' toward death."

"_ _ _ _ _ _ _ _ _ _"

4. "Discontinue that so-called Polonaise jumble you've been playing for days!"

"_ _ _ _ _ _ _ _ _ _ _ _ _"

115

5. "Crap-shoot is a matter of individual enterprise. Crap-shoot makes this country great!"

   "___ _____"

6. "And that's the kind of hairpin I am!"

   "___ _____ _____"

7. "I never dreamed such a mere physical experience could be so exciting."

   "___ _____ _____"

8. "No, sir! And we might as well get together on this 'yielding' business right off the bat. I had some pretty good coaching last night, and I find that if I yield only for a question, a point of order, or a personal privilege, I can hold this floor a little short of doomsday. In other words, I've got a piece to speak—and blow hot or cold, I'm going to speak it."

   "__. _____ ____ __ _____"

9. "I hunt griz."

   "_____ _____"

10. "Job says a woman is beautiful only when she is loved."

    "__. _____"

_____points

(*Answers on page 244*)

57. MORE QUOTABLES—DUFFERS' TEE

Again, we are having some fond memories with dialogue we've enjoyed from a number of well-known films. And once again, we're asking you to identify the films, which we've listed out of order in Column Two. Select the film which included the line of dialogue we've dredged up for you, and match it to the correct quote. For each correct pairing, you receive 15 points!

1. "Speak! You have a civil tongue in your head! I ought to know—I sewed it there!"

    a. "High Sierra"

2. "You handle a sword like a devil from hell!"

    b. "Jeremiah Johnson"

3. "Remember what Johnny Dillinger said about guys like you and him . . . he said you're just rushin' toward death. That's it—you're just rushin' toward death."

    c. "The Strawberry Blonde"

4. "Discontinue that so-called Polonaise jumble you've been playing for days!"

    d. "The Candidate"

5. "Crap-shoot is a matter of individual enterprise. Crap-shoot makes this country great!"

    e. "Mr. Smith Goes to Washington"

6. "And that's the kind of hairpin I am!"

    f. "A Song to Remember"

7. "I never dreamed such a mere physical experience could be so exciting."

    g. "Mr. Skeffington"

8. "No, sir! And we might as well get together on this 'yielding' business right off the bat. I had some pretty good coaching last night, and I find that if I yield only for a question, a point of order, or a personal privilege, I can hold this floor a little short of doomsday. In other words, I've got a piece to speak—and blow hot or cold, I'm going to speak it."

    h. "The African Queen"

9. "I hunt griz."

    i. "I Was a Teenage Frankenstein"

10. "Job says a woman is beautiful only when she is loved."

    j. "The Mark of Zorro"

_____points

(*Answers on page 244*)

117

58. MORE QUOTABLES: BONUS!

Well, we presume you did very, very well on that last quiz. So well, in fact, that you're no doubt ready to take a few bonus points. In this quiz, we're dealing with the same films and the same lines of dialogue. All you have to do is tell us the name of the player who spoke the line of memorable dialogue. It's not a snap, we know, so we're letting you add 20 points to your score for each player you can identify.

1. "Speak! You have a civil tongue in you head! I ought to know—I sewed it there!"

   ____ _____

2. "You handle a sword like a devil from hell!"

   _. _____ _____

3. "Remember what Johnny Dillinger said about guys like you and him . . . he said you're just rushin' toward death. That's it— you're just rushin' toward death."

   _____ ____

4. "Discontinue that so-called Polonaise jumble you've been playing for days!"

   _____ _____

5. "Crap-shoot is a matter of individual enterprise. Crap-shoot makes this country great!"

   _____ _____

6. "And that's the kind of hairpin I am!"

   _____ _____

7. "I never dreamed such a mere physical experience could be so exciting."

   _____
   _____

8. "No sir! And we might as well get together on this 'yielding' business right off the bat. I had some pretty good coaching last night, and I find that if I yield only for a question, a point of order, or a personal privilege, I can

hold this floor a little
short of doomsday. In
other words, I've got a
piece to speak—and blow
hot or cold, I'm going to
speak it."

9. "I hunt griz." _____ _____

10. "Job says a woman is beautiful
only when she is loved." _____ _____

_____points

(*Answers on page 245*)

58. MORE QUOTABLES: BONUS!—DUFFERS' TEE

We presume you did very, very well on that last quiz, and no doubt took every bloomin' point we offered. Now we're letting you have the opportunity to rack up a few bonus points. In this quiz, we're dealing with the same films and the same lines of dialogue. But there's a little wrinkle which makes this quiz different. In this one, we're asking you to select the name of the player from the list we've most thoughtfully provided in Column Two who spoke the line of dialogue in the film. Merely match the player to the line, and you may add 20 points for each correct answer. Do put on your thinking cap —because frankly, my dear, we do give a damn!

1. "Speak! You have a civil tongue in your head! I ought to know—I sewed it there!"
   a. Katharine Hepburn

2. "You handle a sword like a devil from hell!"
   b. Robert Redford

3. "Remember what Johnny Dillinger said about guys like you and him . . . he said you're just rushin' toward death. That's it—you're just rushin' toward death."
   c. J. Edward Bromberg

4. "Discontinue that so-called Polonaise jumble you've been playing for days!"
   d. Henry Hull

5. "Crap-shoot is a matter of individual enterprise. Crap-shoot makes this country great!"
   e. James Stewart

119

6. "And that's the kind of hairpin I am!"   f. Will Geer
7. "I never dreamed such a mere physical   g. Whit Bissell
   experience could be so exciting."
8. "No, sir! And we might as well get   h. Merle Oberon
   together on this 'yielding' business
   right off the bat. I had some pretty
   good coaching last night, and I find
   that if I yield only for a question,
   a point of order, or a personal
   privilege, I can hold this floor a little
   short of doomsday. In other words,
   I've got a piece to speak—and blow
   hot or cold, I'm going to speak it."
9. "I hunt griz."   i. Bette Davis
10. "Job says a woman is beautiful only when j. James Cagney
    she is loved."

_____points

(*Answers on page 245*)

59. YOU CAN'T HARDLY GET THERE FROM HERE

Many excellent films have been made on the premise that "you can't hardly get there from here." The perils of a long, arduous trip have made for great cinema fare for a number of years. Below, in Column One, we provide the take-off point and the intended destination of some memorable cinematic trips. Complete the titles of the films in Column Two in which these famous journeys were so important to the plot, and take 15 points for each answer you complete correctly.

1. New York to Lake
   Tanganyika, Africa   "S _ _ _ _ _ _ a _ _
                           L _ _ _ _ _ _ _ _ _ _"

2. The Reform Club,
   London, to the
   Reform Club,
   London   "A _ _ _ _ _ _ t _ _ W _ _ _ _ i _
                          E _ _ _ _ _ _ D _ _ _"

3. New York to Paris   "T _ _ G _ _ _ _ _ R _ _ _"

4. Roosevelt Field, New
   York, to Le Bourget
   Field, France

   "T_ _ _ S_ _ _ _ _ _ o_ S_.
   L_ _ _ _"

5. Southampton, England,
   to New York   "T_ _ _ _ _ _ _"
6. Vera Cruz, Mexico, to
   Bremerhaven,
   Germany   "S_ _ _ o_ F_ _ _ _"
7. Nauvoo, Illinois, to the
   Great Salt Lake   "B_ _ _ _ _ _ _ Y_ _ _ _
                        —F_ _ _ _ _ _ _ _ _ _ _"

8. The U.N., New York, to
   Mount Rushmore   "N_ _ _ _ _ b_ N_ _ _ _ _ _ _ _"
9. Plymouth, England, to
   Cape Cod Bay   "P_ _ _ _ _ _ _ _ A_ _ _ _ _ _ _ _"
10. Spithead, England, to
    Otaheite (Tahiti)   "M_ _ _ _ _ o_ t_ _ B_ _ _ _ _"
11. Istanbul to Calais   "M_ _ _ _ _ o_ t_ _ O_ _ _ _ _
                         E_ _ _ _ _ _"
12. Frankfurt, Germany, to
    Lakehurst, New
    Jersey, U.S.A.   "T_ _ H_ _ _ _ _ _ _ _ _"

_____points

(*Answers on page 245*)

59. YOU CAN'T HARDLY GET THERE FROM HERE— DUFFERS' TEE

As we told the Buffs, many excellent films have been made on the premise that "you can't hardly get there from here." The perils of a long, arduous trip have made for great cinema fare for a number of years. Below, in Column One, we provide the take-off point and the intended destination of some memorable cinematic trips. Match these with the correct film in which each trip was so important to the plot, and take 15 points for each correct pairing.

1. New York to Lake Tanganyika,   a. "Brigham Young
   Africa   —Frontiersman"

2. The Reform Club, London, to the Reform Club, London
3. New York to Paris
4. Roosevelt Field, New York, to Le Bourget Field, France
5. Southampton, England, to New York
6. Vera Cruz, Mexico, to Bremerhaven, Germany
7. Nauvoo, Illinois, to the Great Salt Lake
8. The U.N., New York, to Mount Rushmore
9. Plymouth, England, to Cape Cod Bay
10. Spithead, England, to Otaheite (Tahiti)
11. Istanbul to Calais
12. Frankfurt, Germany, to Lakehurst, New Jersey, U.S.A

b. "Murder on the Orient Express"
c. "Titanic"
d. "Stanley and Livingstone"
e. "Plymouth Adventure"
f. "The Hindenburg"
g. "Mutiny on the Bounty"
h. "Around the World in Eighty Days"
i. "The Spirit of St. Louis"
j. "The Great Race"
k. "Ship of Fools"
l. "North by Northwest"

_____points

(*Answers on page 245*)

60. PENCILED IN: FEMALES

We've had a couple of quizzes about those stars who were at one time announced for a role in a feature film, only to be replaced for some reason or other prior to the film's production and release. Now we're turning once more to the ladies who underwent the experience. Column One lists those female players who had originally been cast in the films listed in Column Two. Your task is to tell us who finally played each role in the final release version. Take 25 points for each name you can correctly provide.

1. Shirley Deane   "Blondie"   _____
2. Margaret Marquis   "Love Finds Andy Hardy"   _____
3. Gloria DeHaven   "Good News"   _____
4. Susan Peters   "Gentle Annie"   _____

122

5.	Edna May Oliver	"The Wizard of Oz"	_____
6.	Dinah Shore	"Show Boat"	_____
7.	Patricia Morison	"The Glass Key"	_____
8.	Judy Garland	"The Barkleys of Broadway"	_____
9.	Miriam Hopkins	"Devotion"	_____
10.	Geraldine Fitzgerald	"Captain Horatio Hornblower"	_____

_____points

(*Answers on page 246*)

60. PENCILED IN: FEMALES—DUFFERS' TEE

We've had a couple of quizzes about these stars who were at the outset announced for a role in a major feature film, only to be replaced in the role before production was completed and the film released. Now once again we're turning to the ladies who had the experience. Column One lists a feature which had a female performer changed from the one originally announced. Column Two provides the identity of the original female performer. And once again, we've provided the names of the replacement stars—though out of order—in Column Three. Select the replacement talent from Column Three, and match it correctly with the feature of Column One and the replaced actress of Column Two. Get it right, and take 20 points for each correct matching.

	Column One	Column Two	Column Three
1.	"Blondie"	Shirley Deane	a. Margaret Hamilton
2.	"Love Finds Andy Hardy"	Margaret Marquis	b. Ginger Rogers
3.	"Good News"	Gloria DeHaven	c. Ava Gardner
4.	"Gentle Annie"	Susan Peters	d. Olivia de Havilland
5.	"The Wizard of Oz"	Edna May Oliver	e. Virginia Mayo
6.	"Show Boat"	Dinah Shore	f. Veronica Lake
7.	"The Glass Key"	Patricia Morison	g. Penny Singleton
8.	"The Barkleys of Broadway"	Judy Garland	h. Donna Reed

9. "Devotion"   Miriam Hopkins   i. Ann Rutherford
10. "Captain Horatio   Geraldine Fitzgerald   j. Patricia
      Hornblower"   Marshall

                                            _____ points

                                    (*Answers on page 246*)

61. NAMES IN COMMON

Below, we list pairs of players who have appeared in films and who have the same surname. You'll note, however, that we've failed to give you the surname, but we will tell you that some of these couples *are* related while the rest have only the commonality of the same surname for reasons which are "strictly coincidental." As the first part of your quiz, you are to come up with the correct surname. For each one with which you are successful, you may take 5 points. In addition, you are to enter in either of the columns at the right your answer as to whether the couples are related or unrelated. If they *are* related, you must provide the relationship. For each correct answer regarding the relationship or non-relationship, you may have another 10 points. That's a possible 300 points on this quiz alone!

	RELATED	UNRELATED
1. Chester and Adrian		
2. Teresa and Will _ _ _ _ _ _		
3. Evelyn and George _ _ _ _ _ _		
4. Gene and Joyce		
5. Winifred and Artie _ _ _ _ _		
6. Louise and Mel _ _ _ _ _ _ _		
7. Antonio and Rita _ _ _ _ _ _ _		
8. Frank and Matt _ _ _ _ _ _ _		
9. Steve and Sally _ _ _ _ _ _ _ _		
10. Olive and Harry _ _ _ _ _ _		
11. John and David		
12. Nancy and Jack _ _ _ _ _ _		
13. Marjorie and Fritz		
14. Joan and Gloria		

124

15. Robert and R. G.
_ _ _ _ _ _ _ _ _
16. John and Deborah _ _ _ _
17. Jennifer and L. Q. _ _ _ _ _ _
18. James and Russell
_ _ _ _ _ _ _
19. Sidney and Dennis _ _ _ _ _ _
20. Danny and Frankie
_ _ _ _ _ _

_____points

(*Answers on page 247*)

61. NAMES IN COMMON—DUFFERS' TEE

Below in Column One, we have listed pairs of players who have the same surname. In the two columns at the right of the page, we ask you to tell us if there is or is not a relationship. If you can distinguish correctly, you may have 5 points. In those cases where there is some relationship, you can win another 5 points by telling us what the relationship is.

RELATED   UNRELATED

1. Chester and Adrian Morris
2. Teresa and Will Wright
3. Evelyn and George Brent
4. Gene and Joyce Reynolds
5. Winifred and Artie Shaw
6. Louise and Mel Brooks
7. Antonio and Rita Moreno
8. Frank and Matt McHugh
9. Steve and Sally Forrest
10. Olive and Harry Carey
11. John and David Carradine
12. Nancy and Jack Kelly
13. Marjorie and Fritz Weaver
14. Joan and Gloria Blondell
15. Robert and R. G. Armstrong
16. John and Deborah Kerr
17. Jennifer and L. Q. Jones
18. James and Russell Gleason
19. Sidney and Dennis James
20. Danny and Frankie Thomas

_____points

(*Answers on page 247*)

62. FIRST, THE WORD

Undeniably, the best films begin with a good script, and—happily—Hollywood has done some magnificent screen treatments of the more contemporary writers, as well as of the classics. Below, we list in Column One two films which trace their origin to the same writer. Here the question is two-part: (a) You must identify the author—and for each correct identification, you get 10 points; and (b) from the three films listed in Column Two, you are to select the film also attributable to the same author. For this, take 10 points for each correct title. And we must insist that you get both parts right in order to claim any score. We never said we wouldn't be hard-nosed about this . . .

1. "Goodbye, Mr. Chips"

   "Random Harvest"

   ———————————

   a. "Our Hearts Were Young and Gay"
   b. "Lost Horizon"
   c. "Good Morning, Miss Dove"

2. "The Thin Man"
   "The Glass Key"

   ———————————

   a. "Shane"
   b. "Manhattan Melodrama"
   c. "The Maltese Falcon"

3. "The Blue Dahlia"
   "Lady in the Lake"

   ———————————

   a. "The Big Sleep"
   b. "The Last Gangster"
   c. "Harper"

4. "Little Caesar"
   "Scarface"

   ———————————

   a. "Bullets or Ballots"
   b. "Serenade"
   c. "High Sierra"

5. "Journey into Fear"

   "Topkapi"

   ———————————

   a. "Kiss the Blood Off My Hands"
   b. "The Enforcer"
   c. "The Mask of Dimitrios"

6. "The Night of June 13th"
   "Private Scandal"

   ———————————

   a. "Julie"
   b. "Laura"
   c. "Vicki"

7. "The Specter of the Rose"
   "Notorious"

   ———————————

   a. "Mr. Lucky"
   b. "The Red Shoes"
   c. "Spellbound"

8. "Midnight Lace"
   "The Voice of Bugle Ann"

   ———————————

   a. "Portrait in Smoke"
   b. "The Best Years of Our Lives"
   c. "Ruthless"

9. "The Ipcress File"
   "Billion Dollar Brain"

   ———————————

   a. "Strangers on a Train"
   b. "Funeral in Berlin"
   c. "One, Two, Three"

10. "The Old Dark House"	a. "Invasion of the Body Snatchers"
"Laburnum Grove"	b. "Sleuth"
_____	c. "An Inspector Calls"
11. "The Fall of the House of Usher"	a. "Dr. Praetorious"
"The Raven"	b. "People Will Talk"
_____	c. "The Pit and the Pendulum"
12. "Double Indemnity"	a. "Ruby Gentry"
"The Postman Always Rings Twice"	b. "Stella Dallas"
_____	c. "Mildred Pierce"

_____points

(*Answers on page 247*)

62. FIRST, THE WORD—DUFFERS' TEE

Many literary classics have been adapted into films, and the effort has resulted in some equally memorable movies. But at the same time, Hollywood has not overlooked more contemporary writers as a source of screenplays. Below, in Column One, we list two films which have come from the same writer. In Column Two, we list (out of order) the authors in question. And in Column Three, we list (also out of order) another list of films which sprang from the same pens. Make your proper selections from Columns Two and Three to correspond with the films of Column One, and take 10 points for each correct answer—or 20 points per question. If you get only one part of the answer correct, you may take credit for that *half* answer —and we're being more liberal with you than we were with the Buffs! That low rumble you hear is the sulking of the Buffs!

1. "Goodbye, Mr. Chips" "Random Harvest"	A. W. R. Burnett	a. "Laura"
2. "The Thin Man" "The Glass Key"	B. Ben Hecht	b. "Funeral in Berlin"
3. "The Blue Dahlia" "Lady in the Lake"	C. J. B. Priestley	c. "Mildred Pierce"
4. "Little Caesar" "Scarface"	D. James Hilton	d. "The Best Years of Our Lives"

5. "Journey into Fear" "Topkapi"	E. Raymond Chandler	e. "Spellbound"
6. "The Night of June 13th" "Private Scandal"	F. Len Deighton	f. "Lost Horizon"
7. "The Specter of the Rose" "Notorious"	G. Edgar Allan Poe	g. "The Maltese Falcon"
8. "Midnight Lace" "The Voice of Bugle Ann"	H. Dashiell Hammett	h. "The Pit and the Pendulum"
9. "The Ipcress File" "Billion Dollar Brain"	I. Eric Ambler	i. "The Big Sleep"
10. "The Old Dark House" "Laburnum Grove"	J. Vera Caspary	j. "The Mask of Dimitrios"
11. "The Fall of the House of Usher" "The Raven"	K. James M. Cain	k. "An Inspector Calls"
12. "Double Indemnity" "The Postman Always Rings Twice"	L. MacKinlay Kantor	l. "High Sierra"

_____points

(*Answers on page 248*)

63. MORE THAN A BIT!

We believe that the real film fan is as interested in the bit players as he is in the stars of a film. For years, the same familiar and loved faces have added to our enjoyment of hundreds of films. Though they rarely attain stardom, or even *featured* status, many players of minor parts in films have gained recognition for their contributions. Below, we list sixteen such personalities, and from the clues given, you should be able to evoke some delightful memories just by recalling their names. Merely fill in the blanks correctly, and take 10 points for each correct name you can recall. Also, hidden in the answers is the name of another well-known actress—and by ferreting out her name, you can add 40 points to your score. You not only get an increase in your points—you might even learn where the wolf-bane grows!

1	J. Pat O'	– – – – –
2	Thurston H	– – –
3	Emory P	– – – – – –
4	Iris A	– – – – –
5	John Q	– – – – –
6	Wade B	– – – – – –
7	Byron F	– – – – – –
8	Elmira S	– – – – – – –
9	Murray A	– – – –
10	Bess F	– – – – – –
11	Luis A	– – – – – –
12	Hal K. D	– – – – –
13	Cliff C	– – – –
14	John W	– – – – – –
15	Steven G	– – – –
16	Milton P	– – – – – –

———— points

(*Answers on page 248*)

63. MORE THAN A BIT!—DUFFERS' TEE

We believe that the real film fan is as interested in the bit players as he is in the stars of a film. (Everyone knows that Paul Hurst was a star of "Gone With the Wind.") For years, the same familiar and loved faces have added to our enjoyment of hundreds of films, though they never rose to stardom, or even *featured* status. Many players of minor parts in films over the years have gained recognition for their contributions. Below, we list clues relating to sixteen such personalities. Identify the player by matching the last name from Column Two with the first names we provide in Column One. You may have 10 points for each correct pairing. If you do it properly, you can add another 40 points to your score by deducing the name of yet another well-known actress. You might even discover where the wolfbane grows.

129

1.	J. Pat	— — — — — —	a. Adrian
2.	Thurston	— — — —	b. Alberni
3.	Emory	— — — — — — —	c. Alper
4.	Iris	— — — — —	d. Boteler
5.	John	— — — — — —	e. Clark
6.	Wade	— — — — — — —	f. Dawson
7.	Byron	— — — — — —	g. Flowers
8.	Elmira	— — — — — — — —	h. Foulger
9.	Murray	— — — — —	i. Geray
10.	Bess	— — — — — —	j. Hall
11.	Luis	— — — — — — —	k. O'Malley
12.	Hal K.	— — — — — —	l. Parnell
13.	Cliff	— — — — —	m. Parsons
14.	John	— — — — — — —	n. Qualen
15.	Steven	— — — — —	o. Sessions
16.	Milton	— — — — — — —	p. Wengraf

——— points

(*Answers on page 249*)

64. THE OTHER WOMAN

It is usually the case with film freaks that mention of the title will prompt one to recall the stars who played the male and female leads. Occasionally, too, a third or fourth star, or even a supporting player, is remembered. Looking back, we've come up with a number of films in which the stars are easily remembered, but which also had "another woman" in the cast whom we'd nearly forgotten. These other women sometimes played the "other woman" in a romantic triangle —but all were names of stature. Below, we list a dozen films, plus the two leads in each film. See if you can recall the name of the actress who was the "other woman" in each film. Take 15 points for each name you recall.

1. "An American in Paris"
   Gene Kelly and Leslie
   Caron _____ a _____ h

2. "Only Angels Have Wings"
   Cary Grant and Jean
   Arthur _____ a _____ h

3. "The Carpetbaggers"
   George Peppard and
   Carroll Baker ___a___ ___r___

4. "The Strange Love of
   Martha Ivers"
   Barbara Stanwyck and
   Kirk Douglas ___h___ ___t___

5. "Teacher's Pet"
   Clark Gable and Doris
   Day ___e___ ___n___

6. "Cass Timberlane"
   Spencer Tracy and Lana
   Turner ___y___ ___r___

7. "The Spoilers"
   John Wayne and Marlene
   Dietrich ___t___ ___y___

8. "Homecoming"
   Clark Gable and Lana
   Turner ___e___ ___r___

9. "Daddy Long Legs"
   Fred Astaire and Lesile
   Caron ___y___ ___e___

10. "Red River"
    John Wayne and Joanne
    Dru ___n___ ___y___

11. "Dr. Jekyll and Mr. Hyde"
    Spencer Tracy and Ingrid
    Bergman ___a___ ___r___

12. "The Seven Year Itch"
    Marilyn Monroe and Tom
    Ewell ___n___ ___s___

See what we mean?

_____points

(*Answers on page 249*)

64. THE OTHER WOMAN—DUFFERS' TEE

It is usually the case with film freaks (even Duffers!) that mention of a title will prompt one to recall the stars who played the male and female leads. Occasionally, too, a third or fourth star, or even a supporting player, is remembered. Looking back, we've come up with a number of films in which the stars are easily remembered, but which also had "another woman" in the cast whom we'd nearly forgotten. These other women sometimes played the "other woman" in a romantic triangle—but all were names of stature. Below, we list a dozen films, plus the male and female leads. Listed out of order in Column Two are those actresses who played "the other woman." Make your selection from Column Two, and pair her with the proper title-star combination. Take 15 points for each correct pairing.

1. "An American in Paris"
   Gene Kelly and Leslie Caron
2. "Only Angels Have Wings"
   Cary Grant and Jean Arthur
3. "The Carpetbaggers"
   George Peppard and Carroll Baker
4. "The Strange Love of Martha Ivers"
   Barbara Stanwyck and Kirk Douglas
5. "Teacher's Pet"
   Clark Gable and Doris Day
6. "Cass Timberlane"
   Spencer Tracy and Lana Turner
7. "The Spoilers"
   John Wayne and Marlene Dietrich
8. "Homecoming"
   Clark Gable and Lana Turner
9. "Daddy Long Legs"
   Fred Astaire and Leslie Caron
10. "Red River"
    John Wayne and Joanne Dru
11. "Dr. Jekyll and Mr. Hyde"
    Spencer Tracy and Ingrid Bergman
12. "The Seven Year Itch"
    Marilyn Monroe and Tom Ewell

a. Lizabeth Scott

b. Terry Moore

c. Margaret Lindsay

d. Anne Baxter

e. Rita Hayworth

f. Colleen Gray

g. Nina Foch

h. Mary Astor

i. Martha Hyer

j. Mamie Van Doren

k. Evelyn Keyes

l. Lana Turner

_____points

(*Answers on page 249*)

65. ODD MAN OUT

This quiz is a two-part job. In this book's predecessor, we listed a number of cinematic crime-fighters and asked the reader to identify who played those uprights of the law. As we all know, the crime-fighter has long been glorified in films, but there are so many versions of different detective epics that we now ask *not* who played So-and-so but rather, *who did not!* Below, in each question we list four players. Three of them portrayed a particular cinematic crime-fighter. For one part of your quiz, we ask you to eliminate the player who never played the particular crime-fighter in question. Find the ODD MAN OUT, and take 5 points for each one you detect. But identify the crime-fighter played by the three players who *do* belong, and make an additional 10 points per correct answer. Here's a possible increase to your score of 150 points—if you can find the ODD MAN OUT.

1. Lewis Wilson	Robert Lowery	John Ridgeley	Adam West
2. Bert Lytell	Lionel Barrymore	Chester Morris	William Gargan
3. George Sanders	Tom Conway	Hugh Marlowe	John Calvert
4. George Brent	Ronald Colman	Jack Buchanan	John Howard
5. Raymond Burr	Warren William	Ricardo Cortez	Donald Woods
6. Claude Dauphin	Austin Trevor	Tony Randall	Albert Finney
7. Jim Bannon	Louis Hayward	George Sanders	Hugh Sinclair
8. Robert Kent	Jack Holt	Francis Lederer	Gerald Mohr
9. Robert Warwick	"Chick" Chandler	Roger Pryor	Dennis O'Keefe
10. Warner Oland	Sidney Toler	Sessue Hayakawa	George Kuwa

_____points

(*Answers on page 250*)

65. ODD MAN OUT—DUFFERS' TEE

In this book's predecessor, *The Compleat Motion Picture Quiz Book,* we listed a number of crime-fighters from the screen and asked the reader to identify who played those dauntless heroes. The crime-fighter has long been glorified in films, and there are so many versions of different detective epics that we now ask *not* who played So-and-so, but rather, *who did not!* Below, we list a well-known cinematic crime-fighter, followed by the names of four players. Three

133

of them played the character at one time or another—while the fourth did not. Isolate for us the ODD MAN OUT, and take 15 points for each correct answer.

1. BATMAN	Lewis Wilson	Robert Lowery	John Ridgeley	Adam West
2. BOSTON BLACKIE	Bert Lytell	Lionel Barrymore	Chester Morris	William Gargan
3. THE FALCON	George Sanders	Tom Conway	Hugh Marlowe	John Calvert
4. BULLDOG DRUMMOND	George Brent	Ronald Colman	Jack Buchanan	John Howard
5. PERRY MASON	Raymond Burr	Warren William	Richardo Cortez	Donald Woods
6. HERCULE POIROT	Claude Dauphin	Austin Trevor	Tony Randall	Albert Finney
7. THE SAINT	Jim Bannon	Louis Hayward	George Sanders	Hugh Sinclair
8. THE LONE WOLF	Robert Kent	Jack Holt	Francis Lederer	Gerald Mohr
9. JIMMY VALENTINE	Robert Warwick	"Chick" Chandler	Roger Pryor	Dennis O'Keefe
10. CHARLIE CHAN	Warner Oland	Sidney Toler	Sessue Hayakawa	George Kuwa

_____points

(*Answers on page 250*)

66. TELL US WHO PART II

Below, in each question, we list two incidents or plot points from two films in which the same player—male or female—appeared. From your memory, tell us the name of the player we are seeking. Take 15 points for each correct identification. But if you can also correctly name the titles of the two films from which the incidents are taken, you may add *another* 10 points. You must, however, name *both* of the films to take advantage of the bonus 10 points.

1. He beat Alan Ladd in a vicious fight, and he was himself beaten and thrown from a lifeboat by Walter Slezak.
2. Gene Tierney visited him while he was in his bathtub, and—as a baby-sitter for parents Robert Young and Maureen O'Hara—he retaliated for a toddler's wrongdoing by pouring cereal on the head of his charge.
3. He took Jean Simmons to Havana for dinner, and—after a vicious lashing, administered by Karl Malden—his hand was smashed.
4. He attempted to defraud Taylor Holmes by presenting Coleen Gray as the spirit of Holmes's dead fiancée, and he feigned pain as Everett Sloane pretended to gouge out his eyes.
5. He went swimming at night with Katharine Hepburn, and he fought off a murderous Raymond Burr by popping flashbulbs in his attacker's face.
6. He led a wagon train of pioneers from Illinois to the Great Salt Lake, and he was an ineffective law officer in the employ of Robert Ryan.
7. He helped raise a stage curtain to reveal Debbie Reynolds singing for Jean Hagen, and he physically attacked Skip Homeier following the shooting of Gregory Peck.
8. He tromped through the wilds of Africa with Duncan Renaldo, and —as Vice-President of the United States—he allowed James Stewart to conduct a filibuster.
9. He posed for a portrait as Bette Davis pleaded for him to aid Brian Aherne, and he planned to escape to Brazzaville with Humphrey Bogart.
10. He was a noisy drunk in a diner, annoying Robert Walker and Judy Garland, and he shot the face off a Coca-Cola machine in order to get a coin for a pay phone.

_____points

(*Answers on page 251*)

66. TELL US WHO PART II—DUFFERS' TEE

Below, we list in each question two incidents or plot points from two films in which the same player appeared. From your memory, tell us the name of the player we're seeking. We've provided the names—out of order—in Column Two, so for each player you can match with incidents in his cinematic career, you may have 15 points. If you can *also* tell us *both* film titles represented, you may add another 10 points per question. So put on your thinking cap, and good luck for a possible 250-point addition to your score.

1. He beat Alan Ladd in a vicious fight, and he was himself beaten and thrown from a lifeboat by Walter Slezak.   a. Clifton Webb

2. Gene Tierney visited him while he was in his bathtub, and—as a baby-sitter for parents Robert Young and Maureen O'Hara—he retaliated for a toddler's wrongdoing by pouring cereal on the head of his charge.   b. Keenan Wynn

3. He took Jean Simmons to Havana for dinner, and—after a vicious lashing, administered by Karl Malden—his hand was smashed.   c. Tyrone Power

4. He attempted to defraud Taylor Holmes by presenting Coleen Gray as the spirit of Holmes's dead fiancée, and he feigned pain as Everett Sloane pretended to gouge out his eyes.   d. Claude Rains

5. He went swimming at night with Katharine Hepburn, and he fought off a murderous Raymond Burr by popping flashbulbs in his attacker's face.   e. William Bendix

6. He led a wagon train of pioneers from Illinois to the Great Salt Lake, and he was an ineffective law officer in the employ of Robert Ryan.   f. Millard Mitchell

7. He helped raise a stage curtain to reveal Debbie Reynolds singing for Jean Hagen, and he physically attacked Skip Homeier following the shooting of Gregory Peck.   g. Marlon Brando

8. He tromped through the wilds of Africa
   with Duncan Renaldo, and—as
   Vice-President of the United States
   —he allowed James Stewart to
   conduct a filibuster.   h. James Stewart

9. He posed for a portrait as Bette Davis
   pleaded for him to aid Brian Aherne,
   and he planned to escape to Brazzaville
   with Humphrey Bogart.   i. Dean Jagger

10. He was a noisy drunk in a diner, annoying
    Robert Walker and Judy Garland, and
    he shot the face off a Coca-Cola
    machine in order to get a coin for
    a pay phone.   j. Harry Carey

                                            _____points

                                            (*Answers on page 251*)

67. FILMS IN COMMON PART II

Again, we're looking at films which have something in common
with other films, and this version of FILMS IN COMMON is played exactly the same as was the earlier version. The only wrinkle in *this*
version is that the similarity might be something other than plot, so
think carefully as you select the film from Column Two which has
something in common with the two films we've listed in each question of Column One. As before, this test has something in common
with the earlier version, since we're awarding 15 points for each correct answer! Go get 'em!

1. "A Song to Remember"   a. "Hollywood Cavalcade"
   "I'll See You in My Dreams"

2. "Operator 13"   b. "Compulsion"
   "Whistling in Dixie"

3. "One Foot in Heaven"   c. "Saratoga"
   "One Man's Way"

4. "The Devil and the Deep"   d. "This Happy Breed"
   "Destination Tokyo"

5. "The Birth of a Nation"   e. "Operation Petticoat"
   "The Prisoner of Shark Island"

6. "The Odessa File"   f. "A Man Called Peter"
   "Kiss of Death"

7. "Tora, Tora, Tora"	g. "The Red Badge of
"From Here to Eternity"	Courage"
8. "The Big House" (1930)	h. "Prince of Players"
"Birdman of Alcatraz"	
9. "In Cold Blood"	i. "In Harm's Way"
"The Girl in the Red Velvet Swing"	
10. "Marty"	j. "White Heat"
"Days of Wine and Roses"	
11. "The Son-Daughter"	k. "Brute Force"
"Dragon Seed"	
12. "Private Lives"	l. "This Land Is Mine"
"In Which We Serve"	
13. "Singin' in the Rain"	m. "Stars and Stripes Forever"
"The Great Waldo Pepper"	
14. "Solomon and Sheba"	n. "The Catered Affair"
"My Son John"	
15. "The Moon Is Down"	o. "The Good Earth"
"The Chetniks"	

_____points

(*Answers on page 252*)

67. FILMS IN COMMON PART II—DUFFERS' TEE

It's time again to look at films which have something *in common* with other films, and this version of FILMS IN COMMON is played exactly the same as was the earlier version. The only wrinkle in *this* version is that the similarity might be something other than plot, so think carefully before you make your selection. As before, we list two films in each question of Column One. Following, in Column Two, we provide you a choice of three films—only one of which has something *in common* with the two films in Column One. Select the one film from Column Two which has something strongly in common with the two films of Column One, and take 15 points for each correct grouping. Go get 'em!

1. "A Song to Remember"	a. "Anchors Aweigh"
"I'll See You in My Dreams"	b. "Stars and Stripes Forever"
	c. "Wife Versus Secretary"

2. "Operator 13"

    "Whistling in Dixie"

a. "The Red Badge of Courage"

b. "Two Years Before the Mast"

c. "China"

3. "One Foot in Heaven"
    "One Man's Way"

a. "The Devil Is a Sissy"

b. "Little Lord Fauntleroy"

c. "A Man Called Peter"

4. "The Devil and the Deep"
    "Destination Tokyo"

a. "Operation Petticoat"

b. "Air Force"

c. "Airport"

5. "The Birth of a Nation"
    "The Prisoner of Shark Island"

a. "The Prisoner"

b. "Riot in Cell Block 11"

c. "Prince of Players"

6. "The Odessa File"
    "Kiss of Death"

a. "White Heat"

b. "I Can Get It for You Wholesale"

c. "Broken Lance"

7. "Tora, Tora, Tora"

    "From Here to Eternity"

a. "The House Across the Bay"

b. "In Harm's Way"

c. "The Old Dark House"

8. "The Big House" (1930)
    "Birdman of Alcatraz"

a. "Born Free"

b. "Brute Force"

c. "The Lion"

9. "In Cold Blood"
    "The Girl in the Red Velvet Swing"

a. "Compulsion"

b. "Pete Kelly's Blues"

c. "Intermezzo"

10. "Marty"
    "Days of Wine and Roses"

a. "The Lost Weekend"

b. "Julie"

c. "The Catered Affair"

11. "The Son-Daughter"
    "Dragon Seed"

a. "Dragonwyck"

b. "The High Window"

c. "The Good Earth"

12. "Private Lives"
    "In Which We Serve"

a. "Black Beauty"

b. "This Happy Breed"

c. "Chitty Chitty Bang Bang"

13. "Singin' in the Rain"	a. "All About Eve"
"The Great Waldo Pepper"	b. "Hollywood Cavalcade"
	c. "King Solomon's Mines"

14. "Solomon and Sheba"	a. "David and Lisa"
"My Son John"	b. "Saratoga"
	c. "The Devil at Four O'Clock"

15. "The Moon Is Down"	a. "The Moon and Sixpence"
"The Chetniks"	b. "Winter Carnival"
	c. "This Land Is Mine"

_____points

(*Answers on page 253*)

68. RULE, BRITANNIA!

This crisscross deals with those actors and actresses who have come to us through the courtesy of the British Isles. The diagram following can be completed—and your score can be 500 points greater —by filling in the blanks with the correct surnames—and be sure each surname is of a proper length. Since you are Buffs, we've omitted giving you the names to be used, but thought we'd let you fend for yourselves. (Bet you could learn to hate us!) We'll give you one important clue—and it breaks our heart to do it: our favorite Britisher, Mr. Charles Laughton, is not in the quiz. But enough of this pampering. Buckle down—stiff upper lip and all that.

THREE-LETTER NAMES
This Bernard was 007's boss!
FOUR-LETTER NAMES
This Edna was a superlative.
Bugs Bunny must've loved this Lumsden.
She was Ronnie's wife—and we don't mean Reagan.
This Geoffrey is usually a businessman, a police inspector, or an army officer.
Her name is spelled the same, but it's pronounced differently from America's John.
This Montagu's last name sometimes means "nothing."
This Kenneth is by no means "Less."
This Reginald was our favorite Scrooge.
He is related to Sir Carol.
Michael or Susannah . . .

140

Heather was a passenger on the "Lifeboat."

She was Chaplin's ballerina.

Dr. Watson, of course . . .

This Colin's creation set off a string of sequels.

In "Gunga Din," he got tipsy on punch.

He won an Oscar for being a good Welsh father.

Another Reginald.

The original Mr. Chips.

Edith was a classy Dame.

A pretty blond Cockney was Virginia.

This Archie began as a stilt-walker.

This Nigel kept track of "The Ipcress File."

Hedy was once his bride.

The Moon's His Balloon!

Unlike his first starring role, his talent was not visible.

C. Aubrey . . .

This was a "Man Who Could Work Miracles!"

He was the Emperor of Mexico, with a golden beard!

Though a Britisher, he portrayed Alexander Hamilton and Voltaire.

Good old Felix!

" 'Tis a far, far better thing I do . . ."

Melville or Gladys.

Dear Noel!

This June was Ernie Mott's love.

This Richard was a star for Darryl F.

Trevor or Leslie.

This Ian was once Richard the Lion-Hearted.

She went from playing neurotic women to become a director.

This Aubrey usually played butlers, though his face was cherubic.

Tall, gray, and suave—he belonged in tweeds . . . did this Alan!

She was Sir Laurence's Cathy.

This Cecil was perfect as the harried Britisher.

Tommy was a leprechaun.

Dame May—

This Constance was perfect as the Grande Dame.

007.

The satanic and evil were well portrayed by this Henry.

Sir John.

His real name is the same as our Mr. Smith's.

Not Kate, but Audrey.

Raymond or G. P.

This Kay was one of "Les Girls."

He lost a weekend.

The pompous and fraudulent was this Alan's forte.

She was "Frankie's ma"—and the Monster terrified her.

Some have called this "Sir" the world's greatest English-speaking actor.

Dr. Strangelove.

This Arthur is Barry's brother.

This Frederick is not a warlock—but close!

EIGHT-LETTER NAMES

His friends called him Bramwell.

This Reggie, as Beverly Carlton, visited Mr. Whiteside.

He played a king, a Pope, and a conqueror.

"Get Me to the Church on Time."

He ran a restaurant with Lana Turner . . . and then along came Garfield!

His Gypo won an Oscar!

Few knew this Herbert had a wooden leg.

This Philip was Gladys Cooper's husband.

This Laurence was Archesilaus when Liz was Cleo.

One address for him was 221-B Baker Street.

Lynn and Vanessa called him "Father."

The classic "gentleman's gentleman."

His friends know him as Emlyn.

NINE-LETTER NAMES

This Cedric once spent a lot of time in a tree.

Wilfrid sang and danced with Rex and Audrey.

TEN-LETTER NAMES

She was a well-remembered "Bride."

He once played Sir Boss.

ELEVEN-LETTER NAME

A young lad, he received sage counsel from Mr. Micawber.

TWELVE-LETTER NAME

This Richard started as a teen-ager, and soon went to character roles.

_____points

(*Answers on page 254*)

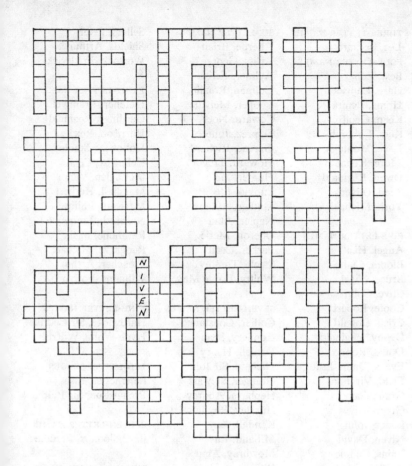

68. RULE, BRITANNIA!—DUFFERS' TEE

This RULE, BRITANNIA! crisscross, as contained in the preceding diagram, can be completed by filling in the last names of well-known players from British cinema. Complete the diagram, and add 350 points to your score, by inserting the correct names (each of the appropriate length) so that the entire diagram interlocks. These British players all fit nicely (though we nearly went bananas figuring out the diagram)—and we apologize most profusely for being unable to include Mr. Laughton. We suggest you use logic, deduction, and a pencil with a large eraser—though if you have even a smidgen of the indomitable British spirit, you'll charge right in with a ballpoint. So have at it—for Harry, England, and St. George!

143

_____points

(*Answers on page 256*)

69. HEY, WASN'T THAT . . . ?

There have been a number of films which include well-known personalities appearing as "themselves." In this quiz, we have attempted to avoid those star-studded spectacles wherein every performer under contract was used in a "cameo." Rather, the questions in this quiz focus on appearances by celebrities well-known in *other* fields apart from motion pictures. Below, we list twenty such personalities, and ask you to tell us the title of the films in which they appeared as "Himself" or "Herself." Take 15 points for each title you complete.

1. Cecil B. DeMille   "S _ _ _ _ _ _ B _ _ _ _ _ _ _ _ _"
2. Louis Armstrong   "T _ _ F _ _ _ P _ _ _ _ _ _ _"
3. Babe Ruth   "P _ _ _ _ _ o _ t _ _ Y _ _ _ _ _ _ _"
4. John Ringling North   "T _ _ G _ _ _ _ _ _ _ _ _ S _ _ _ o _
     E _ _ _ _"
5. H. V. Kaltenborn   "M _. S _ _ _ _ _ G _ _ _ t _
     W _ _ _ _ _ _ _ _ _"
6. Nat "King" Cole   "T _ _ B _ _ _ _ G _ _ _ _ _ _ _ _"
7. Tony Zale   "S _ _ _ _ _ _ _ _ U _ T _ _ _ _ _
     L _ _ _ _ M _"
8. Walter Winchell   "W _ _ _ U _ a _ _ L _ _ _ _"
9. Jascha Heifetz   "T _ _ _ S _ _ _ _ _ H _ _ _ _
     M _ _ _ _"
10. Fanny Brice   "T _ _ G _ _ _ _ _ Z _ _ _ _ _ _ _ _"
11. Bill Dickey   "T _ _ S _ _ _ _ _ _ _ _ S _ _ _ _"
12. Sam Snead   "F _ _ _ _ _ t _ _ S _ _"
13. Mitzi Mayfair   "F _ _ _ J _ _ _ _ _ i _ a J _ _ _"
14. Walter Catlett   "L _ _ _ f _ _ t _ _ S _ _ _ _ _
     L _ _ _ _ _"
15. Don Budge   "P _ _ a _ _ M _ _ _ _"
16. Cary Middlecoff   "F _ _ _ _ _ t _ _ S _ _"
17. Gene Krupa   "T _ _ G _ _ _ _ M _ _ _ _ _ _
     S _ _ _ _"
18. Paul Whiteman   "S _ _ _ _ _ _ U _ t _ _ B _ _ _ _"
19. Emmett Kelly   "T _ _ G _ _ _ _ _ _ _ _ _ S _ _ _ o _
     E _ _ _ _"
20. Babe Didrikson   "P _ _ a _ _ M _ _ _ _"

_____points

(*Answers on page 256*)

69. HEY, WASN'T THAT . . . ?—DUFFERS' TEE

There have been a number of films which include appearances by well-known personalities appearing as "themselves." In this quiz, we have attempted to avoid those star-studded spectacles wherein every performer under contract was used in a "cameo." Rather, the questions in this quiz focus on appearances by celebrities well-known in

145

other fields apart from motion pictures. Below, we ask you to match the twenty celebrities with the films in which they appeared. These, of course, are the titles in Column Two, which, as always, are listed out of order. Take 15 points for each correct matching of the personality with the film in which that person appeared as "Himself" or "Herself."

1. Cecil B. DeMille		a.	"Look for the Silver Lining"
2. Louis Armstrong		b.	"Follow the Sun"
3. Babe Ruth		c.	"Pat and Mike"
4. John Ringling North		d.	"The Blue Gardenia"
5. H. V. Kaltenborn		e.	"The Stratton Story"
6. Nat "King" Cole		f.	"Sunset Boulevard"
7. Tony Zale		g.	"Pride of the Yankees"
8. Walter Winchell		h.	"They Shall Have Music"
9. Jascha Heifetz		i.	"Follow the Sun"
10. Fanny Brice		j.	"Pat and Mike"
11. Bill Dickey		k.	"The Five Pennies"
12. Sam Snead		l.	"Mr. Smith Goes to Washington"
13. Mitzi Mayfair		m.	"The Greatest Show on Earth"
14. Walter Catlett		n.	"The Greatest Show on Earth"
15. Don Budge		o.	"The Great Ziegfeld"
16. Cary Middlecoff		p.	"Somebody Up There Likes Me"
17. Gene Krupa		q.	"Strike Up the Band"
18. Paul Whiteman		r.	"Wake Up and Live"
19. Emmett Kelly		s.	"Four Jills in a Jeep"
20. Babe Didrikson		t.	"The Glenn Miller Story"

_____points

(*Answers on page 256*)

70. LA RONDE: COMEDIANS AND THEIR LADIES

We're certain you all know how LA RONDE works by now. Remember the Marjorie Main/Gertrude Lawrence example? Well, this is exactly the same, although it's bigger and more complex. If your memory fails, just look back to LA RONDE, and you'll be in good shape for this one. Here, in the diagram following, we ask you to start at the beginning and wend your way slowly *back* to the beginning.

This is our salute to the durable, long-suffering actresses who have appeared opposite some of the great screen comedians—although we decided to let Mme. Dumont go undisturbed, her dignity unruffled. To complete this LA RONDE puzzle, supply the appropriate titles in the spaces we've designated for the symbols A through X. Do this completely and correctly—and you'll not only have completed the circle, but you'll also have added 500 points to your score.

A. Eddie Cantor and
    Constance Moore   "_ _ _ _ _ _ _ _ _ _ _ _ _"

B. Constance Moore and
    W. C. Fields   "_ _ _ _ _ _ , _ _ _ _ _ _ _
    _ _ _ _ _ _ _ _ _"

C. W. C. Fields and
    Maureen O'Sullivan   "_ _ _ _ _ _ _ _ _ _ _ _ _ _"

D. Maureen O'Sullivan and
    the Marx Bros.   "_ _ _ _ _ _ _ _ _ _ _ _ _"

E. The Marx Bros. and
    Marilyn Monroe   "_ _ _ _ _ _ _ _ _"

F. Marilyn Monroe and
    Mickey Rooney   "_ _ _ _ _ _ _ _ _ _ _"

G. Mickey Rooney and
    Ann Rutherford   "_ _ _ _ _ _ _ _ _ _ _ _ _ _ _
    _ _ _ _ _"

H. Ann Rutherford and
    Danny Kaye   "_ _ _ _ _ _ _ _ _ _ _ _ _ _
    _ _ _ _ _ _ _ _ _ _"

I. Danny Kaye and
    Katharine Hepburn   "_ _ _ _ _ _ _ _ _ _ _ _
    _ _ _ _ _ _ _"

J. Katharine Hepburn and
    Bob Hope   "_ _ _ _ _ _ _ _ _ _ _ _ _ _"

K. Bob Hope and Martha
    Raye   "_ _ _ _ _ _ _ _ _ _ _ _ _
    _ _ _ _ _"

L. Martha Raye and
    Jimmy Durante   "_ _ _ _ _"

M. Jimmy Durante and
    Lupe Velez   "_ _ _ _ _ _ _ _ _ _ _ _ _ _ _"

N. Lupe Velez and Wheeler
    & Woolsey   "_ _ _ _ _ _ _ _ _"

O. Wheeler & Woolsey and
    Betty Grable   "_ _ _ _ _ _ _ _ _"

P. Betty Grable and Joe
   Penner   "___ ___ ___ _____
   ____"

Q. Joe Penner and Lucille
   Ball   "__. _____ _____"

R. Lucille Ball and Red
   Skelton   "_____ ___ _ ____"

S. Red Skelton and Ginger
   Rogers   "_____ _____
   ____"

T. Ginger Rogers and Joe
   E. Brown   "___ _____"

U. Joe E. Brown and
   Kathryn Grayson   "____ _____"

V. Kathryn Grayson and
   Abbott & Costello   "___ ____"

W. Abbott & Costello and
   Joan Davis   "____ ____ _____"

X. Joan Davis and Eddie
   Cantor   "__ ___ ____ _____"

_____points

(*Answers on page 257*)

70. LA RONDE COMEDIANS AND THEIR LADIES—DUFFERS' TEE

We're certain that *both* Buffs and Duffers know how LA RONDE works by now. Remember the Marjorie Main/Gertrude Lawrence example? Well, this is exactly the same, although it's bigger and perhaps just a bit more complex. If your memory fails, just look back to LA RONDE, and you'll be in good shape for this one. Here, in the diagram on the next page, we ask you to start at the beginning and wend your way slowly *back* to the beginning.

This quiz is a salute to the durable, long-suffering actresses who have appeared opposite some of the great screen comedians—and out of the deepest respect, we decided to let Margaret Dumont (bless her haughty soul!) go undisturbed, her dignity unruffled. To complete the wheel, select the appropriate titles suggested by the symbols A through X. For this Duffers' Tee, we've supplied the titles, out of order, in Column Two. Your task is to unscramble the order and

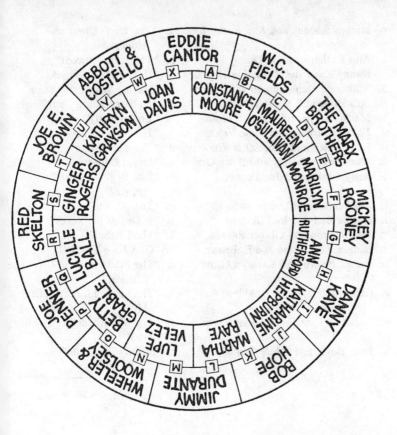

match the correct title with the correct star combination. You receive no score at all unless you use all the titles, once and once only. But get them all correct and your ever increasing score is fatter by 475 points!

A. Eddie Cantor and Constance Moore

B. Constance Moore and W. C. Fields

C. W. C. Fields and Maureen O'Sullivan

D. Maureen O'Sullivan and the Marx Bros.

E. The Marx Bros. and Marilyn Monroe

F. Marilyn Monroe and Mickey Rooney

a. "Show Boat"

b. "The Day the Bookies Wept"

c. "Jumbo"

d. "High Flyers"

e. "Rio Rita"

f. "Show Business"

149

G. Mickey Rooney and Ann Rutherford   g. "You Can't Cheat an Honest Man"

H. Ann Rutherford and Danny Kaye   h. "The Iron Petticoat"

I. Danny Kaye and Katharine Hepburn   i. "If You Knew Susie"

J. Katharine Hepburn and Bob Hope   j. "Having Wonderful Time"

K. Bob Hope and Martha Raye   k. "Dubarry Was a Lady"

L. Martha Raye and Jimmy Durante   l. "Love Happy"

M. Jimmy Durante and Lupe Velez   m. "Hold That Ghost"

N. Lupe Velez and Wheeler & Woolsey   n. "The Tenderfoot"

O. Wheeler & Woolsey and Betty Grable   o. "David Copperfield"

P. Betty Grable and Joe Penner   p. "Life Begins for Andy Hardy"

Q. Joe Penner and Lucille Ball   q. "The Nitwits"

R. Lucille Ball and Red Skelton   r. "A Day at the Races"

S. Red Skelton and Ginger Rogers   s. "The Fireball"

T. Ginger Rogers and Joe E. Brown   t. "Go Chase Yourself"

U. Joe E. Brown and Kathryn Grayson   u. "The Madwoman of Chaillot"

V. Kathryn Grayson and Abbott & Costello   v. "The Secret Life of Walter Mitty"

W. Abbott & Costello and Joan Davis   w. "The Big Broadcast of 1938"

X. Joan Davis and Eddie Cantor   x. "Strictly Dynamite"

_____points

(*Answers on page 257*)

71. WHO SANG . . . ? PART II

Below, in Column One, we list a number of song titles—and, as before, we caution that not all of these songs were given big, splashy presentations. In Column Two, you'll find (out of order) the player or players who performed the songs, and in Column Three (also out of order) you'll find clues relating to the titles of the films in which the songs were seen. So match the song to the performer—and then to the film in which it was performed. You may have 5 points for each part completed correctly—so here's a possible addition of 150 points to your score.

1. "I'll Build a Stairway to Paradise!"   A. Virginia O'Brien   a. "C____ D____"

2. "Is It a Crime?"   B. Gene Raymond   b. "J____ A____"

3. "You and I"   c. Ricardo   c. "I__ O__
                       Montalban   C____"
                       and Esther
                       Williams

4. "Baby, It's Cold   D. Debbie   d. "G____ N____"
    Outside"   Reynolds and
                       Carleton
                       Carpenter

5. "Pass That Peace   E. Betty Hutton   e. "H____ S____"
    Pipe"

6. "Aba Daba   F. Dorothy   f. "Z____ F____"
    Honeymoon"   Lamour

7. "True Love"   G. Tyrone Power g. "R____"

8. "Blue Room"   H. Nelson Eddy   h. "M__ M__ i__
                                   S__. L____"

9. "Bring On the   I. Judy Holliday i. "N____'__
    Wonderful Men"   D____"

10. "I've Taken Quite a J. Leon Ames   j. "W____ a__
    Fancy to You"   and Mary   M____"
                       Astor

11. "Dancing for Nickels K. Joan   k. "T__ B____ A__
    and Dimes"   McCracken   R____"

12. "Don't Sit Under the L. Alice Faye   l. "A__ A____ i__
    Apple Tree"   P____"

13. "I Wake Up in the M. Georges   m. "T__ W____
    Morning Feeling   Guetary   w__ L____"
    Fine"

14. "In the Still of the N. Perry Como   n. "S____ M____"
    Night"

15. "All I Do Is Dream O. Bing Crosby   o. "R__, H__ a__
    of You"   and Grace   B__"
                     Kelly

____points

(*Answers on page 258*)

71. WHO SANG . . . ? PART II—DUFFERS' TEE

Below, in Column One, we list a number of song titles—and, as before, we caution you that not all of these songs were given big, splashy presentations. In Column Two, you'll find (out of order) the player or players who performed the songs, and in Column Three (also out of order) you'll find the films in which these songs were performed. Your task is to match the song to the performer, and then to the film in which it was performed. You'll be awarded 5 points for each part answered correctly—so with fifteen questions at a possible 10 points each, you can soon be 150 points richer!

1. "I'll Build a Stairway to Paradise"	A. Virginia O'Brien	a. "Crash Dive"
2. "Is It a Crime?	B. Gene Raymond	b. "Johnny Apollo"
3. "You and I"	C. Ricardo Montalban and Esther Williams	c. "In Old Chicago"
4. "Baby, It's Cold Outside"	D. Debbie Reynolds and Carleton Carpenter	d. "Good News"
5. "Pass That Peace Pipe"	E. Betty Hutton	e. "High Society"
6. "Aba Daba Honeymoon"	F. Dorothy Lamour	f. "Ziegfeld Follies"
7. "True Love"	G. Tyrone Power	g. "Rosalie"
8. "Blue Room"	H. Nelson Eddy	h. "Meet Me in St. Louis"
9. "Bring On the Wonderful Men"	I. Judy Holliday	i. "Neptune's Daughter"
10. "I've Taken Quite a Fancy to You"	J. Leon Ames and Mary Astor	j. "Words and Music"
11. "Dancing for Nickels and Dimes"	K. Joan McCracken	k. "The Bells Are Ringing"
12. "Don't Sit Under the Apple Tree"	L. Alice Faye	l. "An American in Paris"
13. "I Wake Up in the Morning Feeling Fine"	M. Georges Guetary	m. "Two Weeks with Love"

14. "In the Still of   N. Perry Como   n. "Sadie McKee"
     the Night"

15. "All I Do Is Dream   o. Bing Crosby and   o. "Red, Hot and
     of You"   Grace Kelly   Blue"

_____points

(*Answers on page 258*)

72. THE BIG BULB: PAIRS

Once again we're looking at instances where actors and actresses who were long-familiar faces in feature films moved over to television. In some cases, new "teams" were created and their newfound popularity on the small screen was often greater than it had ever been in feature films. Below, we list a number of pairs of actors and/or actresses and ask you to place them in the proper TV series by completing the series titles suggested in Column Two. Take 15 points for each correct completion.

1. Guy Madison and Andy
   Devine   "W _ _ _ _   B _ _ _ _   H _ _ _ _ _ _"
2. George Brent and Dane
   Clark   "W _ _ _ _   S _ _ _ _ _ _ _"
3. Alan Mowbray and Frank
   Jenks   "C _ _ _ _ _ _ _   F _ _ _ _ _"
4. James Dunn and Michael
   O'Shea   "I _ _'_ a _ _ _ _ _ _   L _ _ _"
5. Barbara Britton and Richard
   Denning   "_ _. a _ _ _ _ _.   N _ _ _ _"
6. Tom Tully and Warner
   Anderson   "_ _ _   L _ _ _ _-_ _"
7. Wendell Corey and Marsha
   Hunt   "P _ _ _ _'_   B _ _   G _ _ _ _"
8. Howard Duff and Ida Lupino   "_ _. _ _ _ _ _ _   a _ _   E _ _"
9. Ronald Colman and Benita
   Hume   "T _ _   H _ _ _ _ _   _ _   I _ _"
10. Jimmie Lydon and Mitzi
    Green   "S _ T _ _ _ _   I _
                   H _ _ _ _ _ _ _ _"
11. Anne Jeffreys and Robert
    Sterling   "_ _ _ _ _ _"
12. Richard Jaeckel and John
    Derek   "F _ _ _ _ _ _ _ _   C _ _ _ _ _"

(*Answers on page 259*)   _____points

72. THE BIG BULB: PAIRS—DUFFERS' TEE

Once again we're looking at instances where actors and actresses who were long-familiar faces in feature films moved over to television. In some cases, new "teams" were created and their newfound popularity on the small screen was often greater than it had ever been in feature films. Below, we list a dozen pairs of actors and/or actresses, and ask you to place them in the proper TV series by pairing them with the out-of-order list provided in Column Two. Match the pair to the proper series and take 15 points for each correct pairing. Here's a possible 180 points for your ever growing score.

1. Guy Madison and Andy Devine
2. George Brent and Dane Clark
3. Alan Mowbray and Frank Jenks
4. James Dunn and Michael O'Shea
5. Barbara Britton and Richard Denning
6. Tom Tully and Warner Anderson
7. Wendell Corey and Marsha Hunt
8. Howard Duff and Ida Lupino
9. Ronald Colman and Benita Hume
10. Jimmie Lydon and Mitzi Green
11. Anne Jeffreys and Robert Sterling
12. Richard Jaeckel and John Derek

a. "Peck's Bad Girl"
b. "Topper"
c. "So This Is Hollywood"
d. "Wild Bill Hickok"
e. "Mr. Adams and Eve"
f. "Colonel Flack"
g. "Frontier Circus"
h. "Wire Service"
i. "It's a Great Life"
j. "The Line-up"
k. "Mr. and Mrs. North"
l. "The Halls of Ivy"

_____points

(*Answers on page 259*)

73. MISCELLANY

Here are some miscellaneous questions which really don't fit into any particular category, but we're going to give them to you anyway. The point values vary, so with each question, we'll advise what each answer is worth. Okay? Go!

1. In the mid-to-late 1960s, there were five American-made newsreels being shown in U.S. theaters. They were Pathé News, Paramount News, Fox Movietone News, News of the Day (made by Hearst Metrotone News for M-G-M release), and . . . which other one? (Take 20 points for the correct answer.)
2. In which year did the last remaining newsreel, releasing newsreels on

a regular basis, terminate operations? (Take 15 points for the correct answer.)

3. Helen Hayes, Ingrid Bergman, and Jack Lemmon have the distinction —at this writing—of being the only performers to win Oscars both as "Best Actress (or Actor)" and "Best Supporting Actress (or Actor)." Another performer had the opportunity to join this distinguished company in 1944. Name the person, and the two films which might have made this honor possible. (And take 20 points for *each* of the three answers you might get correct.)

4. Referring to Question 3 above, nearly forty years elapsed between Helen Hayes's first Oscar and her second—making her one of the oldest winners of an Oscar. Two other performers of advanced years won "Best Supporting" Oscars in 1947 and 1968. They were seventy years and seventy-two years of age, respectively, at the time of their triumph. Name both the players and the films involved—and take 25 points for each correct answer, or a possible 100 points on this question.

5. Who was the first child to be nominated as "Best Actor"? You may have 20 points for naming the child, 30 points for naming the film in which the nominated performance was included, and 50 points for naming the year.

6. One of the most delightful film musicals for M-G-M's "Golden Era" was "Seven Brides for Seven Brothers." Name four of the seven actors who portrayed the "Brothers" of the title. You may have 15 points apiece *if* you name at least four.

7. One of the big hits of 1967 was Robert Aldrich's "The Dirty Dozen" —an exciting war story about twelve army misfits who were given special training and sent on a raid behind Nazi lines. Name *six* of the "Dirty Dozen" (or a "Dirty Half Dozen," if you will) and take 20 points for each one you get correct.

8. Which of the following do *not* belong in this group, and why (take 30 points, if you get *both* answers correct): (a) Orry-Kelly, (b) Edith Head, (c) Adrian, (d) Chico Day, and (e) Helen Rose.

9. Identify the following . . . and take 20 points for each correct identification: (a) Grayson Hall, (b) Robert Rich, (c) Billy and Bobby Mauch, (d) Jon Whiteley and Vincent Winter, and (e) Bess Flowers.

10. Identify the "firsts" represented by these films. Score 25 points for each correct identification: (a) "The Robe," (b) "The Lights of New York," (c) "Flowers and Trees," (d) "Becky Sharp."

_____points

(*Answers on page 260*)

73. MISCELLANY—DUFFERS' TEE

Here are some miscellaneous questions which really don't fit into any particular category, but we're going to give them to you anyway. The point values vary, so with each question, we'll advise you what the answer is worth. Okay? Go!

1. In the mid-to-late 1960s, there were five American-made newsreels being shown in U.S. theaters. Three of them were: Pathé News, Fox Movietone News, and Paramount News. Which one of the following was *not* a bona fide newsreel: (a) Universal Newsreel, (b) News on the March, (c) News of the Day? (Take 20 points for the correct answer.)

2. The last year in which a newsreel was released on a regular basis . . . was it: (a) 1966, (b) 1967, (c) 1968, or (d) 1969? (Take 15 points for the correct answer.)

3. Helen Hayes, Jack Lemmon, and Ingrid Bergman are the only performers—as of this writing—to have won Oscars both as "Best Actress (or Actor)" and "Best Supporting Actress (or Actor)." Another performer had the opportunity to join this distinguished company in 1944. Would that person have been: (a) Dorothy Malone, (b) Harold Russell, (c) Jennifer Jones, (d) Dorothy McGuire, or (e) Gig Young? (Take 30 points for the correct answer.)

4. Referring to Question 3 above, nearly forty years elapsed between Helen Hayes's first Oscar and her second—making her one of the oldest Oscar winners. Two other performers of advanced years won "Best Supporting" Oscars in 1947 and 1968. They were seventy years and seventy-two years of age, respectively, at the time of their triumph. The two performers involved were: (a) Judith Anderson, (b) Tom Tully, (c) Edmund Gwenn, (d) Warner Anderson, (d) Ruth Gordon, (e) Maria Ouspenskaya. (Take 20 points for *each* answer.)

5. The *first* child to be nominated as "Best Actor" (or "Best Actress") was: (a) Jackie Searle, (b) Jackie Coogan, (c) Jackie Cooper, (d) Shirley Temple, (e) Marcia Mae Jones, (f) Juanita Quigley. (Take 40 points for the correct answer.)

6. One of the most delightful film musicals of M-G-M's "Golden Era" was "Seven Brides for Seven Brothers." Of the eight performers listed below, pick four who appeared as the "Brothers" (score 15 points each): (a) George Chakiris, (b) Russ Tamblyn, (c) Jeff Richards, (d) Tony Musante, (e) Bob Fosse, (f) Matt Mattox, (g) Jacques d'Amboise, (h) Royce Blackburn.

7. One of the big hits of 1967 was Robert Aldrich's "The Dirty Dozen" —an exciting war story about twelve army misfits who were given special training and sent on a raid behind Nazi lines. Of the twelve

performers listed below, six did *not* appear in the film—however, six did. Select the six who did, and take 20 points for each one you get correct: (a) Jim Brown, (b) David Hemmings, (c) Trini Lopez, (d) George Peppard, (e) Leslie Nielsen, (f) Donald Sutherland, (g) Chad Everett, (h) Keir Dullea, (i) Gary Lockwood, (j) Clint Walker, (k) Charles Bronson, (l) John Cassavetes.

8. Which of the following do *not* belong in this group, and why (take 30 points if you get both answers correct): (a) Lew Lehr, (b) Andre Baruch, (c) John Nesbitt, (d) Ed Thorgerson, (e) Ed Herlihy, (f) Lowell Thomas.

9. Identify the following . . . and take 20 points for each correct identification: (a) Nadia Gray, (b) George O'Hanlon, (c) Cyril Delevanti, (d) Yakima Canutt, and (e) Billy Bitzer.

10. Identify the "firsts" represented by these films. Score 50 points for each correct identification: (a) "The Robe," (b) "The Lights of New York," (c) "Flowers and Trees," (d) "Becky Sharp."

_____points

(*Answers on page 261*)

74. SEEING DOUBLE

We've met long-time movie fans who still cannot explain to us what a "cue mark" is, or who cannot define "carbon pencil," "trailer," or "canopy." But they all seem to know what a *dual role* is —and that's what we're concerned with in this quiz. Below, in Column One, we list titles of films which included a dual role—that is, two roles played by the same player. In Column Two, we list the characters portrayed by this person, and in Column Three, we ask you to tell us who portrayed the dual roles. Some of these are admittedly difficult—so don't be reluctant to take 30 points for each correct answer.

1. "The Masquerader"	Sir John Chilicote John Loder	_____
2. "Passion"	Rosa Melo Tonya Melo	_____
3. "A Stolen Life"	Kate Bosworth Patricia Bosworth	_____
4. "The Great Dictator"	Hynkel A Barber	_____
5. "The House of Rothschild"	Nathan Rothschild Mayer Rothschild	_____

6. "Dead Ringer"	Edith Phillips	
	Margaret Phillips	_____
7. "Thank Your Lucky Stars"	Eddie Cantor	
	Joe Simpson	_____
8. "On the Riviera"	Henri Durand	
	Jack Martin	_____
9. "The Prisoner of Zenda"	Rudolph Rassendyl	
	King Rudolph the Fifth	_____
10. "Here Come the Waves"	Susie Allison	
	Rosemary Allison	_____

_____points

(Answers on page 262)

74. SEEING DOUBLE—DUFFERS' TEE

If you can't explain exactly what a "cue mark" is—or a "trailer" or a "canopy"—don't feel bad. We know a number of Buffs who are in the same boat. But we don't recall ever running across a film fan who didn't know what a *dual role* is—and that's what we're talking about in this quiz, which we've entitled SEEING DOUBLE . . . and that should give you a clue. Below, in Column One, we've listed ten titles which included *dual roles* as part of their plots. Immediately following, in Column Two, you'll find the names of the two characters represented by these dual roles. Out of order in Column Three are those players who played both the roles. Select the appropriate player, and match him or her with the titles and characters of Columns One and Two. You may have 25 points for each correct grouping.

1. "The Masquerader"	Sir John Chilicote John Loder	a. Charlie Chaplin
2. "Passion"	Rosa Melo Tonya Melo	b. Bette Davis
3. "A Stolen Life"	Kate Bosworth Patricia Bosworth	c. Betty Hutton
4. "The Great Dictator"	Hynkel A Barber	d. Keenan Wynn
5. "The House of Rothschild"	Nathan Rothschild Mayer Rothschild	e. Ronald Colman

158

6. "Dead Ringer"	Edith Phillips Margaret Phillips		f.	Yvonne De Carlo
7. "Royal Wedding"	Irving Klinger Edgar Klinger		g.	Danny Kaye
8. "On the Riviera"	Henri Durand Jack Martin		h.	Stewart Granger
9. "The Prisoner of Zenda"	Rudolph Rassendyl King Rudolph the Fifth		i.	George Arliss
10. "Here Come the Waves"	Susie Allison Rosemary Allison		j.	Bette Davis

_____points

(Answers on page 262)

75. MORE LINK-UPS—BUFFS AND DUFFERS

Here, once again, is a quiz which can be played by both Buffs and Duffers. It is the LINK-UP game which you played earlier, and it works exactly the same way. You merely insert the appropriate name in Column Two, and if you're correct, you will have completed the Hollywood personality's name suggested in Column One, and another personality's name suggested in Column Three. If you're confused, remember our example of "Benjamin FRANKLIN Roosevelt," and you'll have no problem. As before, you will receive 5 points for each correct completion.

1. Nigel   _____ Cabot
2. Rose   _____ Cavanaugh
3. Kathryn   _____ Withers
4. Tisha   _____ Hayden
5. Sandy   _____ Hopper
6. Cary   _____ Mitchell
7. Gilbert   _____ Young
8. Esther   _____ Evans
9. Mel   _____ West
10. Jeanette   _____ Carey

_____points

(Answers on page 262)

76. THE MEN FROM THE BOYS PART II

Once again, we're looking at those films in which we watched our hero grow from tiny tot to handsome hero. As before, we list a number of films (Column One), and the young actor who portrayed one of the major characters as a child (Column Two). In Column Three, we provide you with the character name in the film, and in Column Four, you are to provide us with the name of the actor who portrayed the character as a grownup. As before, we're awarding 15 points for each correct identification.

1. "There's No Business Like Show Business"	Donald Bamble	Tim	D_____ O'_____
2. "In Old Chicago"	Gene Reynolds	Dion	T_____ P_____
3. "Citizen Kane"	Buddy Swan	Charles	O_____ W_____
4. "The Sullivans"	Bobby Driscoll	Al	E_____ R_____
5. "The Jolson Story"	Scotty Beckett	Asa	L_____ P_____
6. "In Old Chicago"	Billy Watson	Jack	D_____ A_____
7. "Beau Geste"	Donald O'Connor	Beau	G_____ C_____
8. "Angels with Dirty Faces"	Frankie Burke	Rocky	J_____ C_____
9. "David Copperfield"	Freddie Bartholomew	David	F_____ L_____
10. "Yankee Doodle Dandy"	Douglas Croft	George	J_____ C_____
11. "Public Enemy"	Frank Coghlan, Jr.	Tom	J_____ C_____
12. "In Old Chicago"	Bobs Watson	Bob	T_____ B_____
13. "Heaven Can Wait"	Nino Pipitone, Jr.	Jack	T_____ A_____
14. "Son of Fury"	Roddy McDowall	Ben	T_____ P_____
15. "Beau Geste"	David Holt	Augustus	G___ P___ H_____, Jr.

_____points

(*Answers on page 263*)

76. THE MEN FROM THE BOYS PART II—DUFFERS' TEE

Once again, we're looking at those films in which we watched our hero grow from tiny tot to handsome hero. As before, we list a number of such films in Column One, and the young man who portrayed one of the major characters as a child in Column Two. In Column Three, we provide you with the character name in the film, while in Column Four, we have listed out of order the various (and better-known) actors who portrayed that character as a grownup. Sort out the actors of Column Four, and with the clues of Columns Two and Three, match your choice to the film title of Column One. We're being big about this, and awarding 15 points for each correct selection.

1. "There's No Business Like Show Business"	Donald Bamble	Tim	a. Larry Parks
2. "In Old Chicago"	Gene Reynolds	Dion	b. Frank Lawton
3. "Citizen Kane"	Buddy Swan	Charles	c. James Cagney
4. "The Sullivans"	Bobby Driscoll	Al	d. Tom Brown
5. "The Jolson Story"	Scotty Beckett	Asa	e. James Cagney
6. "In Old Chicago"	Billy Watson	Jack	f. Edward Ryan
7. "Beau Geste"	Donald O'Connor	Beau	g. Tyrone Power
8. "Angels with Dirty Faces"	Frankie Burke	Rocky	h. Tyrone Power
9. "David Copperfield"	Freddie Bartholomew	David	i. Donald O'Connor
10. "Yankee Doodle Dandy"	Douglas Croft	George	j. Tod Andrews
11. "Public Enemy"	Frank Coghlan, Jr.	Tom	k. G. P. Huntley, Jr.
12. "In Old Chicago"	Bobs Watson	Bob	l. Orson Welles
13. "Heaven Can Wait"	Nino Pipitone, Jr.	Jack	m. Don Ameche
14. "Son of Fury"	Roddy McDowall	Ben	n. James Cagney
15. "Beau Geste"	David Holt	Augustus	o. Gary Cooper

_____points

(*Answers on page 263*)

77. WHAT'S THE TITLE? PART II

As before, we list three players who appeared in a film. From this meager clue, you are to name the motion picture we're seeking. In some instances, we omit the obvious stars just to make it more difficult. (We never said this would be easy!) But in other cases, where we have included the stars, you must remember that they may have made more than one film together, and the *third* name becomes the important clue. But if you know your films and have some memory of the casts, you shouldn't be a total failure. And besides, you can get 15 points for each correct answer.

1. Dana Andrews, Vincent Price, Judith Anderson _____
2. Russ Tamblyn, Julie Newmar, Tommy Rall _____
3. Mel Brooks, Madeline Kahn, Harvey Korman _____
4. Akim Tamiroff, Katina Paxinou, Arturo De Cordova _____
5. William Holden, Nancy Olson, Jack Webb _____
6. Lionel Barrymore, Maureen O'Sullivan, W. C. Fields _____
7. Eleanor Parker, Darren McGavin, Arnold Stang _____
8. Robert Walker, Desi Arnaz, Lloyd Nolan _____
9. Akim Tamiroff, Fortunio Bonanova, Anne Baxter _____
10. Fred Astaire, Peter Lawford, Ann Miller _____

_____points

(*Answers on page 264*)

77. WHAT'S THE TITLE? PART II—DUFFERS' TEE

As before, we list three players who appeared in a film. From this meager clue, you are to name the motion picture we're seeking. In some instances, we omit the obvious stars just to make it more difficult (since we never promised you this would be easy!). But in other cases, where we have included the stars, you must remember that they may have made more than one picture together, in which case the *third* name becomes all the more important. But if you know your films and have some memory of the stars in them, you shouldn't be a total failure. And anyway, you can get 20 points for each correct answer, for a possible 200 points on this quiz!

1. Dana Andrews, Vincent Price,
   Judith Anderson   "L _ _ _ _"

2. Russ Tamblyn, Julie Newmar,
   Marc Platt

   "S _ _ _ _ _   B _ _ _ _ _ _
   f _ _ S _ _ _ _
   B _ _ _ _ _ _ _ _"

3. Mel Brooks, Madeline Kahn,
   Harvey Korman

   "B _ _ _ _ _ _ _
   S _ _ _ _ _ _"

4. Akim Tamiroff, Katina Paxinou,
   Arturo De Cordova

   "F _ _ W _ _ _ _ t _ _
   B _ _ _ T _ _ _ _"

5. William Holden, Nancy Olson,
   Jack Webb

   "S _ _ _ _ _ _
   B _ _ _ _ _ _ _ _ _"

6. Lionel Barrymore, Maureen
   O'Sullivan, W. C. Fields

   "D _ _ _ _ _
   C _ _ _ _ _ _ _ _ _ _ _"

7. Eleanor Parker, Darren McGavin,
   Arnold Stang

   "T _ _ M _ _ _ w _ _ _
   t _ _ G _ _ _ _ _
   A _ _"

8. Robert Walker, Desi Arnaz,
   Lloyd Nolan

   "B _ _ _ _ _ _"

9. Akim Tamiroff, Fortunio
   Bonanova, Anne Baxter

   "F _ _ _ _   G _ _ _ _ _
   t _ C _ _ _ _"

10. Fred Astaire, Peter Lawford,
    Ann Miller

   "E _ _ _ _ _ _ P _ _ _ _ _"

   _____points

   (*Answers on page 264*)

78. ONCE AGAIN, NAME THE STAR

Once again, we want you to name the star—so we hope you're not still smarting from the last exercise. Things are getting tougher day by day, and there's no reason our quizzes shouldn't begin to tighten up also. But we think the clues are reasonable ones, and they do offer you a maximum of 400 more points. As before, we're offering you 10 points for each star you can name, using the character clues in Columns One and Two below. And, as before, if you can name the films in which our star played the role, you may have 15 additional points for each title you identify correctly. Cheerio!

1. Ray Biddle	Col. Tom Rossiter
2. Georges Iscovescu	Michael Marnet
3. Grandma Leckie	Sister Mary Teresa Vauzous
4. Hank Tesling	Cos Erickson
5. Ellen Berent	Isabel Bradley
6. Richard Dadier	Lieut. Max Siegel
7. The Marquess of Trinton	Tony Preston
8. Terry Brennan	Melvin R. Foster
9. De Bois-Guilbert	Cosmo Constantine
10. Zeb Rawlings	Paul Varjak

_____points

(*Answers on page 264*)

78. ONCE AGAIN, NAME THE STAR—DUFFERS' TEE

Once again, we're asking you to name the star—and believe us, the clues *are* a little more liberal here than with the Buffs . . . though we admit the general outlook is getting tougher. But you can again add 400 points to your score. We are again offering 10 points for each star you can name using the character names we've provided in the two columns below. And, also as before, if you can put your finger on the correct titles represented by the two character names, you can reap another 15 points for each correct title. Go get 'em, tiger!

1. Will Slattery	Lafe Evans
2. Monod	Duc de Praslin
3. Sophie Patourel	Alice, Duchess de Brancourt
4. Joseph Wladislaw	Danny Velinski
5. Baketamon	Belle Starr
6. Johnny Farrell	Gen. Omar Bradley
7. Stephen Fox	Saladin
8. Butch Schmidt	Herr Preysing
9. The Saran of Gaza	Addison De Witt
10. Jonas Cord	Bruno Stachel

_____points

(*Answers on page 265*)

79. IN A BIG WAY

Hollywood has long had a mania for "bigness"—and this trait influences not only films, but many of their titles. Below, we list a number of films which were considered *big* ones, and ask you to provide us with the star. You may have 10 points apiece for playing it BIG!

1. "The Big Circus"   V _ _ _ _ _ M _ _ _ _ _
2. "The Big Carnival"   K _ _ _ _ D _ _ _ _ _ _
3. "The Big Parade"   J _ _ _ _ G _ _ _ _ _ _ _
4. "The Big House"   W _ _ _ _ _ _ _ B _ _ _ _ _
5. "The Big Heat"   G _ _ _ _ _ F _ _ _
6. "The Big Operator"   M _ _ _ _ _ R _ _ _ _ _ _
7. "The Big Street"   H _ _ _ _ _ F _ _ _ _ _
8. "The Big Shot"   H _ _ _ _ _ _ _ _ B _ _ _ _ _ _
9. "The Big Sleep"   H _ _ _ _ _ _ _ _ B _ _ _ _ _ _
10. "The Big Lift"   M _ _ _ _ _ _ _ _ _ _ _ C _ _ _ _ _
11. "The Big Hangover"   V _ _ J _ _ _ _ _ _ _
12. "The Big Clock"   R _ _ M _ _ _ _ _ _ _
13. "The Big Caper"   R _ _ _ _ C _ _ _ _ _ _ _
14. "The Big Steal"   R _ _ _ _ _ _ M _ _ _ _ _ _ _
15. "The Big Mouth"   J _ _ _ _ _ _ L _ _ _ _ _
16. "The Big Boodle"   E _ _ _ _ _ F _ _ _ _ _
17. "The Big Sky"   K _ _ _ _ D _ _ _ _ _ _ _
18. "The Big Cat"   L _ _ M _ _ _ _ _ _ _ _ _ _ _
19. "The Big Store"   T _ _ M _ _ _ _ B _ _ _ _ _ _ _ _
20. "The Big Country"   C _ _ _ _ _ _ _ _ _ H _ _ _ _ _

_____points

(Answers on page 265)

79. IN A BIG WAY—DUFFERS' TEE

Hollywood has long had a mania for "bigness"—and this trait influences not only films, but many of their titles. Below, in Column One, we have listed a number of films which were considered *big* ones (witness their titles). In Column Two, we have listed a star from each of these films, out of order. Your task is to match the star from Column Two with the appropriate title in Column One. Do so, and you may claim 10 points for each correct matching! BIG deal!

1. "The Big Circus"		a.	The Marx Brothers
2. "The Big Carnival"		b.	Robert Mitchum
3. "The Big Parade"		c.	Van Johnson
4. "The Big House"		d.	Lon McCallister
5. "The Big Heat"		e.	Mickey Rooney
6. "The Big Operator"		f.	Jerry Lewis
7. "The Big Street"		g.	Charlton Heston
8. "The Big Shot"		h.	Ray Milland
9. "The Big Sleep"		i.	Kirk Douglas
10. "The Big Lift"		j.	Rory Calhoun
11. "The Big Hangover"		k.	Victor Mature
12. "The Big Clock"		l.	Montgomery Clift
13. "The Big Caper"		m.	Errol Flynn
14. "The Big Steal"		n.	Humphrey Bogart
15. "The Big Mouth"		o.	Humphrey Bogart
16. "The Big Boodle"		p.	Henry Fonda
17. "The Big Sky"		q.	Glenn Ford
18. "The Big Cat"		r.	John Gilbert
19. "The Big Store"		s.	Kirk Douglas
20. "The Big Country"		t.	Wallace Beery

_____points

(*Answers on page 265*)

80. Y'ALL REMEMBER WORLD WAR II? PART II

It's ration-point-and-gas-stamps time again as we transport you back to the romantic days of World War II! Tucked in between newsreel shots of GIs doing the Lambeth Walk (one-two-three-oihh!) in a British dance hall and a Robert Benchley short on the misadventures of a bumbling air raid warden in the midst of a practice blackout were a number of exciting features with war themes. Below we have provided "suggestions" for fifteen titles which should evoke memories of defense stamps, Liberty Ships, and "Heil, Heil, Right in Der Fuehrer's Face!" Besides a partial cast listing, we provide you with the year of release, which should be a catalyst for those memory cells having to do with war films. You come up with the title, and for each one you put your finger on, take 15 points!

1. Brian Donlevy, Robert Preston, William Bendix, Macdonald Carey (1943)
2. Robert Taylor, Desi Arnaz, Lloyd Nolan, Kenneth Spencer (1943)

3. John Wayne, John Agar, Forrest Tucker, Adele Mara (1949)
4. Richard Widmark, Jack Palance, Karl Malden, Richard Boone (1951)
5. Van Johnson, John Hodiak, James Whitmore, Ricardo Montalban, Denise Darcel (1949)
6. Errol Flynn, Ronald Reagan, Arthur Kennedy, Alan Hale (1942)
7. Spencer Tracy, Van Johnson, Robert Mitchum, Robert Walker (1944)
8. Paul Muni, Anna Lee, Lillian Gish, Sir Cedric Hardwicke (1943)
9. Dana Andrews, Richard Conte, John Ireland (1946)
10. John Payne, Maureen O'Hara, Randolph Scott (1942)
11. John Wayne, Anthony Quinn, Beulah Bondi, Richard Loo (1945)
12. Robert Montgomery, John Wayne, Ward Bond, Jack Holt (1945)
13. John Wayne, Susan Hayward, Dennis O'Keefe, William Frawley (1944)
14. William Bendix, Lloyd Nolan, Anthony Quinn (1943)
    And what list would be complete without . . .
15. Otto Kruger, Elissa Landi, Donald Woods (1943)

_____points

(*Answers on page 266*)

80. Y'ALL REMEMBER WORLD WAR II? PART II —DUFFERS' TEE

It's ration-point-and-gas-stamps time again as we transport you back to the romantic days of World War II! Tucked in between newsreel shots of GIs doing the Lambeth Walk in a British dance hall and a Robert Benchley short on the misadventures of a bumbling air raid warden in the midst of a practice blackout were a number of exciting features with war themes. Below, in Column One, we've suggested a number of these films by giving you some cast members and the year of release. Your task, again, is to come up with the titles we're looking for in Column Two. Fill in the blanks for the correct titles, and take 15 points for each correct answer. Keep 'em flying!

1. Brian Donlevy, Robert
   Preston, William
   Bendix, Macdonald
   Carey (1943)   "_ _ _ _   _ _ _ _ _ _"

2. Robert Taylor, Desi
   Arnaz, Lloyd
   Nolan, Robert
   Walker, Kenneth
   Spencer (1943)   "_ _ _ _ _ _"
3. John Wayne, John Agar,
   Forrest Tucker,
   Adele Mara (1949)   "_ _ _ _ _ _ _ _ _ _ _ _ _ _ _"
4. Richard Widmark, Jack
   Palance, Karl
   Malden, Richard
   Boone (1951)   "_ _ _ _ _ _ _ _ _
                                 _ _ _ _ _ _ _ _ _"
5. Van Johnson, John
   Hodiak, James
   Whitmore, Ricardo
   Montalban, Denise
   Darcel (1949)   "_ _ _ _ _ _ _ _ _ _ _"
6. Errol Flynn, Ronald
   Reagan, Arthur
   Kennedy, Alan
   Hale (1942)   "_ _ _ _ _ _ _ _ _ _ _ _ _ _"
7. Spencer Tracy, Van
   Johnson, Robert
   Mitchum, Robert
   Walker (1944)   "_ _ _ _ _ _ _ _ _ _ _ _ _ _ _
                                 _ _ _ _ _"
8. Paul Muni, Anna Lee,
   Lillian Gish, Sir
   Cedric Hardwicke
   (1943)   "_ _ _ _ _ _ _ _ _ _ _ _
                                 _ _ _ _ _ _ _ _ _"
9. Dana Andrews, Richard
   Conte, John Ireland
   (1946)   "_ _ _ _ _ _ _ _ _ _ _ _ _"
10. John Payne, Maureen
    O'Hara, Randolph
    Scott (1942)   "_ _ _ _ _ _ _ _ _ _ _ _
                                 _ _ _ _ _ _ _"
11. John Wayne, Anthony
    Quinn, Beulah
    Bondi, Richard Loo
    (1945)   "_ _ _ _ _ _ _ _ _ _ _"
12. Robert Montgomery,
    John Wayne, Ward
    Bond, Jack Holt
    (1945)   "_ _ _ _ _ _ _ _
                                 _ _ _ _ _ _ _ _ _"

13. John Wayne, Susan
      Hayward, Dennis
      O'Keefe, William
      Frawley (1944)   "___ _____

                              _____"

14. William Bendix, Lloyd
      Nolan, Anthony
      Quinn (1943)   "_____ _____"

And we just had to
      include . . .

15. Otto Kruger, Elissa
      Landi, Donald
      Woods (1943)   "_____"

                                    _____points

                              (*Answers on page 266*)

81. ANYTHING SHE CAN DO, I CAN DO BETTER

This quiz takes the same form of similar quizzes earlier in the
book, but if you read the title closely, you've no doubt surmised that
we're dealing in this quiz with *female* players exclusively. Below,
there are two columns of motion picture actress names. Each actress
represented in Column One portrayed a historical character in one of
her films. The same historical characters were also portrayed by the
actresses listed in Column Two. Your task is to pair the actresses
from Columns One and Two who portrayed the same historical
character—and by so doing, you may have 5 points for each correct
pairing. You may win another 10 points for correctly identifying the
historical character—and if you're *really* with it, you may have another 10 points for each film title you can name which included these
historic portrayals. So that's a possible 35 points per question—and
ten questions to try your smarts on.

		CHARACTER	TITLE	TITLE
1. Ingrid Bergman	A. Spring Byington	_____	_____	_____
2. Ethel Barrymore	B. Elisabeth Bergner	_____	_____	_____
3. Ginger Rogers	C. Nina Foch	_____	_____	_____

169

4. Merle Oberon	D. Una Merkel	_____ ____ _____
5. Norma Shearer	E. Jean Seberg	_____ ____ _____
6. Mary Howard	F. Janet Suzman	_____ ____ _____
7. Elizabeth Taylor	G. Ava Gardner	_____ ____ _____
8. Lillian Bond	H. Elaine Stewart	_____ ____ _____
9. Bette Davis	I. Bette Davis	_____ ____ _____
10. Flora Robson	J. Vivien Leigh	_____ ____ _____

_____points

(Answers on page 266)

81. ANYTHING SHE CAN DO, I CAN DO BETTER— DUFFERS' TEE

This is another one of those ANYTHING YOU CAN DO quizzes, only this time it's ANYTHING *she* CAN DO. That should be a tip-off that we're dealing with female players exclusively. Remember the bit about each actress playing the same historical character? Well, again you match the actress in Column Two to the appropriate actress in Column One. Get it right, and grab 15 points per correct pairing. Then select the film from Column Three in which the portrayal of the Column Two actress was included. There's another fast 15 points. So, with a possible 30 points a question, and ten questions waiting for your nimble brain, you can't help but increase your score. Hardly.

1. Ingrid Bergman; Jeanne d'Arc in "Joan of Arc"	A. Spring Byington	a. "Abraham Lincoln"
2. Ethel Barrymore; Czarina Alexandra in "Rasputin and the Empress"	B. Elisabeth Bergner	b. "Caesar and Cleopatra"
3. Ginger Rogers; Dolly Madison in "The Magnificent Doll"	c. Nina Foch	c. "The Life and Times of Judge Roy Bean"

4. Merle Oberon; Anne Boleyn   D. Una Merkel   d. "Scara-
in "The Private Life of   mouche"
Henry VIII"

5. Norma Shearer; Marie   E. Jean Seberg   e. "Young
Antoinette in "Marie   Bess"
Antoinette"

6. Mary Howard; Ann Rutledge   F. Janet Suzman   f. "The
in "Abe Lincoln in   Buccaneer"
Illinois"

7. Elizabeth Taylor; Cleopatra   G. Ava Gardner   g. "Nicholas
in "Cleopatra"   and
                                                 Alexandra"

8. Lillian Bond; Lily Langtry   H. Elaine Stewart   h. "The Private
in "The Westerner"   Lives of
                                                 Elizabeth
                                                 and Essex"
                                                 or "The
                                                 Virgin
                                                 Queen"

9. Bette Davis; Catherine of   I. Bette Davis   i. "St. Joan"
Russia in "John Paul
Jones"

10. Flora Robson; Queen   J. Vivien Leigh   j. "Catherine
Elizabeth I in "Fire over   the Great"
England"

_____points

(*Answers on page 267*)

82. VERY IMPORTANT PROPS PART II

As we said earlier, a number of films have titles which emphasize the importance of a single prop or item. If you can come up with the Very Important Prop—or Props—in the following titles, you'll complete the film title we're seeking, and will earn 10 points for each such title.

1. "The Black _ _ _ _ _"
2. "Aladdin and His _ _ _ _ _"
3. "The Band _ _ _ _ _ _"
4. "Behind the Iron _ _ _ _ _ _ _ _"
5. "Kitten with a _ _ _ _ _"
6. "The Glass _ _ _"
7. "Apache _ _ _ _ _ _"
8. "Battle _ _ _ _ _"
9. "Red _ _ _ _ _ _ _ _ _"
10. " _ _ _ _ _ _ _ _ _ _ _ Potemkin"
11. "The Big _ _ _ _ _ _"
12. " _ _ _ _ _ on My Knee"
13. "Golden _ _ _ _ _ _ _ _ _ _"
14. "Oil for the _ _ _ _ _ _ of China"
15. "The Fuzzy Pink _ _ _ _ _ _ _ _ _ _ _"

_____points

(*Answers on page 268*)

82. VERY IMPORTANT PROPS PART II—DUFFERS' TEE

As we said earlier, a number of films have titles which emphasize the importance of a single prop or item. If you can come up with the Very Important Prop—or Props—in the following titles, you'll complete the film title we're seeking, and will earn 10 points for each such title.

1. "The Black _____"	a. Earrings
2. "Aladdin and His _____"	b. Key
3. "The Band _____"	c. Lamps
4. "Behind the Iron _____"	d. Whip
5. "Kitten with a _____"	e. Battleship
6. "The Glass _____"	f. Curtain
7. "Apache _____"	g. Book
8. "Battle _____"	h. Banjo
9. "Red _____"	i. Drums
10. "_____ Potemkin"	j. Wagon
11. "The Big _____"	k. Taxi
12. "_____ on My Knee"	l. Lamp
13. "Golden _____"	m. Tomahawk
14. "Oil for the _____ of China"	n. Nightgown
15. "The Fuzzy Pink _____"	o. Knife

(*Answers on page 268*)   _____points

83. HERE'S LOOKIN' AT YOU, BOGIE! PART II

Here is another quiz which pays tribute to that screen legend, Mr. Humphrey DeForest Bogart. As in Part I earlier, we list in Column One below a number of the screen characters portrayed by Bogie, and ask you to complete the titles suggested in Column Two which are the films that gave birth to Bogie's well-remembered characters. You may have 15 points for each title correctly completed. Okay, shweetheart?

1. Dixon Steele   "_ _ _ L_ _ _ _ _ _ _ _ _ _ _ _"
2. Eddie Willis   "_ _ _ H_ _ _ _ _ _ T_ _ _ _ _ _ _ _"
3. "Rocks" Valentine   "_ _ _ A_ _ _ _ _ _ _ _ _.
                           C_ _ _ _ _ _ _ _ _ _ _ _ _"
4. George Halley   "_ _ _ R_ _ _ _ _ _ _ T_ _ _ _ _ _ _ _ _"
5. "Gloves" Donahue   "_ _ _ T_ _ _ _ _ _ _ _ t_ _ N_ _ _ _"
6. James Frazier   "_ _ _ _ _ _ _ _ _ _ _ _ _ _ _ _ _
                           _ _ _ _ _"
7. Chuck Martin   "I_ _ _ _ _ _ _ _ _ _ S_ _ _ _ _ _ _"
8. Pete Martin   "R_ _ _ _ _ _ B_ _ _ _ _ _ _"
9. Martin Ferguson   "_ _ _ E_ _ _ _ _ _ _ _ _"
10. Mark Braden   "C_ _ _ _ _ S_ _ _ _ _ _"
11. Joe "Red"
         Kennedy   "S_ _ Q_ _ _ _ _ _ _"
12. Vincent Parry   "D_ _ _ _ P_ _ _ _ _ _ _"
13. Frank McCloud   "K_ _ L_ _ _ _"

                                         _____points

(*Answers on page 269*)

83. HERE'S LOOKIN' AT YOU, BOGIE! PART II— DUFFERS' TEE

Here is another quiz which pays tribute to that screen legend, Mr. Humphrey DeForest Bogart. As in Part I earlier, we list in Column One below a number of screen characters portrayed by Bogie, and ask you to complete the titles suggested in Column Two which are the films that gave birth to Bogie's well-remembered characters. You may have 15 points for each title correctly completed. As was the case earlier, the characters in this Duffers' version are a bit more well-known than those we used in the Buffs' version, so you have a good opportunity to increase your score. Okay, shweetheart?

1. Glenn Griffin   "____ D_____ H_____"
2. Andrew Morton   "K_____ __ A__ D____"
3. Billy Dannreuther   "B___ ___ D_____"
4. Jim Carmody   "___ L___ H____ __ ___"
5. Linus Larrabee   "S_____"
6. "Duke" Mantee   "___ P_____ F_____"
7. "Baby Face"
      Martin   "D___ E__"
8. Rick Blaine   "C_____"
9. "Whip" McCord   "___ O_____ K__"
10. Rick Leland   "A_____ ___ P_____"
11. John Murrell   "V_____ C____"
12. "Chips" McGuire   "__ ___ ____ ____"
13. Sgt. Joe Gunn   "S_____"

_____points

(*Answers on page 269*)

84. THE BIG BULB: OATERS

One more BIG BULB quiz—and we promise you that this is the last!
But we've been through males, females, and teams—so we couldn't
leave without a nod to that staple of features *and* TV, the Western
(or, as *Variety* would call them, the "oaters"). As you know by now,
these BIG BULB quizzes look at those well-established film players
who moved over into television and became stars of various TV
series. We assume you kept track of the whereabouts of your good
cinema friends and recognized their talents during many hours of television. In this quiz, we list a number of well-established film players
in Column One, and in Column Two, we provide clues to the TV
series in which they starred. Your task is to complete the TV series
titles in Column Two—in which your old Hollywood friend starred
—by filling in the blanks. Take 15 points for each correct answer—
and remember, all of the answers we're looking for in this quiz have
to do with the Western!

1. Stanley Andrews   "_____ _____ _____"
2. Tris Coffin   "2_ M__"
3. Willard Parker   "T_____ __ ___T_____
                          R_____"
4. Dick Powell   "____ ____ T_____"
5. Audie Murphy   "W_____ S_____"

174

6. Richard Egan   "_ _ _ _ _ _"

7. Rory Calhoun   "T _ _ T _ _ _ _ _"

8. George
   Montgomery   "C _ _ _ _ _ _ _ _ C _ _ _ _"

9. William Bendix   "O _ _ _ _ _ _ _ _ T _ _ _ _ _"

10. Edgar Buchanan   "T _ _ A _ _ _ _ _ _ _ _ _ _ o _
    J _ _ _ _ R _ _ B _ _ _"

11. Duncan Renaldo
    and Leo
    Carrillo   "_ _ _ _ _ _ _ _ _ _ _"

12. Russell Hayden
    and Jackie
    Coogan   "C _ _ _ _ _ _ G- _ _ _ _"

13. Henry Fonda   "T _ _ D _ _ _ _ _ _"

14. Walter Brennan   "T _ _ G _ _ _ _ o _
    W _ _ _ _ S _ _ _ _ _ _ _"

15. Richard Carlson   "M _ _ _ _ _ _ _ _ _ _ _ ' _ R _ _ _ _ _ _ _"

16. John Payne   "T _ _ R _ _ _ _ _ _ _ _ _ G _ _"

17. Scott Brady   "S _ _ _ _ _ _ _ _ S _ _ _ _"

18. Barry Sullivan   "T _ _ T _ _ _ _ M _ _"

19. Leif Erickson and
    Cameron
    Mitchell   "H _ _ _ _ C _ _ _ _ _ _ _ _ _"

20. Jeffrey Hunter   "T _ _ _ _ _ _ H _ _ _ _ _ _ _"

_____points

(*Answers on page 269*)

84. THE BIG BULB: OATERS—DUFFERS' TEE

One more BIG BULB quiz—and we solemnly promise that this one is the last. But after having been through males, females, and teams —well, we just couldn't ignore that staple of features *and* TV, the Western (or, as *Variety* would call them, the "oaters"). As you certainly know by now, the BIG BULB quizzes look at those Hollywood players who moved over into television and became stars of a number of TV series. And we assume you kept track of your favorite Hollywood names and are knowledgeable about their TV activities. In this quiz, we list a number of well-established Hollywood names in Column One. In Column Two, we list (out of order) those TV series in which they starred. Your task is to match the series titles

175

from Column Two with the star-names of Column One—and you may add 15 points to your score for each correct pairing. Remember, they went thataway!

1. Stanley Andrews
2. Tris Coffin
3. Willard Parker
4. Dick Powell
5. Audie Murphy
6. Richard Egan
7. Rory Calhoun
8. George Montgomery
9. William Bendix
10. Edgar Buchanan
11. Duncan Renaldo and Leo Carrillo
12. Russell Hayden and Jackie Coogan
13. Henry Fonda
14. Walter Brennan
15. Richard Carlson

16. John Payne
17. Scott Brady
18. Barry Sullivan

19. Leif Erickson and Cameron Mitchell
20. Jeffrey Hunter

a. "Zane Grey Theatre"
b. "Temple Houston"
c. "The Restless Gun"
d. "The Tall Man"
e. "The Deputy"
f. "High Chaparral"
g. "MacKenzie's Raiders"
h. "The Cisco Kid"
i. "Whispering Smith"
j. "The Guns of Will Sonnett"
k. "Cowboy G-Men"

l. "26 Men"
m. "Empire"
n. "Death Valley Days"
o. "Tales of the Texas Rangers"
p. "Overland Trail"
q. "The Texan"
r. "The Adventures of Judge Roy Bean"

s. "Cimarron City"
t. "Shotgun Slade"

_____points

(*Answers on page 269*)

85. MORE TYPE-CASTING

Once again, we're looking at the varied types Hollywood players are called upon to act during their careers. Below, we list four different types played by the same player in four of his or her films. From the clues we provide, we ask you to identify the actor or actress in question. If you're correct, you may have 15 points for the identification. Moreover, if you can name the films suggested by the clues, we'll award an additional 10 points for each correct film title

176

you get. That's a possible 55 points (!) a question, or a potential 550-point addition to your score. Incredible!

1. Sea captain; inventor; sports writer; fisherman.
2. Defrocked priest; actor; British flyer; spy.
3. Pianist-orchestra leader; pirate; bullfighter; Canadian Mountie.
4. Psychiatrist; traveling companion; missionary; guerilla.
5. Nun; heiress; Roman empress; army nurse.
6. Lawyer; naval captain; gold prospector; charter boat operator.
7. Movie actor; movie scriptwriter; naval captain; playwright-composer.
8. Night club entertainer; dope addict; hotel operator; assassin.
9. Broadway lyricist; wood sprite; Japanese eccentric; Western Union messenger.
10. Insurance investigator; eccentric inventor; philandering business executive; naval officer.

_____points

(*Answers on page 270*)

85. MORE TYPE-CASTING—DUFFERS' TEE

Again, we're looking at the varied types Hollywood players are called upon to act during their careers. Below, we list four different types played by the same player in four of his or her films. From the clues we provide, we ask you to identify the actor or actress in question. Select the appropriate player from Column Two, and match him or her with the proper grouping from Column One. Award yourself 15 points for each correct pairing. And if you can name at least three of the films suggested in the grouping of Column One, you may add 40 bonus points for that question. That's ten questions, with a possible score of 55 points per question—or 550 points. Mercy, how they do pile up!

Column One	Column Two
1. Sea captain; inventor; sports writer; fisherman.	a. Mickey Rooney
2. Defrocked priest; actor; British flyer; spy.	b. Fred MacMurray
3. Pianist-orchestra leader; pirate; bullfighter; Canadian Mountie.	c. James Cagney
4. Psychiatrist; traveling companion; missionary; guerilla.	d. Frank Sinatra
5. Nun; heiress; Roman empress; army nurse.	e. Ingrid Bergman
6. Lawyer; naval captain; gold prospector; charter boat operator.	f. Richard Burton

7. Movie actor; movie scriptwriter; naval captain; playwright-composer.   g. Tyrone Power

8. Night club entertainer; dope addict; hotel operator; assassin.   h. Claudette Colbert

9. Broadway lyricist; wood sprite; Japanese eccentric; Western Union messenger.   i. Humphrey Bogart

10. Insurance investigator; eccentric inventor; philandering business executive; naval officer.   j. Spencer Tracy

_____points

(Answers on page 270)

86. FIRST, THE WORD PART II

As before, we're looking at those films which came from the more contemporary authors, as we did in the earlier FIRST, THE WORD. Below, in Column One, we list two films which are the brainchildren of the *same* writer; and, as before, the question is in two parts: (a) you must identify the author—and for each such identification you get correct, you may have 10 points—and (b) from the three films listed in Column Two, you are to select the film also attributable to the same author. For this, take 10 more points for each correct answer. Unlike our tender, loving treatment to the Duffers, we're insisting you get *both* parts right in order to claim any score. Sure, Marty —you can do it!

1. "The Night Walker"
"The Deadly Bees"
R   B
_____
a. "Trog"
b. "My Name Is Julia Ross"
c. "Psycho"

2. "Ride the Pink Horse"
"The Fallen Sparrow"
D   B. H
_____
a. "I Married a Zombie"
b. "In a Lonely Place"
c. "Phantom of the Opera"

3. "Odds Against Tomorrow"
"The Caper of the Golden Bulls"
W   M
_____
a. "The Big Heat"
b. "The Big Town"
c. "The Big House"

4. "Above Suspicion"
"The Venetian Affair"
H   M
_____
a. "Desperate Journey"
b. "The Conspirators"
c. "Assignment in Brittany"

178

5. "And Then There Were None"

   "Murder on the Orient Express"
       A   C _____

   a. "Witness for the
      Prosecution"
   b. "No Blade of Grass"
   c. "The Bishop Misbehaves"

6. "Rope"
   "Hangover Square"
       P   H _____

   a. "Rear Window"
   b. "Payment on Demand"
   c. "Gaslight"

7. "This Gun for Hire"
   "Our Man in Havana"
       G   G _____

   a. "The Third Man"
   b. "The Great McGinty"
   c. "China"

8. "Mrs. O'Malley and Mr. Malone"
   "The Lucky Stiff"
       C   R _____

   a. "The Big Street"
   b. "Brother Orchid"
   c. "Having Wonderful Crime"

9. "Miss Pinkerton"
   "The Nurse's Secret"
       M   R   R _____

   a. "Devil Bat"
   b. "Casey at the Bat"
   c. "The Bat Whispers"

10. "The Devil's Mask"
   "The Unknown"
       C _____ E. M _____

   a. "I Love a Mystery"
   b. "The Cat and the Canary"
   c. "Dr. Jekyll and Mr. Hyde"

11. "The Silencers"
   "The Ambushers"

       D   H _____

   a. "Devil Doll"
   b. "In Her Majesty's Secret
      Service"
   c. "Murderers' Row"

12. "A Kiss Before Dying"
   "The Stepford Wives"
       I   L _____

   a. "Yes, Sir, That's My Baby"
   b. "Melancholy Baby"
   c. "Rosemary's Baby"

_____points

(*Answers on page 271*)

86. FIRST, THE WORD PART II—DUFFERS' TEE

As before, we're looking at those films which came from the more contemporary authors, as we did in the earlier FIRST, THE WORD. In Column One below, we list a dozen pairs of films, while in Column Two (listed out of order) are the authors of these films. In Column

Three (also out of order), we list twelve other films which came from the works of the same authors. You are to select the author and "other" film from Columns Two and Three which correspond to the films of Column One. You receive 10 points for each correct selection, or a possible 20 points per question. And you need not get both parts of the question correct in order to win at least *some* score—which is a break we did *not* give the Buffs!

1. "The Night Walker" A. Patrick Hamilton a. "Having Wonderful Crime"
   "The Deadly Bees"

2. "Ride the Pink Horse" B. William McGivern b. "The Bat Whispers"
   "The Fallen Sparrow"

3. "Odds Against Tomorrow" C. Graham Greene c. "Gaslight"
   "The Caper of the Golden Bulls"

4. "Above Suspicion" D. Craig Rice d. "Rosemary's Baby"
   "The Venetian Affair"

5. "And Then There Were None" E. Dorothy B. Hughes e. "Witness for the Prosecution"
   "Murder on the Orient Express"

6. "Rope" F. Carlton E. Morse f. "Psycho"
   "Hangover Square"

7. "This Gun for Hire" G. Ira Levin g. "Assignment in Brittany"
   "Our Man in Havana"

8. "Mrs. O'Malley and Mr. Malone" H. Mary Roberts Rinehart h. "The Big Heat"
   "The Lucky Stiff"

9. "Miss Pinkerton" I. Helen MacInnes i. "The Third Man"
   "The Nurse's Secret"

10. "The Devil's Mask" J. Robert Bloch j. "In a Lonely Place"
    "The Unknown"

11. "The Silencers" K. Donald Hamilton k. "I Love a Mystery"
    "The Ambushers"

12. "A Kiss Before Dying" L. Agatha Christie l. "Murderers' Row"
    "The Stepford Wives"

(*Answers on page 271*)   _____points

180

87. THANK HEAVEN FOR LITTLE GIRLS

As we pointed out in our quiz THE MEN FROM THE BOYS, there have been a number of films where we meet two versions of the hero—as a boy, and later, as a man. And so it is with the female side as well. Below, we list a number of films in which we meet the heroine first as a young lass and later, as a stunning charmer. In Column One below, we give you the titles of a number of films in which this phenomenon occurs. In Column Two, you'll find the names of the young actresses who portrayed each heroine "as a child," and following, in Column Three, you'll find the names of the characters portrayed. In Column Four, we ask you to tell us the name of the actress who played the grown-up version of each character. For each correct answer, take 15 points!

1. "Jane Eyre"	Peggy Ann Garner	Jane	J_____	F_____
2. "The Dolly Sisters"	Evon Thomas	Jenny	B_____	G_____
3. "The Sullivans"	Nancy June Robinson	Genevieve	T_____	M_____
4. "There's No Business Like Show Business"	Linda Lowell	Katy	M_____	G_____
5. "Follow the Sun"	Ann Burr	Valerie	A_____	B_____
6. "Beau Geste"	Ann Gillis	Isobel	S_____	H_____
7. "Yankee Doodle Dandy"	Patsy Lee Parsons	Josie	J_____	C_____
8. "The Dolly Sisters"	Donna Jo Gribble	Rosie	J_____	H_____
9. "Imitation of Life"	Juanita Quigley	Jessie	R_____	H_____
10. "Angels with Dirty Faces"	Marilyn Knowlden	Laury	A_____	S_____
11. "The Ghost and Mrs. Muir"	Natalie Wood	Anna	V_____	B_____
12. "David Copperfield"	Marilyn Knowlden	Emily	M_____	E_____

_____points

(*Answers on page 272*)

87. THANK HEAVEN FOR LITTLE GIRLS—DUFFERS' TEE

As we pointed out in our quiz THE MEN FROM THE BOYS, there have been a number of films where we meet two versions of the hero—as a boy, and later, as a man. And so it is with the female side as well. Below, we list a number of films in which we meet the heroine first as a young lass and later, as a stunning charmer. In Column One below, we give you the titles of the films in which this phenomenon occurs. In Column Two, you'll find the names of the young actresses who played the younger versions, and in Column Three, the names of the characters involved. In Column Four, out of order (of course), you'll find the actresses who portrayed each character as a grownup. Select the appropriate actress from Column Four who groups properly with the clues in Columns One, Two, and Three. You may take 15 points for each selection you get right!

1. "Jane Eyre"	Peggy Ann Garner	Jane	a. Vanessa Brown
2. "The Dolly Sisters"	Evon Thomas	Jenny	b. Madge Evans
3. "The Sullivans"	Nancy June Robinson	Genevieve	c. Rochelle Hudson
4. "There's No Business Like Show Business"	Linda Lowell	Katy	d. Joan Fontaine
5. "Follow the Sun"	Ann Burr	Valerie	e. Ann Sheridan
6. "Beau Geste"	Ann Gillis	Isobel	f. Trudy Marshall
7. "Yankee Doodle Dandy"	Patsy Lee Parsons	Josie	g. Mitzi Gaynor
8. "The Dolly Sisters"	Donna Jo Gribble	Rosie	h. Betty Grable
9. "Imitation of Life"	Juanita Quigley	Jessie	i. Anne Baxter
10. "Angels with Dirty Faces"	Marilyn Knowlden	Laury	j. June Haver

| 11. "The Ghost and Mrs. Muir" | Natalie Wood | Anna | k. Susan Hayward |
| 12. "David Copperfield" | Marilyn Knowlden | Emily | l. Jeanne Cagney |

_____points

(Answers on page 272)

88. THAT OL' GANG OF MINE PART II

You did so well playing this quiz earlier, we're sure you're ripe for another go—and another flock of points being added to your score. As before, we're naming in each question several characters from a film—and they are the *main* (no sneaks we) characters. You have but to tell us the name of the film in which these characters appeared, and take 20 points for each film you correctly identify. You can add 500 points on this one—so have at it!

1. Elizabeth Curtis; Allan Quartermain; John Goode; Van Brun.
2. Ann Redman; Carl Denham; John Driscoll; Captain Englehorn.
3. Ernie Mott; Ma Mott; Aggie Hunter; Twite; Jim Mordinoy.
4. Dusty Rivers; April Logan; Louvette Courbeau; Sgt. Jim Brett.
5. John Wickliff Shawnessy; Susanna Drake; Nell Gaither; Professor Jerusalem Webster Stiles.
6. Gen. James M. Scott; Col. Martin (Jiggs) Casey; President Jordan Lyman; Eleanor Holbrook.
7. Blanche DuBois; Stanley Kowalski; Stella Kowalski; Mitch.
8. Guy Haines; Anne Morton; Bruno Antony; Senator Morton.
9. Robert Conway; Sondra; Alexander P. Lovett; George Conway; Chang.
10. Don Birnam; Helen St. James; Wick Birnam; Nat.
11. Carlotta Vance; Larry Renault; Dan Packard; Kitty Packard.
12. Doc Delaney; Lola Delaney; Marie Loring; Turk Fisher.
13. Billy Dannreuther; Gwendolen Chelm; Maria Dannreuther; Peterson.
14. C. C. (Bud) Baxter; Fran Kubelik; Jeff D. Sheldrake; Joe Dobisch.
15. Jim McLeod; Mary McLeod; Lou Brody; Karl Schneider; Lieut. Monahan.
16. Ari Ben Canaan; Kitty Fremont; Gen. Sutherland; Barak Ben Canaan.
17. Capt. Kinross; Alix Kinross; C.P.O. Hardy; Seaman Shorty Blake.
18. Fred C. Dobbs; Howard; Curtin; Cody; Gold Hat.

19. Joe Gillis; Norma Desmond; Max von Mayerling; Betty Schaefer.
20. Pearl Chavez; Jesse McCanles; Lewt McCanles; Senator McCanles.
21. Rubin Flood; Cora Flood; Lottie; Mavis Pruitt.
22. Katrin Holstrom; Glenn Morley; Mrs. Morley; Clancy.
23. Stanley T. Banks; Ellie Banks; Kay Banks; Buckley Dunstan.
24. Sgt. Milton Warden; Robert E. Lee Prewitt; Karen Holmes; Angelo Maggio.
25. Leslie Lynnton Benedict; Bick Benedict; Jett Rink; Luz Benedict.

_____points

(*Answers on page 273*)

88. THAT OL' GANG OF MINE PART II—DUFFERS' TEE

Would you believe that everybody did so well playing the earlier version of this quiz that we just *had* to trot out another try for you. As before, each question lists several characters from the cast of a single film. The twenty-five films we're looking for are listed out of order (ah, but you *had* come to expect that, hadn't you?) in Column Two. Select the proper title from Column Two and match it with the appropriate list in Column One. Take 20 points for each correct pairing. Give it a good go, now!

1. Elizabeth Curtis; Allan Quartermain; John Goode; Van Brun.

    a. "Lost Horizon"

2. Ann Redman; Carl Denham; John Driscoll; Captain Englehorn.

    b. "Exodus"

3. Ernie Mott; Ma Mott; Aggie Hunter; Jim Mordinoy; Twite.

    c. "Beat the Devil"

4. Dusty Rivers; April Logan; Louvette Corbeau; Sgt. Jim Brett.

    d. "Seven Days in May"

5. John Wickliff Shawnessy; Susanna Drake; Nell Gaither; Professor Jerusalem Webster Stiles.

    e. "A Streetcar Named Desire"

6. Gen. James M. Scott; Col. Martin (Jiggs) Casey; President Jordan Lyman; Eleanor Holbrook.

    f. "The Treasure of the Sierra Madre"

7. Blanche DuBois; Stanley Kowalski; Stella Kowalski; Mitch.

    g. "None But the Lonely Heart"

8. Guy Haines; Anne Morton; Bruno Antony; Senator Morton.

h. "In Which We Serve"

9. Robert Conway; Sondra; Alexander P. Lovett; George Conway; Chang.

i. "Raintree County"

10. Don Birnam; Helen St. James; Wick Birnam; Nat.

j. "Duel in the Sun"

11. Carlotta Vance; Larry Renault; Dan Packard; Kitty Packard.

k. "King Kong"

12. Doc Delaney; Lola Delaney; Marie Loring; Turk Fisher.

l. "The Lost Weekend"

13. Billy Dannreuther; Gwendolen Chelm; Maria Dannreuther; Peterson.

m. "From Here to Eternity"

14. C. C. (Bud) Baxter; Fran Kubelik; Jeff D. Sheldrake; Joe Dobisch.

n. "The Farmer's Daughter"

15. Jim McLeod; Mary McLeod; Lou Brody; Karl Schneider; Lieut. Monahan.

o. "The Dark at the Top of the Stairs"

16. Ari Ben Canaan; Kitty Fremont; Gen. Sutherland; Barak Ben Canaan.

p. "Father of the Bride"

17. Capt. Kinross; Alix Kinross; C.P.O Hardy; Seaman Shorty Blake.

q. "King Solomon's Mines"

18. Fred C. Dobbs; Howard; Curtin; Cody; Gold Hat.

r. "Detective Story"

19. Joe Gillis; Norma Desmond; Max von Mayerling; Betty Schaefer.

s. "Northwest Mounted Police"

20. Pearl Chavez; Jesse McCanles; Lewt McCanles; Senator McCanles.

t. "Dinner at Eight"

21. Rubin Flood; Cora Flood; Lottie; Mavis Pruitt.

u. "The Apartment"

22. Katrin Holstrom; Glenn Morley; Mrs. Morley; Clancy.

v. "Giant"

23. Stanley T. Banks; Ellie Banks; Kay Banks; Buckley Dunstan.

w. "Strangers on a Train"

24. Sgt. Milton Warden; Robert E. Lee Prewitt; Karen Holmes; Angelo Maggio.

x. "Sunset Boulevard"

25. Leslie Lynnton Benedict; Bick Benedict;   y. "Come Back.
    Jett Rink; Luz Benedict.   Little Sheba"

_____points

(*Answers on page 273*)

89. THAT OL' GANG OF MINE PART II: FOLLOW-UP!

Stop! Don't touch that dial. You've just come off the great THAT OL' GANG OF MINE quiz—so while you're hot, grab some more points. Do not pass "Go"—or anything else. Just turn back to the quiz you've just completed and tell us the name of the actor or actress who played the *first character* listed in the group casts of each picture, and you may add 10 points to your score for each player correctly identified.

_____points

(*Answers on page 274*)

89. THAT OL' GANG OF MINE PART II: FOLLOW-UP!— DUFFERS' TEE

We just made an offer to the Buffs that will enable them to increase their score by 250 points—and we're making the same offer to you. After all, what's fair's fair! We've asked the Buffs to identify the actor or actress who played the *first* character in each question of the quiz you've just completed. But you are Duffers, so with our assistance, you might be able to improve your score. Just fill in the blanks correctly, and earn while you learn.

1. Elizabeth Curtis   D _ _ _ _ _ _ _ K _ _ _ _
2. Ann Redman   F _ _ W _ _ _ _
3. Ernie Mott   C _ _ _ G _ _ _ _ _
4. Dusty Rivers   G _ _ _ C _ _ _ _ _ _
5. John Wickliff Shawnessy   M _ _ _ _ _ _ _ _ _ _ C _ _ _ _ _
6. Gen. James M. Scott   B _ _ _ _ L _ _ _ _ _ _ _ _ _ _
7. Blanche DuBois   V _ _ _ _ _ _ L _ _ _ _ _
8. Guy Haines   F _ _ _ _ _ _ G _ _ _ _ _ _ _
9. Robert Conway   R _ _ _ _ _ _ C _ _ _ _ _ _

10. Don Birnam	R _ _ M _ _ _ _ _ _ _
11. Carlotta Vance	M _ _ _ _ _ D _ _ _ _ _ _ _ _
12. Doc Delaney	B _ _ _ L _ _ _ _ _ _ _ _ _
13. Billy Dannreuther	H _ _ _ _ _ _ _ _ B _ _ _ _ _
14. C. C. (Bud) Baxter	J _ _ _ L _ _ _ _ _ _
15. Jim McLeod	K _ _ _ D _ _ _ _ _ _
16. Ari Ben Canaan	P _ _ _ N _ _ _ _ _ _
17. Capt. Kinross	N _ _ _ _ C _ _ _ _ _ _
18. Fred C. Dobbs	H _ _ _ _ _ _ _ _ B _ _ _ _ _
19. Joe Gillis	W _ _ _ _ _ _ _ H _ _ _ _ _
20. Pearl Chavez	J _ _ _ _ _ _ _ _ _ J _ _ _ _
21. Rubin Flood	R _ _ _ _ _ _ P _ _ _ _ _ _
22. Katrin Holstrom	L _ _ _ _ _ _ _ Y _ _ _ _
23. Stanley T. Banks	S _ _ _ _ _ _ _ T _ _ _ _ _
24. Sgt. Milton Warden	B _ _ _ L _ _ _ _ _ _ _ _ _
25. Leslie Lynnton Benedict	E _ _ _ _ _ _ _ _ _ T _ _ _ _ _

_____points

(*Answers on page 274*)

90. CLOSE . . . BUT NO CIGAR

The names of Oscar winners live on through the years—and despite the idea that being *nominated* is tantamount to being a winner, the glory of being nominated often fades fast. Below, we list a number of performers who were nominated—some as "Best Actor" or "Best Actress" and some as "Best Supporting Actor" or "Best Supporting Actress." We're sure you remember the performer, but will you remember the performance for which they were nominated? Fill in the blanks with the title of the film for which the particular performer received an Oscar nomination, and take 15 points for each one you get correct.

1. Elisabeth Bergner (1935)   "E_____ M___
       N_____"

2. Merle Oberon (1935)   "T_____ D_____
       A_____"

3. Marie Dressler (1932)   "E_____"

4. Frank Morgan (1934)   "T_____ A_____ o__
       C_____"

5. Claudette Colbert (1935)   "P_____ W_____"

6. Beulah Bondi (1936)   "T_____ G_____
       H_____"

7. Stuart Erwin (1936)	"P_____ P_____"	
8. Irene Dunne (1937)	"T_____ A_____ T_____"	
9. Andrea Leeds (1937)	"S_____ D_____"	
10. Miliza Korjus (1938)	"T__ G_____ W_____"	
11. Basil Rathbone (1938)	"L__ I W_____ K_____"	
12. Brian Donlevy (1939)	"B_____ G_____"	
13. Jack Oakie (1940)	"T_____ G_____	
	D_____"	
14. James Gleason (1941)	"H_____ C_____ M_____	
	J_____"	
15. Susan Peters (1942)	"R_____ H_____"	
16. Gladys Cooper (1942)	"N_____, V_____"	
17. J. Carroll Naish (1943)	"S_____"	
18. Monty Woolley (1944)	"S_____ Y__ W__ A_____"	
19. Flora Robson (1946)	"S_____ T_____"	
20. Tom Tully (1954)	"T_____ C_____	
	M_____"	

_____points

(*Answers on page 275*)

90. CLOSE . . . BUT NO CIGAR—DUFFERS' TEE

The names of Oscar winners live on through the years—and despite the idea that being *nominated* is tantamount to being a winner, the glory of being nominated often fades fast. Below, in Column One, we list a number of performers who were nominated—some as "Best Actor" or "Best Actress" and some as "Best Supporting Actor" or "Best Supporting Actress." In Column Two, out of order, we list the films in which these Oscar-nominated performances were included, and ask you to match the title of the film with the nominee. To assist you, we've added the year of the Oscar competition—and we're awarding 15 points for each correct pairing!

1. Elisabeth Bergner (1935)	a. "The Great Waltz"
2. Merle Oberon (1935)	b. "Private Worlds"
3. Marie Dressler (1932)	c. "Saratoga Trunk"
4. Frank Morgan (1934)	d. "Beau Geste"
5. Claudette Colbert (1935)	e. "Random Harvest"
6. Beulah Bondi (1936)	f. "Since You Went Away"
7. Stuart Erwin (1936)	g. "Sahara"
8. Irene Dunne (1937)	h. "Now, Voyager"

_____points

(*Answers on page 275*)

91. WHAT A WAY TO GO!

All of the players listed below in Column One, in the films we've specified, played characters who met their death as part of the plot. Some of the methods of death were rather bizarre, and we're asking you to tell us how these characters came to their glorious—or inglorious—end. You will earn 20 points for each answer you get correct. Think about it, now—and agree, when you have the answer, that it's quite a way to go!

1. Gloria Grahame, in "The Bad and The Beautiful" . . .
2. Phyllis Thaxter, in "No Man of Her Own" . . .
3. Tom Powers, in "Double Indemnity" . . .
4. Darryl Hickman, in "Leave Her to Heaven" . . .
5. Anthony Quinn, in "The Ox-Bow Incident" . . .
6. Victor Jory, in "The Adventures of Tom Sawyer" . . .
7. Leo G. Carroll, in "Spellbound" . . .
8. Jeff Corey, in "Brute Force" . . .
9. Shelley Winters, in "The Poseidon Adventure" . . .
10. Spanky McFarland, in "The Trail of the Lonesome Pine" . . .
11. Jennifer Jones, in "The Towering Inferno" . . .
12. Louis Calhern, in "Julius Caesar" . . .
13. Susan Hayward, in "Reap the Wild Wind" . . .
14. Lew Ayres, in "All Quiet on the Western Front" . . .
15. Francis Ford, in "Drums Along the Mohawk" . . .
16. Margaret Hamilton, in "The Wizard of Oz" . . .
17. Roy Thinnes, in "Airport '75" . . .

18. Robert Walker, in "Bataan" . . .
19. Thomas Mitchell, in "Gone With the Wind" . . .
20. Peter Graves, in "Stalag 17" . . .

_____points

(Answers on page 275)

91. WHAT A WAY TO GO!—DUFFERS' TEE

All of the players listed below in Column One, in the films we've specified, portrayed characters who met their death as a part of the plot. In Column Two—out of order—we've listed the various ways in which they came to their violent end. Match the character and title of Column One with the *manner* of death from Column Two, and take 20 points for each correct pairing.

1. Gloria Grahame, in "The Bad and the Beautiful" . . .

a. Machine-gunned by guards while bound to the front of a mine cart during a prison break.

2. Phyllis Thaxter, in "No Man of Her Own" . . .

b. Caught in an explosion.

3. Tom Powers, in "Double Indemnity" . . .

c. Fell to the earth from a tall building after an explosion disabled an exterior elevator.

4. Darryl Hickman, in "Leave Her to Heaven" . . .

d. Stabbed by conspirators.

5. Anthony Quinn, in "The Ox-Bow Incident" . . .

e. Shot by a sniper of the Japanese army.

6. Victor Jory, in "The Adventures of Tom Sawyer" . . .

f. Blown from the cockpit of an airliner as a result of a mid-flight collision.

7. Leo G. Carroll, in "Spellbound" . . .

g. Drowned as an unknowing stowaway on a ship which was deliberately wrecked.

8. Jeff Corey, in "Brute Force" . . .

h. Died of injuries incurred as a result of a fall from a horse.

9. Shelley Winters, in "The Poseidon Adventure" . . .

i. Died in crash of private plane.

190

10. Spanky McFarland, in "The Trail of the Lonesome Pine" . . .

j. Bludgeoned and left for dead alongside a railroad track.

11. Jennifer Jones, in "The Towering Inferno" . . .

k. Died of a heart attack following a strenuous underwater swim.

12. Louis Calhern, in "Julius Caesar" . . .

l. Dissolved in a puff of smoke after being doused with water.

13. Susan Hayward, in "Reap the Wild Wind" . . .

m. Killed in a train wreck.

14. Lew Ayres, in "All Quiet on the Western Front" . . .

n. Drowned while swimming in a lake.

15. Francis Ford, in "Drums Along the Mohawk" . . .

o. Shot by Nazi guards who believed he was trying to escape from a prison camp.

16. Margaret Hamilton, in "The Wizard of Oz" . . .

p. Suicide by gunshot.

17. Roy Thinnes, in "Airport '75" . . .

q. Shot by sniper while trying to catch a butterfly.

18. Robert Walker, in "Bataan" . . .

r. Fell from a precipice during a chase in an underground cavern.

19. Thomas Mitchell, in "Gone With the Wind" . . .

s. Shot by friendly settlers to avoid torture by Indians.

20. Peter Graves, in "Stalag 17" . . .

t. Lynched by an unruly mob.

(*Answers on page*)

(*Answers on page 275*)

92. BE MY GUEST—BUFFS AND DUFFERS

We are blessed with able associates and good friends—many of whom are pretty fair film buffs, and definitely ones to avoid in a shoot-out of movie questioning. We thought it might be a good idea to invite a few of these good friends to pass along their favorite movie questions so you can get some idea of how you stack up against some *real* expertise. One disclaimer, however: some of their questions are deliberately obscure, so we asked our friends not only for the questions . . . but the answers as well. We can't vouch for the latter (since some of our friends are rather sneaky), but we *can* vouch for some real examples of a "fast track" in the field of movie trivia. We trust them implicitly, and hope you have as much fun with their "cup of questions" we borrowed as we had soliciting them. By the way, our friends hold no sympathy for Duffers—so the point value listed with each question is for Buffs and Duffers alike. Good luck, and don't blame us!

From STAN MOGER . . .

[*He's Executive Vice President, SFM Media Service Corp., New York City. Stan's a real pro—not only at his job, but as a Champion Movie Buff. He was most enthusiastic about passing along his prizes, and while we had a tough time selecting the prime of his crop, we were able to winnow a vast array down to a few.*]

1. One of the most distinctive trademarks in films was that of a J. Arthur Rank film. Remember? A well-muscled he-man with glistening biceps swung a huge mallet against a gigantic gong. What was the real name of the man who struck the gong? (Score 175 points.)
2. In the George Stevens film "Gunga Din," it was Eduardo Ciannelli who was the leader of the native assassins, and who beseeched his followers to "Kill! Kill for the love of Kali!" Name the actor who played Ciannelli's son in the film. (Score 170 points.)
3. We spoke of trademarks a moment ago—so name the actress who was used for the Columbia Pictures trademark. She's the one who holds high the torch of liberty in this well-known symbol. (Score 170 points.)

From TONY VERDI . . .

[*He's an excellent television director, and among his credits are the nationally syndicated "Kup's Show" and "The Shari Show," starring Shari Lewis.*]

4. In the film "Bad Day at Black Rock," villain Robert Ryan is seeking information as to the background of John J. MacReedy (Spencer Tracy). Ryan instructs an associate to wire a private detective to conduct an investigation on the mysterious visitor to Black Rock. What was the name of the private detective, and in which hotel of what city could he be reached? (Take 70 points for each correct answer to the three questions, or a total of 210 points.)
5. Referring to the question above: In the same passage of dialogue, Ryan tells what his private detective demands for his services. What was the fee? (Score 75 points.)

From BOB *and* ESTHER MANEWITH . . .

[*He's Editorial Director for the WGN Continental Stations, WGN and WGN-TV; she's an advertising copywriter.*]

6. What do the following performers have in common: Barbara Stanwyck, Peter Lorre, Frank Sinatra, Richard Conte, and Orson Welles? The clue lies in a specific role each one played. (Score 150 points.)

From DAN PECARO . . .

[*He's President and Chief Executive of WGN Continental Broadcasting Co.—and despite the image conjured up by that impressive title, he's also a hell of a film buff. It was with Dan, in a restaurant on the outskirts of Atlanta, that we first were introduced to a game we've included in this book under the title "How Many Can You Get?"*]

7. We're talking about the film "Let 'Em Have It." Name two of the three male stars of the film. (Score 80 each; 160 for getting both.)
8. In the same film, Bruce Cabot plays a wanted criminal, fleeing from government agents. Cabot wants to change his identity, and visits a plastic surgeon to have his face altered. After the operation, Cabot removes the bandages and is horrified to learn that the surgeon has carved his (Cabot's character's) initials on his face! What were the initials, and what name did they represent? (Score 175 points.)

From GARY L. ASH . . .

[*He's Director of Business Affairs for the NBC-TV station in Los Angeles. It's unlikely that Gary could tell you who Hobart Cavanaugh was, or name the first film directed by Stanley Kubrick . . . BUT, we warn you, there's probably no one who has a more encyclopedic knowledge of the Academy Awards and their history than does Gary Ash. Here are the zingers he gave us.*]

9. There were two films which won Oscars as "Best Picture of the Year" whose nomination in this category represented the one and only nomination each film received. Name the two films in question. (Score 90 points for each correct answer.)
10. Twice in Academy history, actresses have been nominated *in the same year* for "Best Actress" in one film and for "Best Supporting Actress" in another. The years in which this happened were 1938 and 1942. Name the actresses *and* the movies involved. (Score 25 points for each actress correctly named and 25 points for each of the four titles involved.)
11. What actor received Oscar nominations for "Best Actor" and "Best Supporting Actor" for the *same* role in the *same* film? This resulted in the Academy's revision of its nominating procedures. (Score 170 points.)
12. Six men have received Oscar nominations as directors and actors, though not necessarily for the same film. Name them. (Score 50 points each; 300 for getting all six.)

From FRAZIER THOMAS . . .

[*Frazier is host of WGN-TV's popular "Bozo's Circus," as well as the creator and star of the long-running and well-loved children's TV show in Chicago, "Garfield Goose." Besides being an avid movie buff and an excellent editor, he seems to have an affinity for friends of the feathered variety.*]

13. In the film "Journey to the Center of the Earth," the Icelandic guide for the expedition brought along his pet duck. What was the name of the duck? (Score 165 points.)

14. Not a duck—but a goose which played such a hilarious supporting role in "Friendly Persuasion," with Gary Cooper and Dorothy McGuire. What was the name of the goose? (Score 165 points.)

From TOM ALDERMAN . . .

[*Tom's an actor, former radio-TV aide to Governor Dan Walker of Illinois, and owns the original "Maltese Falcon" statuette. We've had a soft place in our heart for Tom since we momentarily stumped him during a television interview regarding movie trivia by asking him to name the ship in "The Caine Mutiny"!*]

15. Name five films in which Edmund Purdom appeared. (Score 35 points each, or a total of 175 points.)

From BONNIE *and* CHARLES REMSBERG . . .

[*They're writer-journalists, and friends of long standing. In between writing TV scripts, magazine and newspaper articles, and readying a meticulously researched biography, they were kind enough to send along a couple of their zingers.*]

16. We suggest that a capsule history of U.S. military involvement can be traced by recalling some movie titles. Complete the titles suggested, and you'll see what we mean. (Score 100 points for each title properly completed.)

    a. Tyrone Power and Betty Grable in "A Yank in _____ _____" [1941]

    b. Joan Woodbury and Walter King in "A Yank in _____" [1942]

    c. Laraine Day and Barry Nelson in "A Yank on the _____ _____" [1942]

    d. Lon McCallister and Brett King in "A Yank in _____" [1951]

    e. John Archer and Jean Willes in "A Yank in _____-_____" [1952]

    f. Marshall Thompson and Enrique Magalona in "A Yank in _____ _____" [1964]

17. Each of the following films included the portrayal of a prostitute. Identify the actress who portrayed "the fallen woman." (Score 35 points for each correct identification; 175 points total.)

   a. "Irma La Douce"; b. "Zorba the Greek"; c. "Carnal Knowledge"; d. "Elmer Gantry"; e. "Butch Cassidy and the Sundance Kid."

From MORRY ROTH . . .

[*Morry Roth is a Midwest Bureau Chief for* Variety. *He's an able and honest reporter, a dedicated movie buff, and a good friend of ours for many years.*]

18. "Lonely Are the Brave" was a watershed 1962 *anti-Western*. In it, Kirk Douglas is a contemporary cowboy who is being pursued by Sheriff Walter Matthau across a modern wasteland of tacky housing developments. The movie is intercut with scenes of a semi-trailer hurtling down the highway, a truck that eventually runs down and kills Douglas. The driver of the truck is a character actor who later became the star of an immensely popular TV show. Name him. (Score 100 points.)

From MEL TORMÉ . . .

[*Of course, Mel Tormé is the actor, singer, composer, arranger, writer, and frequently the reviewer of books on cinema for the New York* Times. *He's also an addictive film buff, and all-round nice guy.*]

19. Dumas's "Three Musketeers" have been portrayed in films several times. But for this question, we're turning to the 1935 version, in which Walter Abel played D'Artagnan. Name the three actors who portrayed the Three Musketeers of the title, and to score—you must get all correct. (Score 300 points.)

20. A few years later, Louis Hayward was seen as "The Man in the Iron Mask." Helping him to gain freedom were D'Artagnan and the Three Musketeers. Name the *four* actors who played these roles, and who helped the hero escape his doom. And again, to score—you must get *all four* correct! (Score 300 points.)

_____points

(*Answers on page 277*)

93. HOMESTRETCH—BUFFS AND DUFFERS

It's been a long, hard race—but the band is playing, the colonel is in the stands—rubbin' his rabbit's-foot and a-sippin' on his julep—and if Frankie Darro can withstand the underhanded tricks of that crooked jockey on the black filly, owned by the conniving Douglas Dumbrille, ol' Gallant Heart can stretch his lead to a couple of lengths and come home a winner! We'll not only save the ol' homestead, but young Marse Jeff can finish his education, marry Miz Julie, and open the clinic! Well, not all of that will necessarily happen—but it is the homestretch, and it's your chance to surge home a winner. But you *know* we've saved some killers for this last reel. There are nine questions left, and we suggest you take a seventh-inning stretch before you tackle them. Each question has a different point-value—so get a firm grip on yourself, and don't say it hasn't been fun. Good luck!

1. (Point value: 160, Buffs; 165, Duffers)
   Everyone remembers that in "Yankee Doodle Dandy," James Cagney's sister Jeanne played the part of Josie Cohan, sister to George M. Cohan, played, of course, by James Cagney. But in what *other* film starring James Cagney did his real-life *brother*, William, portray Cagney's screen brother?

2. (Point value: 170, Buffs; 170, Duffers)
   As of this writing, the following four men have one special characteristic in common. They are: Charles Laughton, M-G-M Art Director Cedric Gibbons, Marlon Brando, and Anthony Quinn. Name the characteristic in common, and the four films which exemplify that characteristic.

3. (Point value: 180, Buffs; 180, Duffers)
   Prior to World War I, he was one of Hollywood's major stars. Years later, in the Warner Bros. all-star revue "Thank Your Lucky Stars," screen hero Errol Flynn sang "That's What You Jolly Well Get." Included in this scene, playing the bartender, was the star of 1915. Name him.

4. (Point value: 190, Buffs; 190, Duffers)
   He was one of Hollywood's and Warner Bros.' most prolific producers. A Bob Hope film of 1955 portrayed this man as a child. Obviously, any renown accruing to him at such an early age had nothing to do with his picture-making achievements. Name the Hope film, the producer, and how the character of the child fit into the film.

5. (Point value: 200, Buffs; 200, Duffers)

There were a number of films about the exploits of girl reporter Torchy Blane starring the fast-talking, fast-moving Glenda Farrell. However, the character of Torchy was also portrayed by two other actresses before the series came to an end. Name *both* of them.

6. (Point value: 210, Buffs; 215, Duffers)

Name at least two films in which Humphrey Bogart played a character named Steve.

7. (Point value: 225, Buffs; 225, Duffers)

Speaking of character names, we've often marveled that with the thousands of character names used, the writers seem to come up with fresh and unique names and—unless by design, as in a biographical film—they seldom repeat themselves. Yet this did happen at least once: in 1950, character actor Gregory Ratoff played a lovable eccentric, and two years later, suave Alexander Scourby played a ruthless villain—both characters had the same name. What was the duplicated character name, and in which two films—both starring famous actresses of the cinema—did this occur?

8. (Point value: 250, Buffs; 250, Duffers)

In one of the most famous scenes in one of Hollywood's best-remembered musicals, the following fictional business enterprises were given more than passing exposure. They were: "Mahout Cigarettes," "LaValle Millinery," and "The Mount Hollywood Art School." Describe the scene, and name the film, as well as the star involved.

9. (Point value: 225, Buffs; 260, Duffers)

Aladdin and Sinbad were usually portrayed as picaresque and dashing. Yet in one 1942 spear-and-sandal epic, Sinbad was played as a lazy bumbler by Shemp Howard, later one of the Three Stooges, while an aging Aladdin was played by character actor John Qualen. Name the film.

_____points

(*Answers on page 278*)

ANSWERS

1. CONSUMABLES—BUFFS AND DUFFERS

1. "The (f.) Corn is Green"
2. "Animal (g.) Crackers"
3. "One (j. or m.) Potato, Two (m. or j.) Potato"
4. "The (i.) Doughgirls"
5. "(l.) Tea for Two"
6. "The (n.) Coconuts"
7. "(e.) Dinner at Eight"
8. "Three Bites of the (b.) Apple"
9. "(k.) Breakfast at Tiffany's"
10. "(a.) Duck (d.) Soup"
11. "The (h.) Grapes of Wrath"
12. "(c.) Tobacco Road"

2. VERY IMPORTANT PROPS—BUFFS AND DUFFERS

1. Errol Flynn, Maureen O'Hara, and Anthony Quinn in . . . "Against All (h.) Flags"
2. Rex Harrison and Lilli Palmer in . . . "The (k.) Four Poster"
3. Carole Landis, Kay Francis, Mitzi Mayfair, and Martha Raye in . . . "Four Jills in a (l.) Jeep"
4. Arlene Dahl, Fernando Lamas, and Gilbert Roland in . . . "The (q.) Diamond Queen"
5. John Hodiak, Gene Tierney, and William Bendix in . . . "A (p.) Bell for Adano"
6. Gary Cooper, Phyllis Thaxter, and David Brian in . . . "Springfield (o.) Rifle"
7. John Wayne, Joanne Dru, and John Agar in . . . "She Wore a (j.) Yellow Ribbon"
8. Nelson Eddy and Ilona Massey in . . . "(m.) Balalaika"
9. Spencer Tracy, Richard Widmark, and Katy Jurado in . . . "Broken (r.) Lance"
10. Sterling Hayden, Coleen Gray, and Keith Larsen in . . . "(e) Arrow in the Dust"

11. Gene Kelly, Frank Sinatra, and
     Kathryn Grayson in . . .   "(d.) Anchors Aweigh"
12. Ingrid Bergman, George C. Scott,
     and Rex Harrison in . . .   "The Yellow (n.)
                                             Rolls-Royce"
13. Sean Connery, Dyan Cannon, and
     Martin Balsam in . . .   "The Anderson (t.) Tapes"
14. Sir Laurence Olivier, Robert
     Donat, and Michael
     Redgrave in . . .   "The Magic (c.) Box"
15. Lew Ayres, Gene Evans, and
     Nancy Davis in . . .   "Donovan's (g.) Brain"
16. Fess Parker, Jeffrey Hunter, and
     Claude Jarman, Jr., in . . .   "The Great (s.) Locomotive
                                             Chase"
17. Michael Moriarty, Robert De
     Niro, and Vincent Gardenia
     in . . .   "Bang the (a.) Drum
                                             Slowly"
18. Walter Matthau, Elaine May, and
     Jack Weston in . . .   "A New (b.) Leaf"
19. Rock Hudson, Doris Day, and
     Tony Randall in . . .   "(i.) Pillow Talk"
20. Hurd Hatfield, George Sanders,
     and Donna Reed in . . .   "The (f.) Picture of
                                             Dorian Gray"

3. LOOK WHO'S DANCING WITH MR. SMOOTH—BUFFS AND DUFFERS

1. "Let's Dance"   d. Betty Hutton
2. "Three Little Words"   e. Vera-Ellen
3. "Easter Parade"   h. or o. Ann Miller or Judy Garland
4. "Holiday Inn"   i. Marjorie Reynolds
5. "Yolanda and the Thief"   k. Lucille Bremer
6. "The Sky's the Limit"   a. Joan Leslie
7. "Broadway Melody of
     1940"   l. Eleanor Powell
8. "Easter Parade"   o. or h. Judy Garland or Ann Miller
9. "You Were Never
     Lovelier"   c. Rita Hayworth
10. "The Band Wagon"   n. Cyd Charisse
11. "Royal Wedding"   m. Jane Powell

202

4. SATURDAY NIGHT AT THE FLICKS—BUFFS ONLY

1. "His Other Woman"   "The Desk Set"
2. "Unconventional Linda"   "Holiday"
3. "Melody of Youth"   "They Shall Have Music"
4. "Harmony Parade"   "Pigskin Parade"
5. "The Big Heart"   "Miracle on 34th Street"
6. "The Modern Miracle"   "The Story of Alexander Graham
                               Bell"
7. "If You Feel Like Singing" "Summer Stock"
8. "Everybody's Cheering"   "Take Me Out to the Ball Game"
9. "The Affairs of Sally"   "The Fuller Brush Girl"
10. "Man of Bronze"   "Jim Thorpe—All-American"

4. SATURDAY NIGHT AT THE FLICKS—DUFFERS' TEE

1. "The Desk Set"   c. "His Other Woman"
2. "Holiday"   f. "Unconventional Linda"
3. "They Shall Have Music"   a. "Melody of Youth"
4. "Pigskin Parade"   g. "Harmony Parade"
5. "The Story of Alexander
      Graham Bell"   d. "The Modern Miracle"
6. "Miracle on 34th Street"   b. "The Big Heart"
7. "Take Me Out to the Ball
      Game"   j. "Everybody's Cheering"
8. "Summer Stock"   i. "If You Feel Like Singing"
9. "The Fuller Brush Girl"   h. "The Affairs of Sally"
10. "Jim Thorpe—All-American"   e. "Man of Bronze"

5. BROTH-ER—BUFFS AND DUFFERS

1. "Lust for Life"   Kirk Douglas   b. James Donald
2. "Sabrina"   Humphrey Bogart   c. William Holden

3. "The
   Brotherhood"   Kirk Douglas   b. Alex Cord
4. "Invisible Stripes" George Raft   a. William Holden
5. "Blaze of Noon"   Sterling Hayden   c. William Holden
6. "On the
   Waterfront"   Marlon Brando   c. Rod Steiger
7. "Viva Zapata"   Marlon Brando   b. Anthony Quinn
8. "Jesse James"   Tyrone Power   c. Henry Fonda
9. "The Cardinal"   Tom Tryon   b. Bill Hayes
10. "Champion"   Kirk Douglas   b. Arthur
                                                Kennedy

6. LINK-UPS—BUFFS AND DUFFERS

1. Susan   OLIVER   Reed
2. Leslie   WARREN   Beatty
3. Skye   AUBREY   Mather
4. Heather   ANGEL   Tompkins
5. James   BARTON   MacLane
6. Tina   LOUISE   Allbritton
7. Virginia   MAYO   Methot
8. Christopher GEORGE   Segal
9. Jean   WALLACE   Beery
10. Alex   NICOL   Williamson

7. CAREERS IN COMMON—BUFFS AND DUFFERS

1. Dan Dailey   "Taxi"   Taxicab driver
2. Warner Baxter   "Slave Ship"   Ship's captain
3. Orson Welles   "Moby Dick"   Clergyman
4. James Stewart   "Anatomy of a
                       Murder"   Defense attorney
5. Bette Davis   "The Star"   Movie star
6. George C. Scott "The Flim Flam Man"   Confidence man
7. Marie Wilson   "Boy Meets Girl"   Waitress
8. Zachary Scott   "The Southerner"   Farmer
9. Frank Sinatra   "Suddenly"   Assassin
10. Jack Lemmon   "Some Like It Hot"   Professional musician

8. NAME THE STAR—BUFFS ONLY

1. John Wayne   "Legend of the Lost"   "The Fighting Kentuckian"
2. William Bendix   "Woman of the Year"   "Wake Island"
3. William Holden   "The World of Suzie Wong"   "Boots Malone"
4. Mary Beth Hughes   "Follow the Band"   "Dressed to Kill"
5. Ann Sothern   "Panama Hattie"   "A Letter to Three Wives"
6. Kirk Douglas   "Two Weeks in Another Town"   "The Devil's Disciple"
7. Sonja Henie   "Iceland"   "My Lucky Star"
8. Anne Baxter   "The Spoilers"   "A Walk on the Wild Side"
9. Loretta Young   "And Now Tomorrow"   "China"
10. Ward Bond   "Young Mr. Lincoln"   "They Were Expendable"

8. NAME THE STAR—DUFFERS' TEE

1. John Wayne   "The War Wagon"   "The Green Berets"
2. William Bendix   "The Blue Dahlia"   "Detective Story"
3. William Holden   "Executive Suite"   "The Wild Bunch"
4. Mary Beth Hughes   "The Ox-Bow Incident"   "Young Man with a Horn"
5. Ann Sothern   "The Blue Gardenia"   "Gold Rush Maisie"
6. Kirk Douglas   "Champion"   "Paths of Glory"
7. Sonja Henie   "It's a Pleasure"   "Sun Valley Serenade"
8. Anne Baxter   "The Ten Commandments"   "All About Eve"
9. Loretta Young   "Call of the Wild"   "The Bishop's Wife"
10. Ward Bond   "Wagonmaster"   "The Quiet Man"

9. PENCILED IN—BUFFS ONLY

1. Paulette Goddard   "Destry Rides Again"   Marlene Dietrich
2. Ann Sheridan   "Casablanca"   Ingrid Bergman
3. Judy Garland   "Annie Get Your Gun"   Betty Hutton

4. Miriam Hopkins	"To Be or Not to Be"	Carole Lombard
5. Lee Remick	"Goodbye, Mr. Chips"	Petula Clark
6. Tallulah Bankhead	"Macbeth"	Jeanette Nolan
7. Ann Sheridan	"Strawberry Blonde"	Rita Hayworth
8. Betty Grable	"Guys and Dolls"	Vivian Blaine
9. Vera Zorina	"For Whom the Bell Tolls"	Ingrid Bergman
10. Alice Faye	"Greenwich Village"	Vivian Blaine

9. PENCILED IN—DUFFERS' TEE

1. "Destry Rides Again"	Paulette Goddard	e.	Marlene Dietrich
2. "Casablanca"	Ann Sheridan	g. or d.	Ingrid Bergman
3. "Annie Get Your Gun"	Judy Garland	f.	Betty Hutton
4. "To Be or Not to Be"	Miriam Hopkins	c.	Carole Lombard
5. "Goodbye, Mr. Chips"	Lee Remick	b.	Petula Clark
6. "Macbeth"	Tallulah Bankhead	h.	Jeanette Nolan
7. "Strawberry Blonde"	Ann Sheridan	j.	Rita Hayworth
8. "Guys and Dolls"	Betty Grable	a. or i.	Vivian Blaine
9. "For Whom the Bell Tolls"	Vera Zorina	d. or g.	Ingrid Bergman
10. "Greenwich Village"	Alice Faye	i. or a.	Vivian Blaine

10. PLAY BALL!—BUFFS AND DUFFERS

1. "Angels in the Outfield"	f.	Pittsburgh Pirates
2. "The Kid from Cleveland"	g.	Cleveland Indians
3. "Damn Yankees"	e.	Washington Senators
4. "The Stratton Story"	j.	Chicago White Sox
5. "Fear Strikes Out"	d.	Boston Red Sox
6. "Alibi Ike"	c.	Chicago Cubs
7. "Death on the Diamond"	h.	St. Louis Cardinals
8. "It Happened in Flatbush"	a. or i.	Brooklyn Dodgers

9. "Warming Up"   **b.** New York Yankees
10. "The Jackie Robinson
  Story"   **i. or a.** Brooklyn Dodgers

11. QUOTABLES—BUFFS AND DUFFERS

1. "The first law is . . ."
2. "I haven't the foggiest—"
3. "It profiteth not a man . . ."
4. "The first part of the party of the
  first part . . ."
5. "If there is ever to be law and
  order . . ."
6. "Oh, so?"
7. "You can print it if you want
  to . . ."
8. "You clittering, clattering
  collection of caliginous junk!"
9. "You're no more my mother than a
  toad!"
10. "It is widely held that too much
  wine . . ."

h. "Harry in Your Pocket"
d. "Bridge on the River Kwai"
b. "A Man for All Seasons"

e. "A Night at the Opera"

j. "Jesse James"
a. "Think Fast, Mr. Moto"

i. "Detective Story"

g. "The Wizard of Oz"

c. "The Shanghai Gesture"

f. "Tom Jones"

12. POTSHOTS—BUFFS AND DUFFERS

1. The "Good Witch" in "The Wizard of Oz" was (b) "Glinda."
2. The name of the newspaper owned by Raymond Massey in "The Fountainhead" was (a) The *Banner*.
3. The name of the Japanese farmer Spencer Tracy was seeking in "Bad Day at Black Rock" was (c) Kimoto.
4. The name of the college in "Good News" was (a) Tait College.
5. The school in "Best Foot Forward," attended by the boys—who had invited their dates as house guests for the big dance—was (b) Winsocki—as in "Buckle Down . . ."
6. The name of the auto sold by Douglas Fairbanks, Jr., in "The Young in Heart" was (c) "The Wombat."
7. The name of the boat in "Show Boat" was (c) the *Cotton Blossom*.
8. The single film in which Humphrey Bogart appeared which was produced by Samuel Goldwyn was (c) "Dead End."
9. The song which was fully staged, photographed, and then removed

from "The Wizard of Oz" prior to its release was (b) "The Jitter-bug."

10. The famed Parisian restaurant which was used in "Gigi" was (b) Maxim's.

13. UNIQUE CHARACTERS—BUFFS AND DUFFERS

1. "Cherokee Jim"	g. Charlie Ruggles	(F.) "Incendiary Blonde"
2. "Mosquito"	d. Leo Carrillo	(J.) "Girl of the Golden West"
3. "Pluto"	i. Buddy Hackett	(E.) "God's Little Acre"
4. "Pretty Boy"	f. Skip Homeier	(A.) "The Halls of Montezuma"
5. "Gold Dust"	h. Claire Trevor	(H.) "Honky Tonk"
6. "Moustache"	j. Lou Jacobi	(C.) "Irma La Douce"
7. "Sparrow"	a. Arnold Stang	(I.) "The Man with the Golden Arm"
8. "Regret"	b. Lynne Overman	(G.) "Little Miss Marker"
9. "Southeast"	c. Chill Wills	(D.) "The Westerner"
10. "Odd Job"	e. Harold Sakata	(B.) "Goldfinger"

14. CHICAGO, CHICAGO—BUFFS AND DUFFERS

1. (c) "Take Me Out to the Ball Game"
2. (c) Gene Kelly (O'Brien), Frank Sinatra (Ryan), Jules Munshin (Goldberg)
3. a. "Chicago Calling"   D. Dan Duryea
   b. "Chicago Confidential"   F. Brian Keith
   c. "The Earl of Chicago"   E. Robert Montgomery
   d. "Chicago Deadline"   B. Alan Ladd
   e. "The Chicago Kid"   A. Don Barry
   f. "Chicago Syndicate"   C. Dennis O'Keefe
4. (c) "Nightmare Alley"
5. a. The Great Chicago Fire   E. "In Old Chicago"
   b. The Columbian Exposition of 1894   D. "The Great Ziegfeld"
   c. The St. Valentine's Day massacre   A. "Some Like It Hot"
   d. The building of the Chicago
         Opera House   B. "Citizen Kane"
   e. The Loeb-Leopold trial   C. "Compulsion"
6. (f.) "Pal Joey." Though the stage version *was* set in Chicago, when the film was made (starring Frank Sinatra, Kim Novak, and Rita Hayworth) the site was transferred to San Francisco.

7. (b) Jack Oakie
8. (c) Joe. E. Brown
9. (c) Burt Lancaster
10. 1. Eddie Foy   —   f. Bob Hope ("The Seven Little Foys")

2. John Dillinger   —   g. Lawrence Tierney ("Dillinger")
3. Al Capone   —   h. Rod Steiger ("Al Capone")
4. Grover Cleveland Alexander   —   j. Ronald Reagan ("The Winning Team")
5. Baby Face Nelson   —   c. Mickey Rooney ("Baby Face Nelson")
6. Ruth Etting   —   a. Doris Day ("Love Me or Leave Me")
7. Stephen A. Douglas   —   i. Milburn Stone ("Young Mr. Lincoln")
8. Benny Goodman   —   e. Steve Allen ("The Benny Goodman Story"
9. Little Egypt   —   d. Rhonda Fleming ("Little Egypt")
10. Abraham Lincoln   —   b. Henry Fonda ("Young Mr. Lincoln")

15. ANYTHING YOU CAN DO, I CAN DO BETTER —BUFFS ONLY

1. Tyrone Power	Jesse James	"Jesse James"
J. Wendell Corey		"Alias Jesse James"
2. Robert Taylor	Billy the Kid	"Billy the Kid"
H. Kris Kristofferson		"Pat Garrett and Billy the Kid"
3. James Mason	Field Marshal Erwin Rommel	"The Desert Fox"[1]
F. Erich von Stroheim		"Five Graves to Cairo"
4. George Arliss	Benjamin Disraeli	"Disraeli"
G. Alec Guinness		"The Mudlark"
5. Charlton Heston	Andrew Jackson	"The President's Lady"[2]
A. Hugh Sothern		"The Buccaneer" (1938)
6. William Powell	Florenz Ziegfeld	"The Great Ziegfeld"[3]

[1] "The Desert Rats" would also be acceptable.
[2] "The Buccaneer" (1958) would also be acceptable.
[3] "Ziegfeld Follies" would also be acceptable.

B. Walter Pidgeon		"Funny Girl"
7. George C. Scott	Gen. George Patton	"Patton"
D. Kirk Douglas		"Is Paris Burning?"
8. Charles Laughton	King Henry VIII	"The Private Life of Henry VIII"
I. Robert Shaw		"A Man for All Seasons"
9. Henry Wilcoxon	Richard the Lion-Hearted	"The Crusades"
E. Ian Hunter		"The Adventures of Robin Hood"
10. Howard Keel	Hannibal	"Jupiter's Darling"
C. Victor Mature		"Hannibal"

15. ANYTHING YOU CAN DO, I CAN DO BETTER—DUFFERS' TEE

1. Tyrone Power; Jesse James in "Jesse James"

D. Wendell Corey

g. "Alias Jesse James"

2. Robert Taylor; Billy the Kid in "Billy the Kid"

H. Kris Kristofferson

c. "Pat Garrett and Billy the Kid"

3. James Mason; Field Marshall Rommel in "The Desert Fox"

J. Erich von Stroheim

a. "Five Graves to Cairo"

4. George Arliss; Benjamin Disraeli in "Disraeli"

I. Alec Guinness

j. "The Mudlark"

5. Charlton Heston; Andrew Jackson in "The President's Lady"

F. Hugh Sothern

f. "The Buccaneer"

6. William Powell; Florenz Ziegfeld in "The Great Ziegfeld"

A. Walter Pidgeon

b. "Funny Girl"

7. George C. Scott; Gen. George Patton in "Patton"

C. Kirk Douglas

h. "Is Paris Burning?"

8. Charles Laughton; Henry VIII in "The Private Life of Henry VIII"

B. Robert Shaw

e. "A Man for All Seasons"

9. Henry Wilcoxon; Richard the Lion-Hearted in "The Crusades"

E. Ian Hunter

d. "The Adventures of Robin Hood"

10. Howard Keel; Hannibal in "Jupiter's Darling"

G. Victor Mature

i. "Hannibal"

16. THE "THEY WENT THATAWAY" CRISSCROSS—BUFFS AND DUFFERS

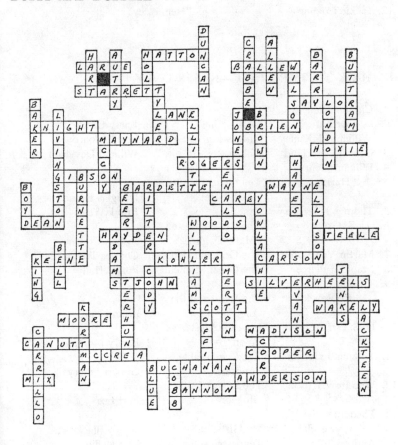

17. THE BIG BULB—BUFFS AND DUFFERS

1. Bill Williams
2. Joel McCrea
3. Ray Milland
4. Roscoe Karns
5. Robert Taylor
6. Broderick Crawford
7. J. Carroll Naish
8. Jeffrey Lynn
9. Stuart Erwin

d. "The Adventures of Kit Carson"
f. "Wichita Town"
e. "Meet Mr. McNutley"
i. "Rocky King, Detective"
c. "The Detectives"
a. "Highway Patrol"
l. "Life with Luigi"
k. "My Son Jeep"
b. "The Trouble with Father"

10. Peter Lawford   j. "Dear Phoebe"
11. Leon Ames   h. "Life with Father"
12. Jackie Cooper   g. "Hennessey"

18. HAIL TO THE CHIEF—BUFFS ONLY

1. Chester Alan Arthur	"Cattle King"	Larry Gates
2. William McKinley	"This Is My Affair"	Frank Conroy
3. Grover Cleveland	"Lillian Russell"	William Davidson
4. William Henry Harrison	"Ten Gentlemen from West Point"	Douglas Dumbrille
5. Thomas Jefferson	"America"	Frank Walsh
6. U. S. Grant	"The Adventures of Mark Twain"	Joseph Crehan
7. Martin Van Buren	"The Gorgeous Hussy"	Charles Trowbridge
8. Franklin Pierce	"The Great Moment"	Porter Hall
9. Theodore Roosevelt	"The Wind and the Lion"	Brian Keith
10. U. S. Grant	"How the West Was Won"	Henry Morgan
11. Thomas Jefferson	"The Remarkable Andrew"	Gilbert Emery
12. Woodrow Wilson	"The Story of Will Rogers"	Earl Lee
13. Theodore Roosevelt	"My Girl Tisa"	Sidney Blackmer
14. Andrew Johnson	"Tennessee Johnson"	Van Heflin
15. Abraham Lincoln	"The Littlest Rebel"	Frank McGlynn (Sr.)

18. HAIL TO THE CHIEF—DUFFERS' TEE

1. Larry Gates	"Cattle King"	g. Chester Alan Arthur
2. Frank Conroy	"This Is My Affair"	h. William McKinley
3. William Davidson	"Lillian Russell"	b. Grover Cleveland

4. Douglas Dumbrille	"Ten Gentlemen from West Point"	c.	William Henry Harrison
5. Frank Walsh	"America"	l. or o.	Thomas Jefferson
6. Joseph Crehan	"The Adventures of Mark Twain"	d. or m.	U. S. Grant
7. Charles Trowbridge	"The Gorgeous Hussy"	k.	Martin Van Buren
8. Porter Hall	"The Great Moment"	i.	Franklin Pierce
9. Brian Keith	"The Wind and the Lion"	a. or j.	Theodore Roosevelt
10. Henry Morgan	"How the West Was Won"	m. or d.	U. S. Grant
11. Gilbert Emery	"The Remarkable Andrew"	o. or l.	Thomas Jefferson
12. Earl Lee	"The Story of Will Rogers"	f.	Woodrow Wilson
13. Sidney Blackmer	"My Girl Tisa"	j. or a.	Theodore Roosevelt
14. Van Heflin	"Tennessee Johnson"	e.	Andrew Johnson
15. Frank McGlynn (Sr.)	"The Littlest Rebel"	n.	Abraham Lincoln

19. SPOT THE BIO: SHOW BIZ—BUFFS AND DUFFERS

1. Dinah Shore	"Till the Clouds Roll By"	f.	Julia Sanderson
2. Judy Guild	"Till the Clouds Roll By"	h.	Marilyn Miller
3. Martin Noble	"Rhapsody in Blue"	g.	Jascha Heifetz
4. Eddie Kane	"The Jolson Story"	c.	Florenz Ziegfeld
5. Betty Hutton	"Incendiary Blonde"	a.	"Texas" Guinan
6. Edwin Maxwell	"The Jolson Story"	i.	Oscar Hammerstein
7. Bing Crosby	"Dixie"	j.	Dan Emmett
8. John Alexander	"Lillian Russell"	e.	Lew Dockstader
9. Ray Daley	"The Five Pennies"	b.	Glenn Miller
10. Eduard Franz	"The Great Caruso"	d.	Giulio Gatti-Casazza

20. TYPE-CASTING?—BUFFS AND DUFFERS

1. _ g. BORIS KARLOFF: "Isle of the Dead"; "Mr. Wong, Detective"; "Unconquered"[1]; "West of Shanghai."

2. _ d. ERROL FLYNN: "Edge of Darkness"; "Northern Pursuit"; "Uncertain Glory"; "Kim."

3. _ b. KIRK DOUGLAS: "The Juggler"; "The Heroes of Telemark"; "Paths of Glory"; "Ulysses."[2]

4. _ f. FREDERIC MARCH: "The Road Back"; "The Affairs of Cellini"; "We Live Again"[3]; "Man on a Tightrope."

5. _ i. CORNEL WILDE: "A Song to Remember"; "High Sierra"; "Sword of Camelot"; "The Greatest Show on Earth."

6. _ j. PAUL MUNI: "The Good Earth"; "Hudson's Bay"; "Counter Attack"; "Juarez."

7. _ h. BASIL RATHBONE: "Captain Blood"; "The Adventures of Marco Polo"; "Anna Karenina"[4]; "The Mark of Zorro."

8. _ a. YUL BRYNNER: "The King and I"; "Taras Bulba"; "Villa Rides"; "The Battle of Neretva."

9. _ e. CHARLES LAUGHTON: "The Hunchback of Notre Dame"; "They Knew What They Wanted"; "Spartacus"; "Rembrandt."

10. _ c. ANTHONY QUINN: "Viva Zapata"; "La Strada"; "The Savage Innocents"; "Lawrence of Arabia."

[1] Sorry if you said "Tap Roots"—but we're going to quibble on this one. In "Tap Roots," he was a Choctaw.
[2] We suppose we'll get letters if we don't allow "Spartacus" also—okay, so be it!
[3] There will be those who'll come up with "Anna Karenina"—but Count Vronsky is hardly a Russian *prince!*
[4] Defining a *bureaucrat* is not easy. For that reason, we'll allow "Tovarich" as an answer. Okay?

214

21. DURABLE, AND DARLING—BUFFS AND DUFFERS

1. Thelma Todd (1932)	r.	"This Is the Night"
2. Marlene Dietrich (1932)	t.	"Blonde Venus"
3. Nancy Carroll (1932)	n.	"Hot Saturday"
4. Sylvia Sidney (1933)	l.	"Thirty Day Princess"
5. Mae West (1933)	a.	"I'm No Angel"
6. Loretta Young (1934)	o.	"Born to Be Bad"
7. Frances Drake (1934)	h.	"Ladies Should Listen"
8. Jean Harlow (1936)	q.	"Suzy"
9. Constance Bennett (1937)	b.	"Topper"
10. Katharine Hepburn (1938)	k.	"Holiday"
11. Jean Arthur (1939)	m.	"Only Angels Have Wings"
12. Carole Lombard (1939)	u.	"In Name Only"
13. Irene Dunne (1940)	p.	"My Favorite Wife"
14. Rosalind Russell (1940)	s.	"His Girl Friday"
15. Joan Fontaine (1941)	c.	"Suspicion"
16. Ginger Rogers (1942)	i.	"Once Upon a Honeymoon"
17. Laraine Day (1943)	B.	"Mr. Lucky"
18. Janet Blair (1944)	C.	"Once Upon a Time"
19. Priscilla Lane (1944)	v.	"Arsenic and Old Lace"
20. Alexis Smith (1946)	d.	"Night and Day"
21. Ingrid Bergman (1946)	w.	"Notorious"
22. Betsy Drake (1948)	x.	"Every Girl Should Be Married"
23. Ann Sheridan (1949)	z.	"I Was a Male War Bride"
24. Jeanne Crain (1951)	j.	"People Will Talk"
25. Deborah Kerr (1953)	e.	"Dream Wife"
26. Grace Kelly (1955)	D.	"To Catch a Thief"
27. Sophia Loren (1957)	y.	"Houseboat"
28. Suzy Parker (1957)	g.	"Kiss Them for Me"
29. Doris Day (1962)	A.	"That Touch of Mink"
30. Audrey Hepburn (1962)	f.	"Charade"

And the star, durable and darling, is Cary Grant!

22. ALMOST A LEGEND—BUFFS AND DUFFERS

1. Warner Oland (1934)	e.	"Mandalay"
2. Warner Baxter (1934)	s.	"Stand Up and Cheer"
3. Spencer Tracy (1934)	i.	"Now I'll Tell"
4. Charles Farrell (1934)	c.	"Change of Heart"
5. Gary Cooper (1934)	r.	"Now and Forever"
6. Lionel Barrymore (1934)	d.	"Carolina"

7. Joel McCrea (1935)	j.	"Our Little Girl"	
8. John Boles (1935)	t.	"Curly Top"	
9. Jack Haley (1936)	a.	"Poor Little Rich Girl"	
10. Robert Young (1936)	n.	"Stowaway"	
11. Victor McLaglen (1937)	p.	"Wee Willie Winkie"	
12. George Murphy (1938)	q.	"Little Miss Broadway"	
13. Randolph Scott (1939)	b.	"Rebecca of Sunnybrook Farm"	
14. Richard Greene (1939)	o.	"The Little Princess"	
15. George Montgomery (1940)	f.	"Young People"	
16. Herbert Marshall (1941)	h.	"Kathleen"	
17. Joseph Cotten (1944)	g.	"Since You Went Away"	
18. Robert Benchley (1945)	k.	"Kiss and Tell"	
19. Franchot Tone (1945)	l.	"Honeymoon"	
20. Cary Grant (1947)	m.	"The Bachelor and the Bobbysoxer"	

And the star is, of course, Miss Shirley Temple!

23. WHO WAS THAT LADY?—BUFFS AND DUFFERS

1. "Anna"	i.	Silvana Mangano
2. "Ada"	o.	Susan Hayward
3. "Billie"	f.	Patty Duke
4. "Emma"	h.	Marie Dressler
5. "Fanny"	l., p., or s.	Leslie Caron
6. "Gidget"	r.	Sandra Dee
7. "Gigi"	p., s., or l.	Leslie Caron
8. "Gypsy"	e.	Natalie Wood
9. "Heidi"	k. or v.	Shirley Temple
10. "Irene"	c.	Anna Neagle
11. "Jennie"	j.	Virginia Gilmore
12. "Jennifer"	u.	Ida Lupino
13. "Jessica"	y.	Angie Dickinson
14. "Josette"	g.	Simone Simon
15. "Judith"	x.	Sophia Loren
16. "Julie"	w.	Doris Day
17. "Kathleen"	v. or k.	Shirley Temple
18. "Kitty"	t.	Paulette Goddard
19. "Laura"	n.	Gene Tierney
20. "Lili"	s., l., or p.	Leslie Caron
21. "Lilith"	q.	Jean Seberg
22. "Maisie"	b.	Ann Sothern
23. "Mickey"	m.	Lois Butler
24. "Nana"	a.	Anna Sten
25. "Zaza"	d.	Claudette Colbert

24. FILMS IN COMMON—BUFFS ONLY

1. "Forbidden Planet"
   "West Side Story"   j. "Joe Macbeth"
   All three films are based on plays by William Shakespeare. "Forbidden Planet" is based on "The Tempest," while "West Side Story" uses "Romeo and Juliet" for its basic plot. The root of "Joe Macbeth" is (obviously) "Macbeth," with this screen version transferring the Scottish king to American gangland.

2. "We Were Strangers"
   "Suddenly"   l. "Executive Action"
   The assassination of a head of state is the common trait. "We Were Strangers" dealt with the attempted assassination of a Cuban dictator, while "Suddenly" was involved with the attempted shooting of a fictional U. S. President. "Executive Action" was speculative fiction which used the Dallas assassination of President John F. Kennedy as its springboard.

3. "Day for Night"
   "The Barefoot Contessa"   m. "Two Weeks in Another Town"
   All three films dealt with the backstage stories of making movies in Europe.

4. "Bullitt"
   "Experiment in Terror"   h. "Barbary Coast"
   All three films were set in San Francisco.

5. "I'll Cry Tomorrow"
   "Love Me Or Leave Me"   k. "With a Song in My Heart"
   The three films were biographical treatments of three American songstresses: Lillian Roth ("I'll Cry Tomorrow"), Ruth Etting ("Love Me or Leave Me"), and Jane Froman ("With a Song in My Heart").

6. "Heaven Can Wait"
   "All That Money Can Buy"   i. "Cabin in the Sky"
   Each of the films had the devil as one of its characters.

7. "Strange Cargo"
   "Papillon"   d. "We're No Angels"
   In each of the films, the main characters were prisoners on Devil's Island.

8. "Executive Suite"
   "The Solid Gold Cadillac"   n. "How to Succeed in Business
                                    Without Really Trying"
   All three films dealt with the machinations of American big business.

9. "The Rogue Song"
   "Mr. Imperium"   o. "Aaron Slick from Punkin Crick"
   Each of the films included in its cast a prominent male opera star: "The Rogue Song," Lawrence Tibbett; "Mr. Imperium," Ezio Pinza; and "Aaron Slick from Punkin Crick," Robert Merrill.

10. "Billy the Kid"
   "This Is Cinerama"   e. "The Robe"
The three films mentioned were each the debut film of a different wide-screen process. "Billy the Kid," in 1930 was in 70 millimeter; "This Is Cinerama" was, of course, the first use of the three-projector Cinerama system; and "The Robe" was the first feature to be produced in the single-projector CinemaScope.

11. "Anatomy of a Murder"
   "Witness for the Prosecution"   f. "Trial"
Each of the plots included lengthy courtroom sequences and trial procedures.

12. "Reap the Wild Wind"
   "Leave Her to Heaven"   b. "A Place in the Sun"
In all three films, drownings were pivotal to the plot.

13. "All the President's Men"
   "30"   c. "Call Northside 777"
The three films focused on the investigative reporting by a large metropolitan newspaper.

14. "Murder on the Orient
      Express"
   "The Narrow Margin"   a. "The Lady Vanishes"
Much of the action in these three films took place aboard a passenger train.

15. "She"
   "The Picture of Dorian
      Gray"   g. "Lost Horizon"
The three films included in their plot phenomena in the aging process.

24. FILMS IN COMMON—DUFFERS' TEE

1. "Forbidden Planet"
   "West Side Story"   b. "Joe Macbeth"
2. "We Were Strangers"
   "Suddenly"   a. "Executive Action"
3. "Day for Night"
   "The Barefoot Contessa"   a. "Two Weeks in Another Town"
4. "Bullitt"
   "Experiment in Terror"   b. "Barbary Coast"
5. "I'll Cry Tomorrow"
   "Love Me or Leave Me"   c. "With a Song in My Heart"
6. "Heaven Can Wait"
   "All That Money Can Buy"   b. "Cabin in the Sky"

218

7. "Strange Cargo"
   "Papillon"   a. "We're No Angels"
8. "Executive Suite"
   "The Solid Gold Cadillac"   a. "How to Succeed in Business
                                            Without Really Trying"
9. "The Rogue Song"
   "Mr. Imperium"   b. "Aaron Slick from Punkin Crick"
10. "Billy the Kid"
    "This Is Cinerama"   c. "The Robe"
11. "Anatomy of a Murder"
    "Witness for the Prosecution"   b. "Trial"
12. "Reap the Wild Wind"
    "Leave Her to Heaven"   c. "A Place in the Sun"
13. "All the President's Men"
    "30"   a. "Call Northside 777"
14. "Murder on the Orient
        Express"
    "The Narrow Margin"   c. "The Lady Vanishes"
15. "She"
    "The Picture of Dorian
        Gray"   c. "Lost Horizon"

For an explanation of the common factor for the three films in each question, please refer to the answer section of the Buffs' version above.

25. ALL WE NEED IS A TITLE—BUFFS AND DUFFERS

1. "The Townsend Harris Story"   f. "The Barbarian and the Geisha"
2. "The Silence of Helen
      McCord"   d. "The Spiral Staircase"
3. "Where Men Are Men"   g. "Fancy Pants"
4. "Man on a Train"   j. "The Tall Target"
5. "The Californian"   h. "The Mark of Zorro"
6. "Tribute to a Bad Man"[1]   e. "The Bad and the Beautiful"
7. "Nearer My God to Thee"   b. "Titanic"
8. "The Dr. Praetorious Story"   c. "People Will Talk"
9. "Chuck-a-Luck"   k. "Rancho Notorious"
10. "The House of
       Dr. Edwardes"   l. "Spellbound"
11. "Pylon"   i. "The Tarnished Angels"
12. "The Fragile Fox"   a. "Attack"

[1] No mistake here. "Tribute to a Bad Man" *was* the original title of the film which ended up being "The Bad and the Beautiful." Apparently, what was suitable for a Hollywood bad man was also appropriate for a Western bad man, so M-G-M found good use for the title a few years later on a film starring James Cagney!

26. THE BIG BULB PART II—BUFFS AND DUFFERS

1. Walter Brennan		h.	"The Tycoon"
2. Reed Hadley		i.	"Public Defender"
3. Wendell Corey		j.	"Harbor Command"
4. Victor Jory		g.	"Manhunt"
5. Charles Bickford		m.	"The Man Behind the Badge"
6. Ralph Bellamy		b.	"Man Against Crime"
7. Boris Karloff		d.	"Colonel March of Scotland Yard"
8. Rod Cameron		n.	"Coronado 9"
9. Kent Taylor		l.	"Boston Blackie"
10. Dennis Morgan		f.	"21 Beacon Street"
11. Louis Jourdan		a.	"Paris Precinct"
12. Stephen McNally		c.	"Target: The Corrupters"
13. Macdonald Carey		o.	"Lock Up"
14. George Raft		k.	"I'm the Law"
15. Everett Sloane		e.	"Official Detective"

27. TELL US WHO—BUFFS AND DUFFERS

1. __ e. Mischa Auer	__	"The Crusades" "My Man Godfrey"
2. __ j. William Powell	__	"Manhattan Melodrama" "Mr. Roberts"
3. __ b. Stewart Granger	__	"Scaramouche" "King Solomon's Mines"
4. __ a. Barbara Stanwyck	__	"Double Indemnity" "Union Pacific"
5. __ h. Robert Shaw	__	"The Sting" "A Man for All Seasons"
6. __ c. James Cagney	__	"A Midsummer Night's Dream" "The Seven Little Foys"
7. __ i. Hume Cronyn	__	"The Cross of Lorraine" "Lifeboat"
8. __ d. Mitzi Gaynor	__	"Les Girls" "South Pacific"
9. __ g. Michael Wilding	__	"Torch Song" "The Glass Slipper"
10. __ f. Bette Davis	__	"A Pocketful of Miracles" "The Man Who Came to Dinner"

28. CASTING DIRECTOR—BUFFS ONLY

1. The evil and cunning Mohammed Khan — g. C. Henry Gordon
2. The wisecracking, "stop-the-presses" reporter — e. Chick Chandler
3. The small-town constable — f. Spencer Charters
4. The top-hatted, white-tied happy drunk — h. Jack Norton
5. The head thug's right-hand man — i. Joe Sawyer
6. The dignified Mittel-European professor — j. Victor Francen
7. The pompous, blustering politician — c. Thurston Hall
8. The big-business tycoon — b. Edward Arnold
9. The cowardly stool pigeon — a. Paul Guilfoyle
10. The weak, unctuous assistant — d. Byron Foulger

28. CASTING DIRECTOR—DUFFERS' TEE

1. The evil and cunning Mohammed Khan — b. C. Henry Gordon
2. The wisecracking, "stop-the-presses" reporter — b. Chick Chandler
3. The small-town constable — c. Spencer Charters
4. The top-hatted, white-tied happy drunk — c. Jack Norton
5. The head thug's right-hand man — a. Joe Sawyer
6. The dignified Mittel-European professor — c. Victor Francen
7. The pompous, blustering politician — a. Thurston Hall
8. The big-business tycoon — b. Edward Arnold
9. The cowardly stool pigeon — c. Paul Guilfoyle
10. The weak, unctuous assistant — c. Byron Foulger

29. RIGHT AFTER THIS MESSAGE—BUFFS ONLY

1. Virginia Christine[1] — f. Coffee
2. Jonathan Winters — e. Garbage bags
3. Gary Merrill — g. Beer
4. Joey Heatherton — i. Mattresses

[1] If the name doesn't ring a bell, besides appearing in "Guess Who's Coming to Dinner," she is also television's meddlesome "Mrs. Olson" . . .

5. Andy Griffith	h. Steak sauce
6. Arthur O'Connell	b. Toothpaste
7. Louis Jourdan	a. Telegraph florists
8. John Williams	j. Recordings
9. Burgess Meredith	d. Canned vegetables
10. Jim Davis	c. Cream substitute

29. RIGHT AFTER THIS MESSAGE—DUFFERS' TEE

1. Jane Withers	j. Drain solvent
2. Edie Adams	g. Cigars
3. Bing Crosby	f. Orange juice
4. Henry Fonda	i. Cameras & floor tile
5. Jane Russell	h. Brassieres
6. Orson Welles	e. Airline travel
7. Sir Laurence Olivier	b. Instant cameras
8. Anna Maria Alberghetti	c. Salad dressing
9. Zsa Zsa Gabor	d. Auto repairs
10. Patricia Neal	a. Instant coffee

30. LA RONDE—BUFFS AND DUFFERS

1. Gary Cooper and Lilli Palmer	(A.) _ h. "Cloak and Dagger"
2. Lilli Palmer and John Garfield	(B.) _ d. "Body and Soul"
3. John Garfield and Shelley Winters	(C.) _ i. "He Ran All the Way"
4. Shelley Winters and Ronald Colman	(D.) _ a. "A Double Life"
5. Ronald Colman and Madeleine Carroll	(E.) _ k. "The Prisoner of Zenda"
6. Madeleine Carroll and Bob Hope	(F.) _ g. "My Favorite Blonde"
7. Bob Hope and Betty Hutton	(G.) _ j. "Let's Face It"
8. Betty Hutton and Fred Astaire	(H.) _ b. "Let's Dance"
9. Fred Astaire and Leslie Caron	(I.) _ c. "Daddy Long Legs"

10. Leslie Caron and Cary
    Grant   (J.) _ e. "Father Goose"
11. Cary Grant and Ingrid
    Bergman   (K.) _ l. "Notorious"[1]
12. Ingrid Bergman and
    Gary Cooper   (L.) _ f. "For Whom the Bell Tolls"

31. SATURDAY NIGHT AT THE FLICKS PART II —BUFFS ONLY

1. "Spirit of the People"	"Abe Lincoln in Illinois"
2. "I Shall Return"	"An American Guerilla in the Philippines"
3. "Polly Fulton"	"B.F.'s Daughter"
4. "The Flaming Torch"	"The Bob Mathias Story"
5. "The Curse of the Allenbys"	"She-Wolf of London"
6. "Get Off My Back"	"Synanon"
7. "The Gay Mrs. Trexel"	"Susan and God"
8. "Chicago, Chicago"	"Gaily, Gaily"
9. "Chicago Masquerade"	"Little Egypt"
10. "Southwest to Sonora"	"The Appaloosa"

31. SATURDAY NIGHT AT THE FLICKS PART II— DUFFERS' TEE

1. "Abe Lincoln in Illinois"	g. "Spirit of the People"
2. "The Appaloosa"	i. "Southwest to Sonora"
3. "Susan and God"	h. "The Gay Mrs. Trexel"
4. "An American Guerilla in the Philippines"	b. "I Shall Return"
5. "Little Egypt"	j. "Chicago Masquerade"
6. "She-Wolf in London"	c. "The Curse of the Allenbys"
7. "Synanon"	a. "Get Off My Back"
8. "The Bob Mathias Story"	f. "The Flaming Torch"
9. "B.F.'s Daughter"	d. "Polly Fulton"
10. "Gaily, Gaily"	e. "Chicago, Chicago"

[1] In the Buffs' version, "Indiscreet" would also be acceptable.

223

32. PENCILED IN: MALES—BUFFS ONLY

1. George Raft	"High Sierra"	Humphrey Bogart
2. Frank Sinatra	"The Only Game in Town"	Warren Beatty
3. Montgomery Clift	"Moby Dick"	Richard Basehart
4. Sammy Davis, Jr.	"Never So Few"	Steve McQueen
5. George Raft	"The Maltese Falcon"	Humphrey Bogart
6. Robert Alda	"Somebody Loves Me"	Ralph Meeker
7. Burt Lancaster	"Les Miserables"	Michael Rennie
8. Tony Randall	"The Young Lions"	Dean Martin
9. Marlon Brando	"The Egyptian"	Edmund Purdom
10. Scott Brady	"Come Back, Little Sheba"	Richard Jaeckel

32. PENCILED IN: MALES—DUFFERS' TEE

1. "High Sierra"	George Raft	f. or g.	Humphrey Bogart
2. "The Only Game in Town"	Frank Sinatra	i.	Warren Beatty
3. "Moby Dick"	Montgomery Clift	d.	Richard Basehart
4. "Never So Few"	Sammy Davis, Jr.	h.	Steve McQueen
5. "The Maltese Falcon"	George Raft	g. or f.	Humphrey Bogart
6. "Somebody Loves Me"	Robert Alda	b.	Ralph Meeker
7. "Les Miserables"	Burt Lancaster	a.	Michael Rennie
8. "The Young Lions"	Tony Randall	j.	Dean Martin
9. "The Egyptian"	Marlon Brando	c.	Edmund Purdom
10. "Come Back, Little Sheba"	Scott Brady	e.	Richard Jaeckel

33. SPOT THE RINGER—BUFFS ONLY

1. Anthony Asquith; "Glory Alley."
2. Ray Enright; "Paint Your Wagon."

3. Don Weis; "Walk East on Beacon."
4. Alfred Werker; "The Stranger."
5. Gordon Douglas; "The Last Time I Saw Archie."
6. Jack Webb; "The King's Pirate."
7. Archie Mayo; "The Spirit of St. Louis."
8. Richard Wallace; "Bordertown."
9. Cy Endfield; "Walk East on Beacon."
10. Sidney Lanfield; "Operation Petticoat."
11. Andre de Toth; "Flaming Feather."
12. Walter Lang; "The Great Impersonation."
13. Julien Duvivier; "D.O.A."
14. Allan Dwan; "Great Expectations."
15. Josef von Sternberg; "The Great Gabbo."

33. SPOT THE RINGER—DUFFERS' TEE

1. William Dieterle; "Indiscreet."
2. Edward Dmytryk; "Trapeze."
3. Elia Kazan; "The High and the Mighty."
4. Stanley Donen; "The War Lord."
5. Raoul Walsh; "The Professionals."
6. Orson Welles; "The Spirit of St. Louis."
7. Blake Edwards; "Crack in the World."
8. William Wellman; "Cool Hand Luke."
9. Robert Wise; "Underworld, U.S.A."
10. Richard Brooks; "Weekend at the Waldorf."
11. John Farrow; "Wee Willie Winkie."
12. Franklin Schaffner; "A Night at the Opera."
13. Billy Wilder; "The Eve of St. Mark."
14. Frank Capra; "Craig's Wife."
15. Josh Logan; "Panic in the Streets."

34. WHO SANG . . . ?—BUFFS AND DUFFERS

1. "I'm Writing a Letter to Daddy"	J. Bette Davis	c. "What Ever Happened to Baby Jane?"
2. "Night and Day"	D. Frank Sinatra	a. "Reveille with Beverly"
3. "Gettin' Corns for My Country"	B. or F. The Andrews Sisters	j. "Hollywood Canteen"

225

4. "I Don't Want to Play in Your Yard"	I. James Cagney	b. "The Oklahoma Kid"
5. "Oh, How I Hate to Get Up in the Morning"	A. Irving Berlin	e. "This Is the Army"
6. "You're a Lucky Fellow, Mr. Smith"	F. or B. The Andrews Sisters	d. "Buck Privates"
7. "Isn't It Kinda Fun?"	E. Vivian Blaine	f. "State Fair"
8. "Arthur Murray Taught Me Dancing in a Hurry"	C. Betty Hutton	h. "The Fleet's In"
9. "Ev'ry Little Movement Has a Meaning All Its Own"	G. Connie Gilchrist Judy Garland	i. "Presenting Lily Mars"
10. "Willy, the Wolf of the West"	H. Cass Daley	g. "Riding High"

35. THE LITTLE WOMAN—BUFFS AND DUFFERS

1. CLAUDETTE COLBERT	"Tovarich"; "Drums Along the Mohawk"; "The Egg and I"[1]
2. BETTE DAVIS	"Juarez"; "Watch on the Rhine"; "The Sisters"
3. INGRID BERGMAN	"Casablanca"; "Gaslight"; "Under Capricorn"
4. JEANNE CRAIN	"A Letter to Three Wives"; "Apartment for Peggy"; "O. Henry's Full House"
5. MAUREEN O'HARA	"Sitting Pretty"; "Buffalo Bill"; "How Do I Love Thee"
6. JOAN FONTAINE	"Darling, How Could You!"; "Suspicion"; "Rebecca"
7. ANNE BAXTER	"Homecoming"; "Follow the Sun"; "My Wife's Best Friend"
8. LORETTA YOUNG	"Bedtime Story"; "The Story of Alexander Graham Bell"; "It Happens Every Thursday"

[1] The title "Maid of Salem" would also be acceptable.

9. GENE TIERNEY	"The Iron Curtain"; "Whirlpool"; "Close to My Heart"
10. LINDA DARNELL	"Unfaithfully Yours"; "A Letter to Three Wives"; "Zero Hour"
11. KATHARINE HEPBURN	"A Long Day's Journey into Night"; "The Lion in Winter"; "Song of Love"
12. IRENE DUNNE	"I Remember Mama"; "Over Twenty-one"; "Life with Father"

36. CONTINUED NEXT WEEK—BUFFS AND DUFFERS

1. "Nyoka and the Tigermen"	d. Kay Aldridge
2. "The Mysterious Dr. Satan"	e. Eduardo Ciannelli
3. "Don Daredevil"	k. Ken Curtis[1]
4. "Commando Cody, Sky Marshal of the Universe"	a. Judd Holden[2]
5. "Federal Operator 99"	o. Marten Lamont
6. "King of the Carnival"	j. Harry Lauter
7. "Man with the Steel Whip"	f. Richard Simmons
8. "King of Jungleland"	n. Clyde Beatty
9. "Panther Girl of the Kongo"	l. Phyllis Coates
10. "King of the Texas Rangers"	b. Sammy Baugh[3]
11. "Zorro's Fighting Legion"	h. Reed Hadley
12. "King of the Rocket Men"	m. Tristram Coffin
13. "The Purple Monster Strikes"	c. Roy Barcroft
14. "Burn 'Em Up Barnes"	g. Jack Mulhall
15. "Zorro Rides Again"	i. John Carroll

37. MORE "NAME THE STAR"—BUFFS ONLY

1. TURHAN BEY	"Bowery to Broadway"	"Ali Baba and the Forty Thieves"
2. CAROLE LOMBARD	"True Confession"	"My Man Godfrey"

[1] Yes—this is the same Ken Curtis from the television series "Gunsmoke."
[2] Judd Holden *did* play Commando Cody in this serial, though the part of Commando Cody also appeared in the serial "Radar Men from the Moon," and was played by George Wallace. (No, not *that* George Wallace!)
[3] Yes—this is the Sammy Baugh also known as "Slingin'" Sammy Baugh of gridiron fame.

3. ADOLPHE		
MENJOU	"Little Miss Marker"	"State of the Union"
4. YUL BRYNNER	"Cast a Giant Shadow"	"The Buccaneer"
5. JEAN PIERRE		
AUMONT	"The Enemy General"	"Hilda Crane"
6. LOUISE		
ALLBRITTON	"The Egg and I"	"Sitting Pretty"
7. HENRY		
TRAVERS	"The Moon Is Down"	"The Bells of St. Mary's"
8. BURGESS		
MEREDITH	"There Was a Crooked Man"	"Hurry Sundown"
9. BORIS KARLOFF	"The Black Cat"	"The House of Rothschild"
10. GENE KELLY	"Inherit the Wind"	"It's a Big Country"

37. MORE "NAME THE STAR"—DUFFERS' TEE

1. TURHAN BEY	"Dragon Seed"	"A Night in Paradise"
2. CAROLE		
LOMBARD	"To Be or Not to Be"	"Nothing Sacred"
3. ADOLPHE		
MENJOU	"Gold Diggers of 1935"	"Paths of Glory"
4. YUL BRYNNER	"The Ten Commandments"	"Taras Bulba"
5. JEAN PIERRE		
AUMONT	"John Paul Jones"	"Assignment in Brittany"
6. LOUISE		
ALLBRITTON	"Pittsburgh"	"The Doolins of Oklahoma"
7. HENRY		
TRAVERS	"It's a Wonderful Life"	"Madame Curie"
8. BURGESS		
MEREDITH	"Advise and Consent"	"The Cardinal"

9. BORIS KARLOFF   "Unconquered"   "Isle of the Dead"
10. GENE KELLY   "For Me and My
                       Gal"   "Singin' in the Rain"

38. WHAT SEEMS TO BE THE PROBLEM?
—BUFFS AND DUFFERS

1. Charles Laughton f. Marty Feldman   Hunchback
   "The Hunchback of   "Young
   Notre Dame"   Frankenstein"

2. Peter Ustinov   h. John Wayne
   "The Egyptian"   "True Grit"[1]   One-eyed

            or   k. Richard Widmark
                         "Alvarez Kelly"   One-eyed

3. Edward Arnold   e. James Cagney
   "The Night Has a   "City for Conquest"   Blind
   Thousand Eyes"

            or   l. Gene Hackman
                         "Young
                         Frankenstein"   Blind

4. Lionel Atwill   i. Wallace Beery
   "Son of   "O'Shaughnessy's
   Frankenstein"   Boy"   One-armed

5. Wallace Beery   a. Sam Jaffe
   "Treasure Island"   "Lost Horizon"   One-legged

6. Gregory Peck   b. Ronald Colman
   "Mirage"   "Random Harvest"   Amnesiac

7. Joan Leslie   d. Boris Karloff
   "High Sierra"   "Tower of London"   Clubfooted[2]

8. Audrey Hepburn   l. Gene Hackman
   "Wait Until Dark"   "Young
                         Frankenstein"   Blind

            or   e. James Cagney
                         "City for Conquest" Blind

9. Marlon Brando   c. Gene Kelly
   "One-Eyed Jacks"   "For Me and My
                         Gal"   Crushed hand

10. Karl Malden   k. Richard Widmark
   "Operation Secret"   "Alvarez Kelly"

            or   h. John Wayne

[1] "Rooster Cogburn" would also be acceptable for the Buffs.
[2] There will be those Buffs who'll insist that James Cagney was clubfooted in "Love Me or Leave Me." This answer is incorrect. In that film, Cagney portrayed Moe Snyder, who was merely crippled, not clubfooted.

	"True Grit"[1]	One-eyed
11. Ray Milland	g. Tyrone Power	
"The Lost Weekend"	"Nightmare Alley"	Alcoholism
12. Dorothy McGuire	j. Jane Wyman	
"The Spiral Staircase"	"Johnny Belinda"	Mute

39. THE BIG BULB PART III—BUFFS AND DUFFERS

1. Fred MacMurray
2. Charlie Ruggles
3. Eddie Albert
4. Brandon de Wilde
5. Marshall Thompson
6. William Demarest
7. Jackie Cooper
8. Pat O'Brien
9. Robert Young
10. William Bendix
11. William Lundigan
12. Richard Greene
13. Robert Stack
14. Edmund Lowe
15. Barry Sullivan
16. Richard Basehart

g. "My Three Sons"
i. "The World of Mr. Sweeney"
k. "Green Acres"
n. "Jamie"
m. "Angel"
a. "Love and Marriage"
b. "The People's Choice"
l. "Harrigan and Son"
o. "Father Knows Best"
p. "The Life of Riley"
d. "Men into Space"
c. "Robin Hood"
j. "The Untouchables"
f. "Front Page Detective"
h. "The Man Called 'X' "
e. "Voyage to the Bottom of the Sea"

40. WILD CARD—BUFFS AND DUFFERS

1. "Hotel Paradiso"
2. "13 Rue Madeleine"
3. "The Night of January 16th"
4. "Dear Ruth"
5. "So This Is Paris"
6. "Having Wonderful Time"
7. "Room at the Top"
8. "Small Hotel"
9. "Room 43"
10. "The Window"
11. "Cafe Metropole"
12. "City Across the River"
13. "The Four Poster"
14. "The Twelve Chairs"
15. "Room for One More"
16. "The Thirteen Chair"
17. "David and Lisa"
18. "Royal Wedding"
19. "The Bride Wore Red"
20. "The Blue Veil"

41. THE MEN FROM THE BOYS—BUFFS AND DUFFERS

1. "Young Man with a Horn"	Orley Lindgren	Rick	d. Kirk Douglas
2. "Blood and Sand"	Rex Downing	Juan	g. or m. Tyrone Power
3. "Lloyds of London"	Freddie Bartholomew	Jonathan	m. or g. Tyrone Power
4. "The Egyptian"	Peter Reynolds	Sinuhe	h. Edmund Purdom
5. "Manhattan Melodrama"	Mickey Rooney	Blackie	k. Clark Gable
6. "The Adventures of Mark Twain"	Jackie Brown	Sam	n. Fredric March
7. "The Light That Failed"	Ronald Sinclair	Dick	l. Ronald Colman

8. "Heaven Can Wait"	Scotty Beckett	Henry	j. Don Ameche
9. "The Great Caruso"	Peter Price	Enrico	e. Mario Lanza
10. "Follow the Sun"	Harold Blade	Ben	a. Glenn Ford
11. "There's No Business Like Show Business"	Billy Chapin	Steve	b. Johnnie Ray
12. "Angels with Dirty Faces"	William Tracy	Jerry	o. Pat O'Brien
13. "Public Enemy"	Frankie Darro	Matt	i. Edward Woods
14. "Beau Geste"	Billy Cook	John	c. Ray Milland
15. "Beau Geste"	Martin Spellman	Dibgy	f. Robert Preston

42. HOW MANY CAN YOU GET?—BUFFS AND DUFFERS

1. "It Happened One Night"
   w. Clark Gable
   k. Claudette Colbert

2. "Mr. Blandings Builds His Dream House"
   z. Cary Grant
   p. Myrna Loy
   t. Melvyn Douglas

3. "Singin' in the Rain"
   j. Gene Kelly
   gg. Debbie Reynolds
   w. Donald O'Connor
   d. Jean Hagen

4. "Beau Geste"
   o. Gary Cooper
   r. Ray Milland
   z. Robert Preston
   s. Brian Donlevy
   g. Susan Hayward

5. "The Last Angry Man"
   t. Paul Muni
   uu. David Wayne
   y. Betsy Palmer
   a. Luther Adler
   q. Claudia McNeil
   d. Joby Baker

6. "Edge of Darkness"
    v. Errol Flynn
   mm. Ann Sheridan
    I. Walter Huston
    l. Nancy Coleman
    r. Helmut Dantine
    b. Judith Anderson
    y. Ruth Gordon

7. "Anatomy of a Murder"
   pp. James Stewart
   ff. Lee Remick
    x. Ben Gazzara
    v. Arthur O'Connell
    c. Eve Arden
    A. Kathryn Grant
    ii. George C. Scott
    E. Murray Hamilton

8. "Lawrence of Arabia"
    x. Peter O'Toole
    c. Alec Guinness
   cc. Anthony Quinn
    F. Jack Hawkins
   kk. Omar Sharif
    u. Jose Ferrer
   dd. Claude Rains
   bb. Anthony Quayle
    K. Arthur Kennedy

9. "From Here to Eternity"
    N. Burt Lancaster
    j. Montgomery Clift
    L. Deborah Kerr
   nn. Frank Sinatra
   ee. Donna Reed
    U. Philip Ober
    ll. Mickey Shaughnessy
    e. Harry Bellaver
    i. Ernest Borgnine
   ss. Jack Warden

10. "Citizen Kane"
  ww. Orson Welles
    p. Joseph Cotten
   tt. Ruth Warrick
    n. Dorothy Comingore
   oo. Everett Sloane
    m. Ray Collins
    q. George Coulouris
    s. Agnes Moorehead
   qq. Paul Stewart
   jj. Harry Shannon
    h. Fortunio Bonanova

11. "Casablanca"

g. Humphrey Bogart
f. Ingrid Bergman
H. Paul Henreid
dd. Claude Rains[1]
rr. Conrad Veidt
B. Sydney Greenstreet
o. Peter Lorre
hh. S. Z. Sakall
vv. Dooley Wilson
aa. John Qualen
M. Leonid Kinskey
r. Helmut Dantine[1]

43. THE MAN—BUFFS AND DUFFERS

1. "The Man in the Net"
2. "The Man on the Eiffel Tower"
3. "The Man Who Came to Dinner"
4. "The Man Who Could Work
    Miracles"
5. "Little Big Man"
6. "The Man in the Gray Flannel
    Suit"
7. "Man in the Attic"
8. "Man of Conquest"
9. "The Man Who Never Was"
10. "The Sheepman"
11. "The Man from Down Under"
12. "The Third Man"
13. "The Best Man"
14. "The Man in the Iron Mask"
15. "The Man in Half Moon Street"
16. "The Illustrated Man"
17. "The Wrong Man"
18. "The Man Who Knew Too Much"
19. "The Man from the Diners' Club"
20. "The Quiet Man"

r. Alan Ladd
i. Franchot Tone[2]
j. Monty Woolley

h. Roland Young
n. Dustin Hoffman

p. Gregory Peck
b. Jack Palance
o. Richard Dix
a. Clifton Webb
c. Glenn Ford
s. Charles Laughton
q. Orson Welles
t. Cliff Robertson
f. Louis Hayward
e. Nils Asther
m. Rod Steiger
d. Henry Fonda
k. James Stewart
l. Danny Kaye
g. John Wayne

[1] We told you two names were used *twice*.
[2] Yes—we're aware of Charles Laughton's appearance in this film—but what will you use as an answer for Question 11?

44. ANYTHING YOU CAN DO, I CAN DO BETTER
PART II—BUFFS ONLY

1. Charles Laughton   Nero   "Sign of the Cross"
   G. Peter Ustinov[1]   "Quo Vadis"
2. Sidney Blackmer   Theodore Roosevelt   "My Girl Tisa"
   H. Brian Keith   "The Wind and the Lion"
3. Thomas Mitchell   Ned Buntline   "Buffalo Bill"
   F. Burt Lancaster   "Buffalo Bill and the Indians, or Sitting Bull's History Lesson"
4. Louis Calhern   Buffalo Bill   "Annie Get Your Gun"
   E. James Ellison   "The Plainsman"
5. Bobby Watson   Adolf Hitler   "The Hitler Gang"
   I. Richard Basehart   "Hitler"
6. Francis McDonald   John Wilkes Booth   "The Prisoner of Shark Island"
   B. John Derek   "Prince of Players"
7. Vincent Price   Sir Walter Raleigh   "The Private Lives of Elizabeth and Essex"
   C. Richard Todd   "The Virgin Queen"
8. Henry Wilcoxon   Marc Antony   "Cleopatra"
   J. Marlon Brando   "Julius Caesar"
9. Ronald Reagan   Gen. George A. Custer   "Santa Fe Trail"
   A. Robert Shaw   "Custer of the West"
10. Dudley Field Malone   Winston Churchill   "Mission to Moscow"
    D. Simon Ward   "Young Winston"

44. ANYTHING YOU CAN DO, I CAN DO BETTER
PART II—DUFFERS' TEE

1. Charles Laughton; Nero in   G. Peter Ustinov   i. "Quo Vadis"
   "Sign of the Cross"

---

[1] We *know* we'll get letters pointing out that matching Charles Laughton's and Robert Shaw's portrayals of Henry VIII would be a possible answer. But since we used that in Part I of ANYTHING YOU CAN DO, I CAN DO BETTER, we didn't think you'd appreciate it another time. Right?

2. Sidney Blackmer; Theodore Roosevelt in "My Girl Tisa"   H. Brian Keith   c. "The Wind and the Lion"

3. Thomas Mitchell; Ned Buntline in "Buffalo Bill"   F. Burt Lancaster   j. "Buffalo Bill and the Indians, or Sitting Bull's History Lesson"

4. Louis Calhern; Buffalo Bill in "Annie Get Your Gun"   E. James Ellison   g. "The Plainsman"

5. Bobby Watson; Adolf Hitler in "The Hitler Gang"   I. Richard Basehart   f. "Hitler"

6. Francis McDonald; John Wilkes Booth in "The Prisoner of Shark Island"   B. John Derek   d. "Prince of Players"

7. Vincent Price; Sir Walter Raleigh in "The Private Lives of Elizabeth and Essex"   C. Richard Todd   h. "The Virgin Queen"

8. Henry Wilcoxon; Marc Antony in "Cleopatra"   J. Marlon Brando   b. "Julius Caesar"

9. Ronald Reagan; Gen. George A. Custer in "Santa Fe Trail"   A. Robert Shaw   e. "Custer of the West"

10. Dudley Field Malone; Winston Churchill in "Mission to Moscow"   D. Simon Ward   a. "Young Winston"

45. BUCKLE MY SWASH!—BUFFS AND DUFFERS

1. Richard Beymer   n. "Adventures of a Young Man"
2. Joan Collins   h. "The Adventures of Sadie"
3. Gary Cooper   l. "The Adventures of Marco Polo"
4. Arturo de Cordova   i. "The Adventures of Casanova"
5. John Derek   g. "The Adventures of Hajji Baba"
6. Robert Donat   a. "The Adventures of Tartu"
7. Errol Flynn   j. "The Adventures of Robin Hood"
8. Errol Flynn   k. "The Adventures of Don Juan"
9. Errol Flynn   c. "The Adventures of Capt. Fabian"

10. Eddie Hodges	d. "The Adventures of Huckleberry Finn"
11. Tommy Kelly	f. "The Adventures of Tom Sawyer"
12. Fredric March	b. "The Adventures of Mark Twain"
13. Kim Novak	o. "The Amorous Adventures of Moll Flanders"
14. Jean Parker	m. "The Adventures of Kitty O'Day"
15. Basil Rathbone	e. "The Adventures of Sherlock Holmes"

46. WHAT'S THE TITLE?—BUFFS AND DUFFERS

1. "Treasure Island"
2. "It All Came True"
3. "Arsenic and Old Lace"
4. "Guys and Dolls"
5. "The Barefoot Contessa"
6. "Fourteen Hours"
7. "Only Angels Have Wings"
8. "Witness for the Prosecution"
9. "Ball of Fire"
10. "Titanic"

47. MIX-UP IN THE TITLING DEPARTMENT—BUFFS AND DUFFERS

1. Produced by . . .	d. Howard Christie
2. Directed by . . .	f. H. Bruce Humberstone
3. Written by . . .	j. Robert Riskin
4. Cinematographer	a. Lee Garmes
5. Score Composed by . . .	l. Bernard Herrmann
6. Art Director	m. Hans Dreier
7. Edited by . . .	c. Anne Bauchens
8. Special Effects by . . .	b. Farciot Edouart
9. Costumes by . . .	k. Edith Head
10. Stuntwork Supervised by . . .	h. Yakima Canutt
11. Montages by . . .	i. Slavko Vorkapich
12. Dance Director	g. Seymour Felix
13. Second Unit Director	n. Andrew Marton
14. Title Design by . . .	e. Saul Bass

48. THE WOMAN—BUFFS AND DUFFERS

1. "The Other Woman"	i.	Cleo Moore
2. "Woman Chases Man"	k.	Miriam Hopkins
3. "The Woman on Pier 13"	f.	Laraine Day
4. "Wicked Woman"	p.	Beverly Michaels
5. "I Take This Woman"	v.	Hedy Lamarr
6. "Woman of the Town"	y.	Claire Trevor
7. "The Tiger Woman"	x.	Adele Mara
8. "This Woman Is Mine"	u.	Carol Bruce
9. "Woman Doctor"	h.	Frieda Inescort
10. "A Woman Alone"	r.	Anna Sten
11. "That Certain Woman"	s.	Bette Davis
12. "This Woman Is Dangerous"	q.	Joan Crawford
13. "That Forsyte Woman"	b.	Greer Garson
14. "The Woman Accused"	e.	Nancy Carroll
15. "That Kind of Woman"	o.	Sophia Loren
16. "Woman in the Window"	d.	Joan Bennett
17. "Woman of the Year"	w.	Katharine Hepburn
18. "A Woman of Affairs"	a.	Greta Garbo
19. "Woman in Hiding"	t.	Ida Lupino
20. "The Woman and the Hunter"	j.	Ann Sheridan
21. "That Hamilton Woman"	m.	Vivien Leigh
22. "Woman Obsessed"	l.	Susan Hayward
23. "A Woman of Straw"	c.	Gina Lollobrigida
24. "Woman Wanted"	n.	Maureen O'Sullivan
25. "Woman Times Seven"	g.	Shirley MacLaine

49. FIND THE TITLE—BUFFS AND DUFFERS

Vertical: (From the left)
Row ⋕1: "Sylvia" [43]; "Aida" [2]; "Angel" [4].
⋕2: "Adventure" [1].
⋕3: "Jaws" [26]; "Chuka" [17]; "Zarak" [50].
⋕4: "Breakout" [13]; "Trial" [45].
⋕5: "Joe" [27].
⋕6: "Attack" [9]; "Konga" [30].
⋕7: "Waco" [48].
⋕8: "WUSA" [49].
⋕9: "She" [39]; "Greed" [24].
⋕10: "Apache" [7].
⋕11: "Niagara" [33]; "Anna" [5].

⚹12: "Breakthrough" [14].
⚹13: "Shakedown" [37]; "Emma" [22].
⚹14: "Copacabana" [19]; "Atlas" [8].
⚹15: "Conquest" [18]; "Sunrise" [42].
⚹16: "America" [3]; "Crashout" [20].

Horizontal: (From the top)
Row ⚹1: "Crisis" [21]; "Fury" [23]; "Jubal" [28].
　　⚹2: "Ben" [11]; "Rebecca" [35].
　　⚹3: "Spartacus" [40]; "Star!" [41]; "Boom!" [12].
　　⚹4: "Shane" [38].
　　⚹5: "Lisa" [32].
　　⚹6: "Vicki" [47].
　　⚹8: "Trog" [46].
　　⚹11: "Anzio" [6].
　　⚹13: "Lenny" [31].
　　⚹14: "Ivy" [25].
　　⚹15: "Kangaroo" [29].
　　⚹16: "Ransom [34]; "Barricade" [10].

Diagonal
　From the "T" of "Spartacus" running downward and to the right:
　　"Texas" [44].
　From the "G" of "Greed" running upward and to the left:
　　"Chang" [16].
　From the "S" of "Sylvia" running downward and to the right:
　　"Saskatchewan" [36].
　From the "C" of "Attack" running downward and to the right:
　　"Candy" [15].
　And the hidden bonus title we were seeking is:

　　"A　　Streetcar　　Named　　Desire"

50. Y'ALL REMEMBER WORLD WAR II?
—BUFFS AND DUFFERS

　　1. "A Wing and a Prayer"
　　2. "Sahara"
　　3. "Objective Burma"
　　4. "Twelve O'Clock High"
　　5. "Air Force"
　　6. "So Proudly We Hail"
　　7. "Command Decision"
　　8. "An American Guerilla in the Philippines"
　　9. "The Story of Dr. Wassell"
　10. "The Moon Is Down"

51. THE BIG BULB: LADIES—BUFFS AND DUFFERS

1. Barbara Hale	k. "Perry Mason"
2. Minerva Urecal	e. "Tugboat Annie"
3. Joan Caulfield	f. or l. "My Favorite Husband" or "Sally"
4. Ann Sothern	h. "Private Secretary"
5. Lucille Ball	d. "I Love Lucy"
6. Joanne Dru	c. "Guestward Ho!"
7. Spring Byington	a. "December Bride"
8. Eve Arden	j. "Our Miss Brooks"
9. Joan Caulfield	l. or f. "Sally" or "My Favorite Husband"
10. Joan Davis	i. "I Married Joan"
11. June Lockhart	g. "Lost in Space"
12. Ellen Corby	b. "The Waltons"

52. HERE'S LOOKIN' AT YOU, BOGIE!—BUFFS ONLY

1. Nick "Bugs" Fenner	"Ballots or Bullets"
2. Frank Taylor	"Black Legion"
3. "Hap" Stuart	"China Clipper"
4. Richard Mason	"Conflict"
5. Joe Barrett	"Tokyo Joe"
6. Maj. Jed Webbe	"Battle Circus"
7. Nick Coster	"The Wagons Roll at Night"
8. Ed Hutchinson	"Deadline, U.S.A."
9. Harry Smith	"Sirocco"
10. Geoffrey Carroll	"The Two Mrs. Carrolls"
11. Frank Wilson	"You Can't Get Away with Murder"
12. Jack Buck	"Brother Orchid"
13. Marshall Quesne	"The Return of Dr. X"
14. Duke Berne	"The Big Shot"

52. HERE'S LOOKIN' AT YOU, BOGIE!—DUFFERS' TEE

1. Roy "Mad Dog" Earle	"High Sierra"
2. Charlie Allnut	"The African Queen"
3. Capt. Philip Francis Queeg	"The Caine Mutiny"

240

4.	Fred C. Dobbs	"The Treasure of the Sierra Madre"
5.	Sam Spade	"The Maltese Falcon"
6.	Philip Marlowe	"The Big Sleep"
7.	Harry Dawes	"The Barefoot Contessa"
8.	Paul Fabrini	"They Drive by Night"
9.	Michael O'Leary	"Dark Victory"
10.	"Turkey" Morgan	"Kid Galahad"
11.	Matrac	"Passage to Marseilles"
12.	Joe Rossi	"Action in the North Atlantic"
13.	Harry Morgan	"To Have and Have Not"
14.	"Rip" Murdock	"Chain Lightning"

53. THAT OL' GANG OF MINE—BUFFS AND DUFFERS

1. __ f. "Camille"
2. __ i. "The Bridges at Toko-Ri"
3. __ k. "Breakfast at Tiffany's"
4. __ h. "Born Yesterday"
5. __ l. "The Big House"
6. __ r. "A Bill of Divorcement"
7. __ q. "Bell, Book, and Candle"
8. __ p. "The Barefoot Contessa"
9. __ y. "The Bad and the Beautiful"
10. __ s. "Bad Day at Black Rock"
11. __ x. "The Best Years of Our Lives"
12. __ o. "Double Indemnity"
13. __ w. "A Face in the Crowd"
14. __ a. "The Fighting 69th"
15. __ n. "Grand Hotel"
16. __ v. "Green Dolphin Street"
17. __ b. "The Great Race"
18. __ u. "The Hucksters"
19. __ t. "Judgment at Nuremberg"
20. __ c. "The Last Hurrah"
21. __ j. "The Mark of Zorro"
22. __ m. "A Night at the Opera"
23. __ d. "On the Waterfront"
24. __ g. "Reap the Wild Wind"
25. __ e. "The Sandpiper"

54. THAT OL' GANG OF MINE: FOLLOW-UP!
—BUFFS AND DUFFERS

1. Margaret Gautier	("Camille")	Greta Garbo
2. Lieut. Harry Brubaker (USNR)	("The Bridges at Toko-Ri")	William Holden
3. Holly Golightly	("Breakfast at Tiffany's")	Audrey Hepburn
4. Billie Dawn	("Born Yesterday")	Judy Holliday
5. John Morgan	("The Big House")	Chester Morris
6. Hillary Fairfield	("A Bill of Divorcement")	John Barrymore[1]
7. Shepherd Henderson	("Bell, Book, and Candle")	James Stewart
8. Harry Dawes	("The Barefoot Contessa")	Humphrey Bogart
9. Georgia Lorrison	("The Bad and the Beautiful")	Lana Turner
10. John J. MacReedy	("Bad Day at Black Rock")	Spencer Tracy
11. Milly Stephenson	("The Best Years of Our Lives")	Myrna Loy
12. Walter Neff	("Double Indemnity")	Fred MacMurray
13. Lonesome Rhodes	("A Face in the Crowd")	Andy Griffith
14. Jerry Plunkett	("The Fighting 69th")	James Cagney
15. Grusinskaya	("Grand Hotel")	Greta Garbo
16. Marianne Patourel	("Green Dolphin Street")	Lana Turner
17. Leslie Gallant III	("The Great Race")	Tony Curtis
18. Victor Albee Norman	("The Hucksters")	Clark Gable
19. Judge Dan Haywood	("Judgment at Nuremberg")	Spencer Tracy
20. Frank Skeffington	("The Last Hurrah")	Spencer Tracy
21. Diego Vega	("The Mark of Zorro")	Tyrone Power
22. Otis B. Driftwood	("A Night at the Opera")	Groucho Marx
23. Terry Malloy	("On the Waterfront")	Marlon Brando
24. Stephen Tolliver	("Reap the Wild Wind")	Ray Milland
25. Laura Reynolds	("The Sandpiper")	Elizabeth Taylor

[1] For the Buffs' version, Adolphe Menjou would also be acceptable.

55. ELEMENTARY, MY DEAR WATSON
—BUFFS AND DUFFERS

1. "Sherlock Holmes" (1922)	D. John Barrymore	c. Roland Young
2. "The Sign of the Four" (1923)	L. Eille Norwood	l. Hubert Willis
3. "The Return of Sherlock Holmes" (1929)	B. or E. Clive Brook	h. H. Reeves-Smith
4. "Sherlock Holmes' Fatal Hour" (1930)	H. or J. Arthur Wontner	g. Ian Fleming
5. "The Speckled Band" (1931)	A. Raymond Massey	k. Athole Stewart
6. "The Sign of the Four" (1932)	J. or H. Arthur Wontner	b. Ian Hunter
7. "The Hound of the Baskervilles" (1932)	C. Robert Rendel	a. Fred Lloyd
8. "Sherlock Holmes" (1932)	E. or B. Clive Brook	i. Reginald Owen
9. "A Study in Scarlet" (1933)	I. Reginald Owen	j. Warburton Gamble
10. "The Adventures of Sherlock Holmes" (1939)	G. Basil Rathbone	f. Nigel Bruce
11. "The Hound of the Baskervilles" (1959)	F. Peter Cushing	e. Andre Morell
12. "The Private Life of Sherlock Holmes" (1969)	K. Robert Stephens	d. Colin Blakely

56. FROM "A" TO "Z"—BUFFS AND DUFFERS

1. "Ada"	c. Susan Hayward
2. "Billy Budd"	q. Terence Stamp
3. "Claudia"	v. Dorothy McGuire
4. "David and Bathsheba"	p. Gregory Peck
5. "Elmer Gantry"	o. Burt Lancaster
6. "Fanny"	u. Leslie Caron
7. "Georgy Girl"	t. Lynn Redgrave
8. "Hannah Lee"	m. Joanne Dru
9. "Irene"	l. Anna Neagle
10. "A Date with Judy"	a. Jane Powell

11. "Kiss Me, Kate"	w. Kathryn Grayson
12. "Lolita"	j. Sue Lyon
13. "Mildred Pierce"	y. Joan Crawford
14. "Nick Carter, Master Detective"	e. Walter Pidgeon
15. "Oliver Twist"	s. John Howard Davies
16. "A Man Called Peter"	n. Richard Todd
17. "Quentin Durward"	z. Robert Taylor
18. "The Daughter of Rosie O'Grady"	f. June Haver
19. "Salome"	i. Rita Hayworth
20. "My Girl Tisa"	g. Lilli Palmer
21. "Ulysses"	b. Kirk Douglas
22. "Valerie"	h. Anita Ekberg
23. "Wee Willie Winkie"	r. Shirley Temple
24. "Yolanda and the Thief"	k. Lucille Bremer
25. "Zorba the Greek"	d. Anthony Quinn

57. MORE QUOTABLES—BUFFS AND DUFFERS

1. "Speak! You have a civil tongue in your head! . . ."

   i. "I Was a Teenage Frankenstein"

2. "You handle a sword like a devil from hell!"

   j. "The Mark of Zorro"

3. "Remember what Johnny Dillinger said about guys like you and him . . ."

   a. "High Sierra"

4. "Discontinue that so-called Polonaise jumble you've been playing for days!"

   f. "A Song to Remember"

5. "Crap-shoot is a matter of individual enterprise . . ."

   d. "The Candidate"

6. "And that's the kind of hairpin I am!"

   c. "The Strawberry Blonde"

7. "I never dreamed such a mere physical experience could be so exciting."

   h. "The African Queen"

8. "No, sir! And we might as well get together on this 'yielding' business right off the bat . . ."

   e. "Mr. Smith Goes to Washington"

9. "I hunt griz."

   b. "Jeremiah Johnson"

10. "Job says a woman is beautiful only when she is loved."

   g. "Mr. Skeffington"

58. MORE QUOTABLES: BONUS!—BUFFS AND DUFFERS

1. "Speak! You have a civil tongue in your head! . . ."
2. "You handle a sword like a devil from hell!"
3. "Remember what Johnny Dillinger said about guys like you and him . . ."
4. "Discontinue that so-called Polonaise jumble you've been playing for days!"
5. "Crap-shoot is a matter of individual enterprise . . ."
6. "And that's the kind of hairpin I am!"
7. "I never dreamed such a mere physical experience could be so exciting."
8. "No, sir! And we might as well get together on this 'yielding' business right off the bat . . ."
9. "I hunt griz."
10. "Job says a woman is beautiful only when she is loved."

g. Whit Bissell

c. J. Edward Bromberg

d. Henry Hull

h. Merle Oberon

b. Robert Redford
j. James Cagney

a. Katharine Hepburn

e. James Stewart
f. Will Geer

i. Bette Davis

59. YOU CAN'T HARDLY GET THERE FROM HERE— BUFFS AND DUFFERS

1. New York to Lake Tanganyika, Africa
2. The Reform Club, London, to the Reform Club, London
3. New York to Paris
4. Roosevelt Field, New York, to Le Bourget Field, Paris
5. Southampton, England, to New York
6. Vera Cruz, Mexico, to Bremerhaven, Germany
7. Nauvoo, Illinois, to the Great Salt Lake

d. "Stanley and Livingstone"

h. "Around the World in Eighty Days"

j. "The Great Race"

i. "The Spirit of St. Louis"

c. "Titanic"

k. "Ship of Fools"

a. "Brigham Young— Frontiersman"

8. The U.N., New York, to Mount
   Rushmore
9. Plymouth, England to Cape Cod
   Bay
10. Spithead, England, to Otaheite
    (Tahiti)
11. Istanbul to Calais

12. Frankfurt, Germany, to Lakehurst,
    New Jersey, U.S.A.

l. "North by Northwest"

e. "Plymouth Adventure"

g. "Mutiny on the Bounty"
b. "Murder on the Orient
   Express"

f. "The Hindenburg"

60. PENCILED IN: FEMALES—BUFFS ONLY

1. Shirley Deane	"Blondie"	Penny Singleton
2. Margaret Marquis	"Love Finds Andy Hardy"	Ann Rutherford
3. Gloria DeHaven	"Good News"	Patricia Marshall
4. Susan Peters	"Gentle Annie"	Donna Reed
5. Edna May Oliver	"The Wizard of Oz"	Margaret Hamilton
6. Dinah Shore	"Show Boat"	Ava Gardner
7. Patricia Morison	"The Glass Key"	Veronica Lake
8. Judy Garland	"The Barkleys of Broadway"	Ginger Rogers
9. Miriam Hopkins	"Devotion"	Olivia de Havilland
10. Geraldine Fitzgerald	"Captain Horatio Hornblower"	Virginia Mayo

60. PENCILED IN: FEMALES—DUFFERS' TEE

1. "Blondie"	Shirley Deane	g. Penny Singleton
2. "Love Finds Andy Hardy"	Margaret Marquis	i. Ann Rutherford
3. "Good News"	Gloria DeHaven	j. Patricia Marshall
4. "Gentle Annie"	Susan Peters	h. Donna Reed
5. "The Wizard of Oz"	Edna May Oliver	a. Margaret Hamilton
6. "Show Boat"	Dinah Shore	c. Ava Gardner
7. "The Glass Key"	Patricia Morison	f. Veronica Lake

8. "The Barkleys of Broadway"	Judy Garland	b. Ginger Rogers
9. "Devotion"	Miriam Hopkins	d. Olivia de Havilland
10. "Captain Horatio Hornblower"	Geraldine Fitzgerald	e. Virginia Mayo

61. NAMES IN COMMON—BUFFS AND DUFFERS

	RELATED	UNRELATED
1. Chester and Adrian Morris	Brothers	
2. Teresa and Will Wright		X
3. Evelyn and George Brent		X
4. Gene and Joyce Reynolds		X
5. Winifred and Artie Shaw		X
6. Louise and Mel Brooks		X
7. Antonio and Rita Moreno		X
8. Frank and Matt McHugh	Brothers	
9. Steve and Sally Forrest		X
10. Olive and Harry Carey	Wife and Husband	
11. John and David Carradine	Father and Son	
12. Nancy and Jack Kelly	Sister and brother	
13. Marjorie and Fritz Weaver		X
14. Joan and Gloria Blondell	Sisters	
15. Robert and R. G. Armstrong		X
16. John and Deborah Kerr		X
17. Jennifer and L. Q. Jones		X
18. James and Russell Gleason		X
19. Sidney and Dennis James[1]		X
20. Danny and Frankie Thomas		X

62. FIRST, THE WORD—BUFFS ONLY

1. James Hilton	b. "Lost Horizon"
2. Dashiell Hammett	c. "The Maltese Falcon"
3. Raymond Chandler	a. "The Big Sleep"
4. W. R. Burnett	c. "High Sierra"
5. Eric Ambler	c. "The Mask of Dimitrios"

[1] And to head off letters telling us that Dennis James is a *television* personality, we agree. He is also a dear friend of ours—but he did appear in at least one film—"Mr. Universe."

247

6. Vera Caspary	b. "Laura"
7. Ben Hecht	c. "Spellbound"
8. MacKinlay Kantor	b. "The Best Years of Our Lives"
9. Len Deighton	b. "Funeral in Berlin"
10. J. B. Priestley	c. "An Inspector Calls"
11. Edgar Allan Poe	c. "The Pit and the Pendulum"
12. James M. Cain	c. "Mildred Pierce"

62. FIRST, THE WORD—DUFFERS' TEE

1. "Goodbye, Mr. Chips" "Random Harvest"	D. James Hilton	f. "Lost Horizon"
2. "The Thin Man" "The Glass Key"	H. Dashiell Hammett	g. "The Maltese Falcon"
3. "The Blue Dahlia" "Lady in the Lake"	E. Raymond Chandler	i. "The Big Sleep"
4. "Little Caesar" "Scarface"	A. W. R. Burnett	l. "High Sierra"
5. "Journey into Fear" "Topkapi"	I. Eric Ambler	j. "The Mask of Dimitrios"
6. "The Night of June 13th" "Private Scandal"	J. Vera Caspary	a. "Laura"
7. "The Specter of the Rose" "Notorious"	B. Ben Hecht	e. "Spellbound"
8. "Midnight Lace" "The Voice of Bugle Ann"	L. MacKinlay Kantor	d. "The Best Years of Our Lives"
9. "The Ipcress File" "Billion Dollar Brain"	F. Len Deighton	b. "Funeral in Berlin"
10. "The Old Dark House" "Laburnum Grove"	C. J. B. Priestley	k. "An Inspector Calls"
11. "The Fall of the House of Usher" "The Raven"	G. Edgar Allan Poe	h. "The Pit and the Pendulum"
12. "Double Indemnity" "The Postman Always Rings Twice"	K. James M. Cain	c. "Mildred Pierce"

248

63. MORE THAN A BIT!—BUFFS AND DUFFERS

1. _ k.   J. Pat O' M alley
2. _ j.   Thurston H A ll
3. _ l.   Emory Pa R nell
4. _ a.   Iris Adr I an
5. _ n.   John Qu A len

6. _ d.   Wade B O teler
7. _ h.   Byron Fo U lger
8. _ o.   Elmira Se S sions
9. _ c.   Murray Al P er
10. _ g.   Bess Flow E rs
11. _ b.   Luis Alber N i
12. _ f.   Hal K. Daw S on
13. _ e.   Cliff Clar K
14. _ p.   John Wengr A f
15. _ i.   Steven Gera Y
16. _ m.   Milton P A rsons

64. THE OTHER WOMAN—BUFFS AND DUFFERS

1. "An American in Paris"
   Gene Kelly and Leslie Caron   g. Nina Foch
2. "Only Angels Have Wings"
   Cary Grant and Jean Arthur   e. Rita Hayworth
3. "The Carpetbaggers"
   George Peppard and Carroll Baker   i. Martha Hyer
4. "The Strange Love of Martha Ivers"
   Barbara Stanwyck and Kirk Douglas   a. Lizabeth Scott
5. "Teacher's Pet"
   Clark Gable and Doris Day   j. Mamie Van Doren
6. "Cass Timberlane"
   Spencer Tracy and Lana Turner   h. Mary Astor
7. "The Spoilers"
   John Wayne and Marlene Dietrich   c. Margaret
                                                     Lindsay
8. "Homecoming"
   Clark Gable and Lana Turner   d. Anne Baxter
9. "Daddy Long Legs"
   Fred Astaire and Leslie Caron   b. Terry Moore
10. "Red River"
    John Wayne and Joanne Dru   f. Colleen Gray

11. "Dr. Jekyll and Mr. Hyde"
    Spencer Tracy and Ingrid Bergman   l. Lana Turner
12. "The Seven Year Itch"
    Marilyn Monroe and Tom Ewell   k. Evelyn Keyes

65. ODD MAN OUT—BUFFS AND DUFFERS

1. BATMAN: John Ridgeley is the ringer here. Honest and upright though he was, Ridgeley never played the masked vigilante. Lewis Wilson played Batman in a Columbia serial, 1943, while Robert Lowery played the role in another Columbia serial six years later. Besides playing the role on television, Adam West appeared in the title role of Twentieth Century-Fox's feature of that title.

2. BOSTON BLACKIE: William Gargan should be eliminated. Bert Lytell was probably the first Boston Blackie, appearing in "Boston Blackie's Little Pal" in 1918. Lionel Barrymore played the detective in 1922's "The Face in the Fog," while the best-remembered Boston Blackie, Chester Morris, began the first of several portrayals with "Meet Boston Blackie" in 1941.

3. THE FALCON: George Sanders was the best-known Falcon, beginning the first of several portrayals with "The Gay Falcon." (How do you like *that* for a title?) His brother, Tom Conway, picked up the role two years later, in 1943, with us finding "The Falcon in Danger." John Calvert played The Falcon in "The Devil's Cargo" in 1948. Eliminate Hugh Marlowe.

4. BULLDOG DRUMMOND: If you eliminated George Brent from this line-up, you've increased your score. Jack Buchanan played Drummond as early as 1925, in "The Third Round." Ronald Colman did the role nine years later in "Bulldog Drummond Strikes Back." John Howard played the role several times, including "Bulldog Drummond Comes Back" in 1937.

5. PERRY MASON: If you haven't spotted the Odd Man Out here— remember, we are *not* concerned with television here, and that eliminates Raymond Burr, even though in this day and age, he is probably the best-known Perry Mason. Warren William portrayed the attorney in "The Case of the Howling Dog" in 1934, while Ricardo Cortez was Mason two years later in "The Case of the Black Cat." Donald Woods was in a 1938 release, "The Case of the Stuttering Bishop," portraying the well-known barrister.

6. HERCULE POIROT: Claude Dauphin doesn't belong. Austin Trevor was Poirot in "Alibi" in 1931, while Tony Randall played the legendary detective in "The Alphabet Murders" thirty-five years

later. And, of course, the most recent was Albert Finney's portrayal, not lost in the all-star cast of "Murder on the Orient Express."

7. THE SAINT: Jim Bannon is a good friend of ours, but he never played the Saint. Louis Hayward appeared in the title role of "The Saint in New York" (1938); and, in the same year, George Sanders had the role in "The Saint Strikes Back." Hugh Sinclair played the role of the crime-fighter in "The Saint's Vacation."

8. THE LONE WOLF: Scratch Robert Kent, who never played the role. Jack Holt was the star of "The Lone Wolf" in 1924, and Francis Lederer was "The Lone Wolf in Paris" fourteen years later. Gerald Mohr was "The Notorious Lone Wolf" in 1946.

9. JIMMY VALENTINE: "Chick" Chandler should be eliminated from this line-up. The dignified Robert Warwick played the picaresque safecracker who skirted both sides of the law in 1915's "Alias Jimmy Valentine." The suave Roger Pryor played the title role in "The Return of Jimmy Valentine," in 1936, while Dennis O'Keefe appeared as the star of 1942's "The Affairs of Jimmy Valentine."

10. CHARLIE CHAN: Students of Earl Derr Biggers' Charlie Chan should know that Sessue Hayakawa did not play the Oriental detective. Warner Oland was probably the best-known, starring in the first of many such roles in "Charlie Chan Carries On" (1931). Sidney Toler came along later and appeared in a number of Chan films, one of which was "Castle in the Desert" (1942). But predating both of them was George Kuwa, who played Chan in "The Chinese Parrot" in 1928.

66. TELL US WHO PART II—BUFFS AND DUFFERS

1.   e. William Bendix   "The Glass Key"
                                          "Lifeboat"

2.   a. Clifton Webb   "Laura"
                                          "Sitting Pretty"

3.   g. Marlon Brando   "Guys and Dolls"
                                          "One-Eyed Jacks"

4.   c. Tyrone Power   "Nightmare Alley"
                                          "Prince of Foxes"

5.   h. James Stewart   "The Philadelphia Story"
                                          "Rear Window"

6.   i. Dean Jagger   "Brigham Young"
                                          "Bad Day at Black Rock"

7.   f. Millard Mitchell   "Singin' in the Rain"
                                          "The Gunfighter"

8.	j.	Harry Carey	"Trader Horn"
			"Mr. Smith Goes to Washington"
9.	d.	Claude Rains	"Juarez"
			"Casablanca"
10.	b.	Keenan Wynn	"The Clock"
			"Dr. Strangelove; or, How I Learned to Stop Worrying and Love the Bomb"

67. FILMS IN COMMON PART II—BUFFS ONLY

1. "A Song to Remember"
   "I'll See You in My Dreams"   m. "Stars and Stripes Forever"
Each of the films was the biography of a well-known composer: "A Song to Remember," Frédéric Chopin; "I'll See You in My Dreams," Gus Kahn; and "Stars and Stripes Forever," John Philip Sousa.

2. "Operator 13"
   "Whistling in Dixie"   g. "The Red Badge of Courage"
The three films all used the Civil War as background.

3. "One Foot in Heaven"
   "One Man's Way"   f. "A Man Called Peter"
Each of the three films' plots revolved around a modern-day clergyman.

4. "The Devil and the Deep"
   "Destination Tokyo"   e. "Operation Petticoat"
In the three films, much of the action took place aboard a submarine.

5. "The Birth of a Nation"
   "The Prisoner of Shark
        Island"   h. "Prince of Players"
There might be some confusion here with Question 2 above; however, each of the three films in this question included a re-enactment of the assassination of President Abraham Lincoln.

6. "The Odessa File"
   "Kiss of Death"   j. "White Heat"
In each of the three films listed, the hero posed as a criminal to infiltrate a gang in order to uncover information concerning illegal activities.

7. "Tora, Tora, Tora"
   "From Here to Eternity"   i. "In Harm's Way"
The three films included a re-enactment of the Japanese attack on Pearl Harbor.

8. "The Big House" (1930)
   "Birdman of Alcatraz"   k. "Brute Force"
The setting for the three films was inside a penitentiary.

252

9. "In Cold Blood"
  "The Girl in the Red Velvet
      Swing"   b. "Compulsion"
The three films in this question were all concerned with the re-enact-
ment of real-life crimes: "In Cold Blood," the Clutter family massacre in
rural Kansas; "The Girl in the Red Velvet Swing," the Harry Thaw-
Stanford White shooting; and "Compulsion," the Bobby Franks murder
case.
10. "Marty"
  "Days of Wine and Roses"   n. "The Catered Affair"
The three films were initially television dramas prior to being filmed as
feature pictures.
11. "The Son-Daughter"
  "Dragon Seed"   o. "The Good Earth"
In the three films, Occidental players portrayed Orientals.
12. "Private Lives"
  "In Which We Serve"   d. "This Happy Breed"
All of the films were written by, or adapted from works by, Noel
Coward.
13. "Singin' in the Rain"
  "The Great Waldo Pepper"   a. "Hollywood Cavalcade"
The three films, or substantial portions thereof, were set in the early
days of Hollywood and film-making.
14. "Solomon and Sheba"
  "My Son John"   c. "Saratoga"
During the production of the three films, a major player died before
filming was completed: "Solomon and Sheba," Tyrone Power; "My Son
John," Robert Walker; and "Saratoga," Jean Harlow.
15. "The Moon Is Down"
  "The Chetniks"   l. "This Land Is Mine"
The three films dealt with life in Nazi-occupied countries during World
War II.

67. FILMS IN COMMON PART II—DUFFERS' TEE

1. "A Song to Remember"
  "I'll See You in My Dreams"   b. "Stars and Stripes Forever"
2. "Operator 13"
  "Whistling in Dixie"   a. "The Red Badge of Courage"
3. "One Foot in Heaven"
  "One Man's Way"   c. "A Man Called Peter"
4. "The Devil and the Deep"
  "Destination Tokyo"   a. "Operation Petticoat"

5. "The Birth of a Nation"
   "The Prisoner of Shark
       Island"   c. "Prince of Players"
6. "The Odessa File"
   "Kiss of Death"   a. "White Heat"
7. "Tora, Tora, Tora"
   "From Here to Eternity"   b. "In Harm's Way"
8. "The Big House" (1930)
   "Birdman of Alcatraz"   b. "Brute Force"
9. "In Cold Blood"
   "The Girl in the Red Velvet
       Swing"   a. "Compulsion"
10. "Marty"
    "Days of Wine and Roses"   c. "The Catered Affair"
11. "The Son-Daughter"
    "Dragon Seed"   c. "The Good Earth"
12. "Private Lives"
    "In Which We Serve"   b. "This Happy Breed"
13. "Singin' in the Rain"
    "The Great Waldo Pepper"   b. "Hollywood Cavalcade"
14. "Solomon and Sheba"
    "My Son John"   b. "Saratoga"
15. "The Moon Is Down"
    "The Chetniks"   c. "This Land Is Mine"

For an explanation of the common factor for the three films in each question, please refer to the answer section of the Buffs' version above.

68. RULE, BRITANNIA!—BUFFS ONLY

THREE-LETTER NAMES	FIVE-LETTER NAMES
Lee, Bernard	Angel, Heather
FOUR-LETTER NAMES	Bloom, Claire
Best, Edna	Bruce, Nigel
Hare, Lumsden	Clive, Colin
Hume, Benita	Coote, Robert
Keen, Geoffrey	Crisp, Donald
Kerr, Deborah	Denny, Reginald
Love, Montagu	Donat, Robert
More, Kenneth	Evans, Dame Edith
Owen, Reginald	Field, Virginia
Reed, Oliver	Grant, Cary
York, Michael or Susannah	Green, Nigel

Loder, John
Niven, David
Rains, Claude
Smith, C. Aubrey
Young, Roland

SIX-LETTER NAMES
Aherne, Brian
Arliss, George
Aylmer, Felix
Colman, Ronald
Cooper, Melville or Gladys
Coward, Noel
Duprez, June
Greene, Richard
Howard, Trevor or Leslie
Hunter, Ian
Lupino, Ida
Mather, Aubrey
Napier, Alan
Oberon, Merle
Parker, Cecil
Steele, Tommy
Whitty, Dame May

SEVEN-LETTER NAMES
Collier, Constance
Connery, Sean
Daniell, Henry
Gielgud, Sir John
Granger, Stewart
Hepburn, Audrey
Huntley, Raymond or G. P.
Kendall, Kay

Milland, Ray
Mowbray, Alan
O'Connor, Una
Olivier, Sir Laurence
Sellers, Peter
Shields, Arthur
Worlock, Frederick

EIGHT-LETTER NAMES
Fletcher, Bramwell
Gardiner, Reginald
Harrison, Rex
Holloway, Stanley
Kellaway, Cecil
McLaglen, Victor
Marshall, Herbert
Merivale, Philip
Naismith, Laurence
Rathbone, Basil
Redgrave, Michael
Treacher, Arthur
Williams, Emlyn

NINE-LETTER NAMES
Hardwicke, Sir Cedric
Hyde-White, Wilfrid

TEN-LETTER NAMES
Lanchester, Elsa
Richardson, Sir Ralph

ELEVEN-LETTER NAME
Bartholomew, Freddie

TWELVE-LETTER NAME
Attenborough, Richard

68. RULE, BRITANNIA!—DUFFERS' TEE

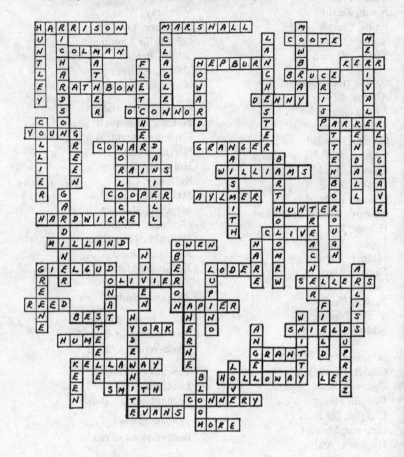

69. HEY, WASN'T THAT . . . ?—BUFFS AND DUFFERS

1. Cecil B. DeMille   f. "Sunset Boulevard"
2. Louis Armstrong   k. "The Five Pennies"[1]
3. Babe Ruth   g. "Pride of the Yankees"
4. John Ringling   m. or n. "The Greatest Show on Earth"
     North
5. H. V. Kaltenborn   l. "Mr. Smith Goes to Washington"
6. Nat "King" Cole   d. "The Blue Gardenia"

[1] Note: we would also accept Louis Armstrong's appearance in "The Glenn Miller Story."

7. Tony Zale — p. "Somebody Up There Likes Me"
8. Walter Winchell — r. "Wake Up and Live"
9. Jascha Heifetz — h. "They Shall Have Music"
10. Fanny Brice — o. "The Great Ziegfeld"
11. Bill Dickey — e. "The Stratton Story"
12. Sam Snead — b. or i. "Follow the Sun"
13. Mitzi Mayfair — s. "Four Jills in a Jeep"
14. Walter Catlett — a. "Look for the Silver Lining"
15. Don Budge — c. or j. "Pat and Mike"
16. Cary Middlecoff — i. or b. "Follow the Sun"
17. Gene Krupa — t. "The Glenn Miller Story"
18. Paul Whiteman — q. "Strike Up the Band"
19. Emmett Kelly — n. or m. "The Greatest Show on Earth"
20. Babe Didrikson — j. or c. "Pat and Mike"

70. LA RONDE: COMEDIANS AND THEIR LADIES— BUFFS AND DUFFERS

A. Eddie Cantor and Constance Moore
B. Constance Moore and W. C. Fields
C. W. C. Fields and Maureen O'Sullivan
D. Maureen O'Sullivan and the Marx Bros.
E. The Marx Bros. and Marilyn Monroe
F. Marilyn Monroe and Mickey Rooney
G. Mickey Rooney and Ann Rutherford
H. Ann Rutherford and Danny Kaye
I. Danny Kaye and Katharine Hepburn
J. Katharine Hepburn and Bob Hope
K. Bob Hope and Martha Raye
L. Martha Raye and Jimmy Durante
M. Jimmy Durante and Lupe Velez

f. "Show Business"
g. "You Can't Cheat an Honest Man"
o. "David Copperfield"
r. "A Day at the Races"
l. "Love Happy"
s. "The Fireball"
p. "Life Begins for Andy Hardy"
v. "The Secret Life of Walter Mitty"
u. "The Madwoman of Chaillot"
h. "The Iron Petticoat"
w. "The Big Broadcast of 1938"
c. "Jumbo"
x. "Strictly Dynamite"

N. Lupe Velez and Wheeler & Woolsey   d. "High Flyers"
O. Wheeler & Woolsey and Betty
     Grable   q. "The Nitwits"
P. Betty Grable and Joe Penner   b. "The Day the Bookies
                                                                Wept"
Q. Joe Penner and Lucille Ball   t. "Go Chase Yourself"
R. Lucille Ball and Red Skelton   k. "Dubarry Was a Lady"
S. Red Skelton and Ginger Rogers   j. "Having Wonderful Time"
T. Ginger Rogers and Joe E. Brown   n. "The Tenderfoot"
U. Joe E. Brown and Kathryn Grayson   a. "Show Boat"
V. Kathryn Grayson and Abbott &
     Costello   e. "Rio Rita"
W. Abbott & Costello and Joan Davis   m. "Hold That Ghost"
X. Joan Davis and Eddie Cantor   i. "If You Knew Susie"

71. WHO SANG . . . ? PART II—BUFFS AND DUFFERS

1. "I'll Build a Stairway to   M. Georges
     Paradise"   Guetary   l. "An
                                                                       American
                                                                       in Paris"

2. "Is It a Crime?"   I. Judy
                                          Holliday   k. "The Bells
                                                                       Are
                                                                       Ringing"

3. "You and I"   J. Leon Ames
                                          and Mary
                                          Astor   h. "Meet Me in
                                                                       St. Louis"

4. "Baby, It's Cold Outside"   C. Ricardo
                                          Montalban
                                          and Esther
                                          Williams   i. "Neptune's
                                                                       Daughter"

5. "Pass That Peace Pipe"   K. Joan
                                          McCracken   d. "Good
                                                                       News"

6. "Aba Daba Honeymoon"   D. Debbie
                                          Reynolds and
                                          Carleton
                                          Carpenter   m. "Two Weeks
                                                                       with Love"

7. "True Love"	o. Bing Crosby and Grace Kelly	e. "High Society"
8. "Blue Room"	N. Perry Como	j. "Words and Music"
9. "Bring On the Wonderful Men"	A. Virginia O'Brien	f. "Ziegfeld Follies"
10. "I've Taken Quite a Fancy to You"	L. Alice Faye	c. "In Old Chicago"
11. "Dancing for Nickels and Dimes"	F. Dorothy Lamour	b. "Johnny Apollo"
12. "Don't Sit Under the Apple Tree"	G. Tyrone Power	a. "Crash Dive"
13. "I Wake Up in the Morning Feeling Fine"	E. Betty Hutton	o. "Red, Hot and Blue"
14. "In the Still of the Night"	H. Nelson Eddy	g. "Rosalie"
15. "All I Do Is Dream of You"	B. Gene Raymond	n. "Sadie McKee"

72. THE BIG BULBS: PAIRS—BUFFS AND DUFFERS

1. Guy Madison and Andy Devine	d. "Wild Bill Hickok"
2. George Brent and Dane Clark	h. "Wire Service"
3. Alan Mowbray and Frank Jenks	f. "Colonel Flack"
4. James Dunn and Michael O'Shea	i. "It's a Great Life"
5. Barbara Britton and Richard Denning	k. "Mr. and Mrs. North"
6. Tom Tully and Warner Anderson	j. "The Line-up"
7. Wendell Corey and Marsha Hunt	a. "Peck's Bad Girl"
8. Howard Duff and Ida Lupino	e. "Mr. Adams and Eve"
9. Ronald Colman and Benita Hume	l. "The Halls of Ivy"
10. Jimmie Lydon and Mitzi Green	c. "So This Is Hollywood"
11. Anne Jeffreys and Robert Sterling	b. "Topper"
12. Richard Jaeckel and John Derek	g. "Frontier Circus"

73. MISCELLANY—BUFFS ONLY

1. Universal Newsreel.
2. 1967.
3. Jennifer Jones; "The Song of Bernadette" (nominated and won as "Best Actress," 1943); "Since You Went Away" (nominated as "Best Supporting Actress" but lost to Ethel Barrymore, "None But the Lonely Heart," 1944).
4. Edmund Gwenn, "Miracle on 34th Street"; Ruth Gordon, "Rosemary's Baby."
5. Jackie Cooper, "Skippy," 1930 (Awards given in 1931). Cooper was beaten by Lionel Barrymore, for his work in "A Free Soul."
6. The "Seven Brothers" were Howard Keel, Russ Tamblyn, Jeff Richards, Marc Platt, Jacques d'Amboise, Matt Mattox, and Tommy Rall.
7. The "Dirty Dozen" were Jim Brown, Tom Busby, Ben Carruthers, Charles Bronson, Stuart Cooper, John Cassavetes, Trini Lopez, Al Mancini, Colin Maitland, Telly Savalas, Donald Sutherland, Clint Walker.
8. Chico Day does not. All of the rest were involved with the costuming of films, while Chico Day was an assistant director.
9. Grayson Hall was the actress nominated for "Best Supporting Actress" Oscar for her work in "The Night of the Iguana." Robert Rich was the pseudonym under which Dalton Trumbo wrote the screenplay for "The Brave One," for which an Oscar was awarded. Billy and Bobby Mauch were identical twins who appeared in the title roles of "The Prince and the Pauper" (with Errol Flynn), as well as in a brief series of "Penrod and Sam" films. Jon Whiteley and Vincent Winter both won miniature Oscar statuettes for their outstanding performances as juveniles in "The Little Kidnappers" (1954). Bess Flowers has been seen in many films. Early in her career, she played small roles, though she was never really featured. Tall, attractive, her gray hair always well-coiffed, she became "Queen of the Dress Extras." It seemed that no fashionable party scene, theater opening, or other posh event depicted in films was complete without her. You might remember her as one of the well-wishers to Eve Harrington (Anne Baxter) as she won the Sarah Siddons Award in "All About Eve."
10. "The Robe" was the first feature film presented in the CinemaScope wide-screen process. "The Lights of New York" was the first all-talking picture. Though "The Jazz Singer" is often credited with this distinction, that film actually had only some songs and a brief passage of dialogue, whereas "The Lights of New York" was *all*-talking! "Flowers and Trees" was a Disney cartoon which was the *first* three-color Technicolor film. "Color films" prior to that time had

been either tinted or photographed in a *two*-color process. "Becky Sharp" was the first feature film to be shot entirely with the *three*-color Technicolor process.

73. MISCELLANY—DUFFERS' TEE

1. News on the March was not a bona fide newsreel, but a fictional one. This was the newsreel which reported on the death of Charles Foster Kane in "Citizen Kane," and whose manager prompted the search for the explanation of *Rosebud!*
2. (b) 1967—December 22, and it was the Universal Newsreel.
3. (c) Jennifer Jones. She had won the "Best Actress" Oscar for "The Song of Bernadette," and was nominated as "Best Supporting Actress" for her performance in Selznick's "Since You Went Away." She was, however, beaten by Ethel Barrymore in this competition for "None But the Lonely Heart."
4. (c) Edmund Gwenn, for "Miracle on 34th Street," and (d) Ruth Gordon, for "Rosemary's Baby."
5. (c) Jackie Cooper.
6. (b) Russ Tamblyn, (c) Jeff Richards, (f) Matt Mattox, (g) Jacques d'Amboise.
7. (a) Jim Brown, (c) Trini Lopez, (f) Donald Sutherland, (j) Clint Walker, (k) Charles Bronson, (l) John Cassavetes.
8. (c) John Nesbitt does not belong. He was the creator of "John Nesbitt's Passing Parade"—an added attraction. The others all narrated newsreels.
9. Nadia Gray was the actress who did the striptease in the party scene of "La Dolce Vita." George O'Hanlon was Joe Doakes in the short subject series—remember his slow emergence from behind the eight ball? Cyril Delevanti was the actor who played the old man in "The Night of the Iguana." Yakima Canutt began his career in Western films, and even played a few cowboy heroes. He became a specialist in trick riding, and thence stunt work. It was he who perfected the trick of falling from between the horses pulling the stagecoach and— after allowing the carriage to pass over him—grasping the rear of the coach and pulling himself back onto the rear. It was Canutt who supervised the stunt work, including the chariot race, for William Wyler's "Ben-Hur" (1959). Billy Bitzer was the cameraman who filmed D. W. Griffith's great films.
10. "The Robe" was the first film produced in the CinemaScope wide-screen process. "The Lights of New York" was the first all-talking picture. Though "The Jazz Singer" is often credited with this distinction, that film actually had only some songs and a brief passage of di-

alogue, whereas "The Lights of New York" was the first *all*-talking feature! "Flowers and Trees" was a Disney cartoon which was the *first* three-color Technicolor film. Prior to that, "color films" were either hand-tinted or photographed in a cruder *two*-color process. "Becky Sharp" was the first feature film to be shot entirely with the *three*-color Technicolor process.

74. SEEING DOUBLE—BUFFS ONLY

1. Ronald Colman
2. Yvonne De Carlo
3. Bette Davis
4. Charlie Chaplin
5. George Arliss

6. Bette Davis
7. Eddie Cantor
8. Danny Kaye
9. Ronald Colman[1]
10. Betty Hutton

74. SEEING DOUBLE—DUFFERS' TEE

1. "The Masquerader"
2. "Passion"
3. "A Stolen Life"
4. "The Great Dictator"
5. "The House of
     Rothschild"
6. "Dead Ringer"
7. "Royal Wedding"
8. "On the Riviera"
9. "The Prisoner of Zenda"
10. "Here Come the Waves"

e. Ronald Colman
f. Yvonne De Carlo
b. or j. Bette Davis
a. Charlie Chaplin

i. George Arliss
j. or b. Bette Davis
d. Keenan Wynn
g. Danny Kaye
h. Stewart Granger[2]
c. Betty Hutton

75. MORE LINK-UPS—BUFFS AND DUFFERS

1. Nigel   BRUCE   Cabot
2. Rose   HOBART   Cavanaugh
3. Kathryn   GRANT   Withers
4. Tisha   STERLING   Hayden

[1] If you're going to be *that* way about it, we'll also accept *Stewart Granger*. And if you really put the press on, we'll also accept *Lewis Stone*—even though *that* version was about thirty years ahead of us.
[2] We'll probably get arguments that we should allow Ronald Colman on this one—but then, what answer would you use for "The Masquerader"?

262

5.	Sandy	DENNIS	Hopper
6.	Cary	GRANT	Mitchell
7.	Gilbert	ROLAND	Young
8.	Esther	DALE	Evans
9.	Mel	BROOKS	West
10.	Jeanette	MACDONALD	Carey

76. THE MEN FROM THE BOYS PART II— BUFFS AND DUFFERS

1.	"There's No Business Like Show Business"	Donald Bamble	Tim	i. Donald O'Connor
2.	"In Old Chicago"	Gene Reynolds	Dion	g. or h. Tyrone Power
3.	"Citizen Kane"	Buddy Swan	Charles	l. Orson Welles
4.	"The Sullivans"	Bobby Driscoll	Al	f. Edward Ryan
5.	"The Jolson Story"	Scotty Beckett	Asa	a. Larry Parks
6.	"In Old Chicago"	Billy Watson	Jack	m. Don Ameche
7.	"Beau Geste"	Donald O'Connor	Beau	o. Gary Cooper
8.	"Angels with Dirty Faces"	Frankie Burke	Rocky	c., e., or n. James Cagney
9.	"David Copperfield"	Freddie Bartholomew	David	b. Frank Lawton
10.	"Yankee Doodle Dandy"	Douglas Croft	George	e., n., or c. James Cagney
11.	"Public Enemy"	Frank Coghlan, Jr.	Tom	n., c., or e. James Cagney

12. "In Old Chicago"	Bobs Watson	Bob		d. Tom Brown
13. "Heaven Can Wait"	Nino Pipitone, Jr.	Jack		j. Tod Andrews
14. "Son of Fury"	Roddy McDowall	Ben	h. or g.	Tyrone Power
15. "Beau Geste"	David Holt	Augustus	k.	G. P. Huntley, Jr.

77. WHAT'S THE TITLE? PART II—BUFFS AND DUFFERS

1. "Laura"
2. "Seven Brides for Seven Brothers"
3. "Blazing Saddles"
4. "For Whom the Bell Tolls"
5. "Sunset Boulevard"
6. "David Copperfield"
7. "The Man with the Golden Arm"
8. "Bataan"
9. "Five Graves to Cairo"
10. "Easter Parade"

78. ONCE AGAIN, NAME THE STAR—BUFFS ONLY

1. RICHARD WIDMARK   "No Way Out"   "Alvarez Kelly"
2. CHARLES BOYER   "Hold Back the Dawn"   "Love Affair"
3. GLADYS COOPER   "The Green Years"   "The Song of Bernadette"
4. CHARLES BRONSON   "Pat and Mike"   "The Sandpiper"
5. GENE TIERNEY   "Leave Her to Heaven"   "The Razor's Edge"
6. GLENN FORD   "The Blackboard Jungle"   "Don't Go Near the Water"
7. REX HARRISON   "The Yellow Rolls-Royce"   "Midnight Lace"
8. WALLACE BEERY   "Tugboat Annie"   "A Date with Judy"

9. GEORGE
   SANDERS   "Ivanhoe"   "Call Me Madam"
10. GEORGE   "How the West Was   "Breakfast at
    PEPPARD   Won"   Tiffany's"

78. ONCE AGAIN, NAME THE STAR—DUFFERS' TEE

1. RICHARD
   WIDMARK   "Slattery's Hurricane"   "The Way West"
2. CHARLES
   BOYER   "Is Paris Burning?"   "All This and Heaven
                                               Too"
3. GLADYS   "Green Dolphin
   COOPER   Street"   "Mrs. Parkington"
4. CHARLES
   BRONSON   "The Dirty Dozen"   "The Great Escape"
5. GENE TIERNEY "The Egyptian"   "Belle Starr"
6. GLENN FORD   "Gilda"   "Is Paris Burning?"
7. REX   "The Foxes of   "King Richard and the
   HARRISON   Harrow"   Crusaders"
8. WALLACE
   BEERY   "The Big House"   "Grand Hotel"
9. GEORGE
   SANDERS   "Samson and Delilah"   "All About Eve"
10. GEORGE
    PEPPARD   "The Carpetbaggers"   "The Blue Max"

79. IN A BIG WAY—BUFFS AND DUFFERS

1. "The Big Circus"   k. Victor Mature
2. "The Big Carnival"   i. or s. Kirk Douglas
3. "The Big Parade"   r. John Gilbert
4. "The Big House"   t. Wallace Beery
5. "The Big Heat"   q. Glenn Ford
6. "The Big Operator"   e. Mickey Rooney
7. "The Big Street"   p. Henry Fonda
8. "The Big Shot"   n. or o. Humphrey Bogart
9. "The Big Sleep"   o. or n. Humphrey Bogart
10. "The Big Lift"   l. Montgomery Clift
11. "The Big Hangover"   c. Van Johnson

12. "The Big Clock"	h. Ray Milland
13. "The Big Caper"	j. Rory Calhoun
14. "The Big Steal"	b. Robert Mitchum
15. "The Big Mouth"	f. Jerry Lewis
16. "The Big Boodle"	m. Errol Flynn
17. "The Big Sky"	s. or i. Kirk Douglas
18. "The Big Cat"	d. Lon McCallister
19. "The Big Store"	a. The Marx Brothers
20. "The Big Country"	g. Charlton Heston

80. Y'ALL REMEMBER WORLD WAR II? PART II— BUFFS AND DUFFERS

1. "Wake Island"
2. "Bataan"
3. "Sands of Iwo Jima"
4. "The Halls of Montezuma"
5. "Battleground"
6. "Desperate Journey"
7. "Thirty Seconds over Tokyo"
8. "The Commandos Strike at Dawn"
9. "A Walk in the Sun"
10. "To the Shores of Tripoli"
11. "Back to Bataan"
12. "They Were Expendable"
13. "The Fighting Seabees"
14. "Guadalcanal Diary"
15. "Corregidor"

81. ANYTHING SHE CAN DO, I CAN DO BETTER —BUFFS ONLY

1. Ingrid Bergman
    E. Jean   "Joan of Arc"
    Seberg   Jeanne d'Arc   "St. Joan"
2. Ethel
    Barrymore   Czarina   "Rasputin and the Empress"
    F. Janet   Alexandra
    Suzman   "Nicholas and Alexandra"

3. Ginger Rogers		"The Magnificent Doll"
A. Spring Byington	Dolly Madison	"The Buccaneer"
4. Merle Oberon		"The Private Life of Henry VIII"
H. Elaine Stewart	Anne Boleyn	"Young Bess"
5. Norma Shearer		"Marie Antoinette"
C. Nina Foch	Marie Antoinette	"Scaramouche"
6. Mary Howard		"Abe Lincoln in Illinois"
D. Una Merkel	Ann Rutledge	"Abraham Lincoln"
7. Elizabeth Taylor		"Cleopatra"
J. Vivien Leigh	Cleopatra	"Caesar and Cleopatra"
8. Lillian Bond		"The Westerner"
G. Ava Gardner	Lily Langtry	"The Life and Times of Judge Roy Bean"
9. Bette Davis		"John Paul Jones"
B. Elisabeth Bergner	Catherine of Russia	"Catherine the Great"
10. Flora Robson		"Fire over England" or "The Sea Hawk"
I. Bette Davis	Elizabeth I of England	"The Private Lives of Elizabeth and Essex," or "The Virgin Queen"

81. ANYTHING SHE CAN DO, I CAN DO BETTER— DUFFERS' TEE

1. Ingrid Bergman; Jeanne d'Arc in "Joan of Arc"

E. Jean Seberg

i. "St. Joan"

2. Ethel Barrymore; Czarina Alexandra in "Rasputin and the Empress"

F. Janet Suzman

g. "Nicholas and Alexandra"

3. Ginger Rogers; Dolly Madison in "The Magnificent Doll"

A. Spring Byington

f. "The Buccaneer"

4. Merle Oberon; Anne Boleyn "The Private Life of Henry VIII"

H. Elaine Stewart

e. "Young Bess"

5. Norma Shearer; Marie Antoinette in "Marie Antoinette"
6. Mary Howard; Ann Rutledge in "Abe Lincoln in Illinois"
7. Elizabeth Taylor; Cleopatra in "Cleopatra"
8. Lillian Bond; Lily Langtry in "The Westerner"
9. Bette Davis; Catherine of Russia in "John Paul Jones"
10. Flora Robson; Queen Elizabeth I in "Fire over England"

c. Nina Foch
D. Una Merkel
J. Vivien Leigh
G. Ava Gardner
B. Elisabeth Bergner
I. Bette Davis

d. "Scaramouche"
a. "Abraham Lincoln"
b. "Caesar and Cleopatra"
c. "The Life and Times of Judge Roy Bean"
j. "Catherine the Great"
h. "The Private Lives of Elizabeth and Essex," or "The Virgin Queen"

82. VERY IMPORTANT PROPS PART II— BUFFS AND DUFFERS

1. "The Black (g.) Book"
2. "Aladdin and His (l.) Lamp"
3. "The Band (j.) Wagon"
4. "Behind the Iron (f.) Curtain"
5. "Kitten with a (d.) Whip"
6. "The Glass (b.) Key"
7. "Apache (i.) Drums"
8. "Battle (k.) Taxi"
9. "Red (m.) Tomahawk"
10. "(e.) Battleship Potemkin"
11. "The Big (o.) Knife"
12. "(h.) Banjo on My Knee"
13. "Golden (a.) Earrings"
14. "Oil for the (c.) Lamps of China"
15. "The Fuzzy Pink (n.) Nightgown"

83. HERE'S LOOKIN' AT YOU, BOGIE! PART II— BUFFS ONLY

1.	Dixon Steele	"In a Lonely Place"
2.	Eddie Willis	"The Harder They Fall"
3.	"Rocks" Valentine	"The Amazing Dr. Clitterhouse"
4.	George Halley	"The Roaring Twenties"
5.	"Gloves" Donahue	"All Through the Night"
6.	James Frazier	"Angels with Dirty Faces"
7.	Chuck Martin	"Invisible Stripes"
8.	Pete Martin	"Racket Busters"
9.	Martin Ferguson	"The Enforcer"
10.	Mark Braden	"Crime School"
11.	Joe "Red" Kennedy	"San Quentin"
12.	Vincent Parry	"Dark Passage"
13.	Frank McCloud	"Key Largo"

83. HERE'S LOOKIN' AT YOU, BOGIE! PART II— DUFFERS' TEE

1.	Glenn Griffin	"The Desperate Hours"
2.	Andrew Morton	"Knock on Any Door"
3.	Billy Dannreuther	"Beat the Devil"
4.	Jim Carmody	"The Left Hand of God"
5.	Linus Larrabee	"Sabrina"
6.	"Duke" Mantee	"The Petrified Forest"
7.	"Baby Face" Martin	"Dead End"
8.	Rick Blaine	"Casablanca"
9.	"Whip" McCord	"The Oklahoma Kid"
10.	Rick Leland	"Across the Pacific"
11.	John Murrell	"Virginia City"
12.	"Chips" McGuire	"It All Came True"
13.	Sgt. Joe Gunn	"Sahara"

84. THE BIG BULB: OATERS—BUFFS AND DUFFERS

1.	Stanley Andrews	n.	"Death Valley Days"
2.	Tris Coffin	l.	"26 Men"
3.	Willard Parker	o.	"Tales of the Texas Rangers"
4.	Dick Powell	a.	"Zane Grey Theatre"

5. Audie Murphy	i.	"Whispering Smith"
6. Richard Egan	m.	"Empire"[1]
7. Rory Calhoun	q.	"The Texan"
8. George Montgomery	s.	"Cimarron City"
9. William Bendix	p.	"Overland Trail"
10. Edgar Buchanan	r.	"The Adventures of Judge Roy Bean"
11. Duncan Renaldo and Leo Carrillo	h.	"The Cisco Kid"
12. Russell Hayden and Jackie Coogan	k.	"Cowboy G-Men"
13. Henry Fonda	e.	"The Deputy"
14. Walter Brennan	j.	"The Guns of Will Sonnett"
15. Richard Carlson	g.	"MacKenzie's Raiders"
16. John Payne	c.	"The Restless Gun"
17. Scott Brady	t.	"Shotgun Slade"
18. Barry Sullivan	d.	"The Tall Man"
19. Leif Erickson and Cameron Mitchell	f.	"High Chaparral"
20. Jeffrey Hunter	b.	"Temple Houston"

85. MORE TYPE-CASTING—BUFFS AND DUFFERS

1. _ j. SPENCER TRACY: "Plymouth Adventure"; "Edison the Man"; "Woman of the Year"; "Captains Courageous."[2]

2. _ f. RICHARD BURTON: "The Night of the Iguana"; "Prince of Players"; "The Longest Day"; "The Spy Who Came In from the Cold."

3. _ g. TYRONE POWER: "The Eddy Duchin Story"; "The Black Swan"; "Blood and Sand"; "Pony Soldier."

4. _ e. INGRID BERGMAN: "Spellbound"; "Murder on the Orient Express"; "The Inn of the Sixth Happiness"; "For Whom the Bell Tolls."

5. _ h. CLAUDETTE COLBERT: "Thunder on the Hill"; "It Happened One Night"; "Sign of the Cross"; "So Proudly We Hail."

6. _ i. HUMPHREY BOGART: "Knock on Any Door"; "The Caine Mutiny"; "The Treasure of the Sierra Madre"; "To Have and Have Not."

7. _ c. JAMES CAGNEY: "Man of a Thousand Faces"; "Boy Meets Girl"; "Mr. Roberts"; "Yankee Doodle Dandy."

[1] In the Buffs' version, the title "Redigo" would also be acceptable.
[2] "The Old Man and the Sea" would also be acceptable.

8. _ d. FRANK SINATRA: "Pal Joey"[1]; "The Man with the Golden Arm"; "A Hole in the Head"; "Suddenly."
9. _ a. MICKEY ROONEY: "Words and Music"; "A Midsummer Night's Dream"; "Breakfast at Tiffany's"; "The Human Comedy."
10. _ b. FRED MACMURRAY: "Double Indemnity"; "The Absent-Minded Professor"[2]; "The Apartment"; "The Caine Mutiny."

86. FIRST, THE WORD PART II—BUFFS ONLY

1. Robert Bloch	c. "Psycho"
2. Dorothy B. Hughes	b. "In a Lonely Place"
3. William McGivern	a. "The Big Heat"
4. Helen MacInnes	c. "Assignment in Brittany"
5. Agatha Christie	a. "Witness for the Prosecution"
6. Patrick Hamilton	c. "Gaslight"
7. Graham Greene	a. "The Third Man"
8. Craig Rice	c. "Having Wonderful Crime"
9. Mary Roberts Rinehart	c. "The Bat Whispers"
10. Carlton E. Morse	a. "I Love a Mystery"
11. Donald Hamilton	c. "Murderers' Row"
12. Ira Levin	c. "Rosemary's Baby"

86. FIRST, THE WORD PART II—DUFFERS' TEE

1. "The Night Walker" "The Deadly Bees" — J. Robert Bloch — f. "Psycho"
2. "Ride the Pink Horse" "The Fallen Sparrow" — E. Dorothy B. Hughes — j. "In a Lonely Place"
3. "Odds Against Tomorrow" "The Caper of the Golden Bulls" — B. William McGivern — h. "The Big Heat"
4. "Above Suspicion" "The Venetian Affair" — I. Helen MacInnes — g. "Assignment in Brittany"
5. "And Then There Were None" "Murder on the Orient Express" — L. Agatha Christie — e. "Witness for the Prosecution"

---

[1] "The Joker Is Wild" would also be acceptable.
[2] "Son of Flubber" would also be acceptable.

6. "Rope" "Hangover Square"	A. Patrick Hamilton	c. "Gaslight"
7. "This Gun for Hire" "Our Man in Havana"	C. Graham Greene	i. "The Third Man"
8. "Mrs. O'Malley and Mr. Malone" "The Lucky Stiff"	D. Craig Rice	a. "Having Wonderful Crime"
9. "Miss Pinkerton" "The Nurse's Secret"	H. Mary Roberts Rinehart	b. "The Bat Whispers"
10. "The Devil's Mask" "The Unknown"	F. Carlton E. Morse	k. "I Love a Mystery"
11. "The Silencers" "The Ambushers"	K. Donald Hamilton	l. "Murderers' Row"
12. "A Kiss Before Dying" "The Stepford Wives"	G. Ira Levin	d. "Rosemary's Baby"

87. THANK HEAVEN FOR LITTLE GIRLS— BUFFS AND DUFFERS

1. "Jane Eyre"	Peggy Ann Garner	Jane	d. Joan Fontaine
2. "The Dolly Sisters"	Evon Thomas	Jenny	h. Betty Grable
3. "The Sullivans"	Nancy June Robinson	Genevieve	f. Trudy Marshall
4. "There's No Business Like Show Business"	Linda Lowell	Katy	g. Mitzi Gaynor
5. "Follow the Sun"	Ann Burr	Valerie	i. Anne Baxter
6. "Beau Geste"	Ann Gillis	Isobel	k. Susan Hayward
7. "Yankee Doodle Dandy"	Patsy Lee Parsons	Josie	l. Jeanne Cagney
8. "The Dolly Sisters"	Donna Jo Gribble	Rosie	j. June Haver
9. "Imitation of Life"	Juanita Quigley	Jessie	c. Rochelle Hudson

10. "Angels with
    Dirty
    Faces"   Marilyn Knowlden   Laury   e. Ann
                                                     Sheridan
11. "The Ghost and
    Mrs. Muir"   Natalie Wood   Anna   a. Vanessa
                                                     Brown
12. "David
    Copperfield"   Marilyn Knowlden   Emily   b. Madge
                                                     Evans

88. THAT OL' GANG OF MINE PART II—
BUFFS AND DUFFERS

1. _ q.   "King Solomon's Mines"
2. _ k.   "King Kong"
3. _ g.   "None But the Lonely Heart"
4. _ s.   "Northwest Mounted Police"
5. _ i.   "Raintree County"
6. _ d.   "Seven Days in May"
7. _ e.   "A Streetcar Named Desire"
8. _ w.   "Strangers on a Train"
9. _ a.   "Lost Horizon"
10. _ l. "The Lost Weekend"
11. _ t. "Dinner at Eight"
12. _ y. "Come Back, Little Sheba"
13. _ c. "Beat the Devil"
14. _ u. "The Apartment"
15. _ r. "Detective Story"
16. _ b. "Exodus"
17. _ h. "In Which We Serve"
18. _ f. "The Treasure of the Sierra Madre"
19. _ x. "Sunset Boulevard"
20. _ j. "Duel in the Sun"
21. _ o. "The Dark at the Top of the Stairs"
22. _ n. "The Farmer's Daughter"
23. _ p. "Father of the Bride"[1]
24. _ m. "From Here to Eternity"
25. _ v. "Giant"

[1] In the Buffs' version, the title "Father's Little Dividend" would also be acceptable.

89. THAT OL' GANG OF MINE PART II: FOLLOW-UP!—BUFFS AND DUFFERS

1. Elizabeth Curtis	("King Solomon's Mines")	Deborah Kerr
2. Ann Redman	("King Kong")	Fay Wray
3. Ernie Mott	("None But the Lonely Heart")	Cary Grant
4. Dusty Rivers	("Northwest Mounted Police")	Gary Cooper
5. John Wickliff Shawnessy	("Raintree County")	Montgomery Clift
6. Gen. James M. Scott	("Seven Days in May")	Burt Lancaster
7. Blanche DuBois	("A Streetcar Named Desire")	Vivien Leigh
8. Guy Haines	("Strangers on a Train")	Farley Granger
9. Robert Conway	("Lost Horizon")	Ronald Colman
10. Don Birnam	("The Lost Weekend")	Ray Milland
11. Carlotta Vance	("Dinner at Eight")	Marie Dressler
12. Doc Delaney	("Come Back, Little Sheba")	Burt Lancaster
13. Billy Dannreuther	("Beat the Devil")	Humphrey Bogart
14. C. C. (Bud) Baxter	("The Apartment")	Jack Lemmon
15. Jim McLeod	("Detective Story")	Kirk Douglas
16. Ari Ben Canaan	("Exodus")	Paul Newman
17. Capt. Kinross	("In Which We Serve")	Noel Coward
18. Fred C. Dobbs	("The Treasure of the Sierra Madre")	Humphrey Bogart
19. Joe Gillis	("Sunset Boulevard")	William Holden
20. Pearl Chavez	("Duel in the Sun")	Jennifer Jones
21. Rubin Flood	("The Dark at the Top of the Stairs")	Robert Preston
22. Katrin Holstrom	("The Farmer's Daughter")	Loretta Young
23. Stanley T. Banks	("Father of the Bride")	Spencer Tracy
24. Sgt. Milton Warden	("From Here to Eternity")	Burt Lancaster
25. Leslie Lynnton Benedict	("Giant")	Elizabeth Taylor

90. CLOSE . . . BUT NO CIGAR—BUFFS AND DUFFERS

1. Elisabeth Bergner	p.	"Escape Me Never"
2. Merle Oberon	s.	"The Dark Angel"
3. Marie Dressler	n.	"Emma"
4. Frank Morgan	j.	"The Affairs of Cellini"
5. Claudette Colbert	b.	"Private Worlds"
6. Beulah Bondi	i.	"The Gorgeous Hussy"
7. Stuart Erwin	m.	"Pigskin Parade"
8. Irene Dunne	q.	"The Awful Truth"
9. Andrea Leeds	o.	"Stage Door"
10. Miliza Korjus	a.	"The Great Waltz"
11. Basil Rathbone	t.	"If I Were King"
12. Brian Donlevy	d.	"Beau Geste"
13. Jack Oakie	k.	"The Great Dictator"
14. James Gleason	r.	"Here Comes Mr. Jordan"
15. Susan Peters	e.	"Random Harvest"
16. Gladys Cooper	h.	"Now, Voyager"
17. J. Carroll Naish	g.	"Sahara"
18. Monty Woolley	f.	"Since You Went Away"
19. Flora Robson	c.	"Saratoga Trunk"
20. Tom Tully	l.	"The Caine Mutiny"

91. WHAT A WAY TO GO!—BUFFS AND DUFFERS

1. Gloria Grahame, in "The Bad and the Beautiful" . . .

   i. Died in crash of private plane.

2. Phyllis Thaxter, in "No Man of Her Own" . . .

   m. Killed in a train wreck.

3. Tom Powers, in "Double Indemnity" . . .

   j. Bludgeoned and left for dead alongside a railroad track.

4. Darryl Hickman, in "Leave Her to Heaven" . . .

   n. Drowned while swimming in a lake.

5. Anthony Quinn, in "The Ox-Bow Incident" . . .

   t. Lynched by an unruly mob.

6. Victor Jory, in "The Adventures of Tom Sawyer" . . .

   r. Fell from a precipice during a chase in an underground cavern.

7. Leo G. Carroll, in "Spellbound" . . .

   p. Suicide by gunshot.

8. Jeff Corey, in "Brute Force" . . .

    a. Machine-gunned by guards while bound to the front of a mine cart during a prison break.

9. Shelley Winters, in "The Poseidon Adventure" . . .

    k. Died of a heart attack following a strenuous underwater swim.

10. Spanky McFarland, in "The Trail of the Lonesome Pine" . . .

    b. Caught in an explosion.

11. Jennifer Jones, in "The Towering Inferno" . . .

    c. Fell to earth from a tall building after an explosion disabled an exterior elevator.

12. Louis Calhern, in "Julius Caesar" . . .

    d. Stabbed by conspirators.

13. Susan Hayward, in "Reap the Wild Wind" . . .

    g. Drowned as an unknowing stowaway on a ship which was deliberately wrecked.

14. Lew Ayres, in "All Quiet on the Western Front" . . .

    q. Shot by sniper while trying to catch a butterfly.

15. Francis Ford, in "Drums Along the Mohawk" . . .

    s. Shot by friendly settlers to avoid torture by Indians.

16. Margaret Hamilton, in "The Wizard of Oz" . . .

    l. Dissolved in a puff of smoke after being doused with water.

17. Roy Thinnes, in "Airport '75" . . .

    f. Blown from the cockpit of an airliner as a result of a mid-flight collision.

18. Robert Walker, in "Bataan" . . .

    e. Shot by a sniper of the Japanese army.

19. Thomas Mitchell, in "Gone With the Wind". . .

    h. Died of injuries incurred as a result of a fall from a horse.

20. Peter Graves, in "Stalag 17"

    o. Shot by Nazi guards who believed he was trying to escape from a prison camp.

92. BE MY GUEST—BUFFS AND DUFFERS

From STAN MOGER . . .
1. "Bombardier" Billy Welles.
2. Abner Biberman.
3. Evelyn Venable.

From TONY VERDI . . .
4. Nick Gandi, the Blake Hotel, Los Angeles.
5. Twenty dollars a day, and expenses.

From BOB and ESTHER MANEWITH . . .
6. Each played a character whose last name was that of a city: Barbara Stanwyck, Stella *Dallas;* Peter Lorre, Joel *Cairo,* "The Maltese Falcon"; Frank Sinatra, Nathan *Detroit,* "Guys and Dolls"; Richard Conte, Martin *Rome,* "Cry of the City"; Orson Welles, Edward *Rochester,* "Jane Eyre." (The Manewiths advise they'd also accept Frank Sinatra's role as Tony *Rome.*)

From DAN PECARO . . .
7. Richard Arlen, Bruce Cabot, and Eric Linden. (Dan points out that Eric Linden was playing "John Beal" before John Beal was.)
8. J.K., for Joe Keefer.

From GARY L. ASH . . .
9. "Wings" (1928), "Grand Hotel" (1932).
10. Fay Bainter, 1938, nominated as "Best Actress" for "White Banners," and as "Best Supporting Actress" for "Jezebel" (which she won); and Teresa Wright, 1942, nominated as "Best Actress" for "Pride of the Yankees," and as "Best Supporting Actress" for "Mrs. Miniver" (which she won).
11. Barry Fitzgerald, for "Going My Way."
12. a. Lionel Barrymore, nominated as "Best Supporting Actor" for "A Free Soul" (which he won), and as "Best Director" for "Madame X" . . .
    b. John Cassavetes, nominated as "Best Supporting Actor" for "The Dirty Dozen," and as "Best Director" for "A Woman Under the Influence" . . .
    c. Charles Chaplin, nominated as "Best Actor" for "The Circus" and "The Great Dictator," and as "Best Director" for "The Circus" . . .
    d. John Huston, nominated as "Best Supporting Actor" for "The Cardinal," and as "Best Director" for "The Asphalt Jungle," "The African Queen," "Moulin Rouge," and "The Treasure of the Sierra Madre" (which he won) . . .

e. Orson Welles, nominated as "Best Actor" and as "Best Director" for "Citizen Kane" . . .

f. Laurence Olivier, nominated as "Best Director" for "Hamlet," and as "Best Actor" for "Wuthering Heights," "Rebecca," "Henry V," "Hamlet" (which he won), "Richard III," "The Entertainer," "Othello," and "Sleuth."

From FRAZIER THOMAS . . .

13. "Journey to the Center of the Earth"—Gertrude
14. "Friendly Persuasion"—Samantha

From TOM ALDERMAN . . .

15. If you named five, you not only qualify as a leading light in the Edmund Purdom Fan Club—you have also run through nearly half of the entire Purdom screen career: "Titanic," "The Student Prince," "The Egyptian," "Athena," "The Prodigal," "The King's Thief," "The Cossacks," "Last of the Vikings," "Lafayette," "Malaga," and "The Yellow Rolls-Royce."

From BONNIE and CHARLES REMSBERG . . .

16. a. "A Yank in the R.A.F."; b. "A Yank in Libya"; c. "A Yank on the Burma Road"; d. "A Yank in Korea"; e. "A Yank in Indo-China"; f. "A Yank in Viet Nam."
17. a. "Irma La Douce," Shirley MacLaine; b. "Zorba the Greek," Lila Kedrova; c. "Carnal Knowledge," Rita Moreno; d. "Elmer Gantry," Shirley Jones; e. "Butch Cassidy and the Sundance Kid," Cloris Leachman.

From MORRY ROTH . . .

18. Carroll O'Connor, the Archie Bunker of "All in the Family."

From MEL TORMÉ . . .

19. "The Three Musketeers" (1935): Paul Lukas, Moroni Olsen, Onslow Stevens.
20. "The Man in the Iron Mask" (1939): Warren William (D'Artagnan), Alan Hale, Miles Mander, Bert Roach.

They are our friends—but we never said they were nice folks when it came to movie trivia!

93. HOMESTRETCH—BUFFS AND DUFFERS

1. The film was a 1950 film entitled "Kiss Tomorrow Goodbye." James Cagney starred as Ralph Cotter. Cagney's brother, William, not only produced the film, but played a small part identified as "Ralph's brother."
2. Gibbons, of course, was Art Director for many great M-G-M films,

and the other three gentlemen each received Oscars for their acting abilities—but also in their credits is the fact they each directed one film: Laughton, "Night of the Hunter"; Brando, "One-Eyed Jacks"; Quinn, "The Buccaneer"; and Gibbons, "Tarzan and His Mate."

3. Monte Blue.

4. The producer was Bryan (Brynie) Foy, and the film was "The Seven Little Foys" (1955). The film was a biographical account of the legendary vaudevillian Eddie Foy and his family. The part of Brynie was played by Billy Gray, who is probably best remembered as the son of Robert Young and Jane Wyatt in the long-running TV series "Father Knows Best." Parenthetically, this was the *second* film in which James Cagney portrayed George M. Cohan, in a brief cameo featuring a charming dance duet with Bob Hope, who played Eddie Foy (Sr.).

5. While Glenda Farrell is best-remembered as Torchy Blane, Lola Lane played the title role in "Torchy Blane in Panama," while Jane Wyman starred in "Torchy Plays with Dynamite."

6. Kind of a trick question—asking you to name two films in which Humphrey Bogart played a character named Steve. It seems as if there were dozens, but there were only two, and both of these early in the Bogart career: "Up the River" (1930) and "A Holy Terror" (1931). Though the character played by Lauren Bacall in "To Have and Have Not" *called* him Steve, Bogart's character in that film was that of Harry Morgan. Tricky?

7. The duplicated character was Max Fabian, played in 1950's "All About Eve" by Gregory Ratoff, in support of Bette Davis. Rita Hayworth starred in "Affair in Trinidad," with Glenn Ford, in 1952—and the villain in this one was Alexander Scourby, as Max Fabian!

8. The next time—and there *will* be a next time—you watch the marvelous Gene Kelly dancing and splashing among the puddles in "Singin' in the Rain," pay a moment or two of attention to the buildings and store windows in the background. There, for millions and millions of enthralled movie buffs to see, are: "Mahout Cigarettes," "LaValle Millinery," and "The Mount Hollywood Art School"___and please, please, don't write asking us who played the bewildered policeman!

9. The film with John Qualen as Aladdin and Shemp Howard as Sinbad was Universal's "Arabian Nights," starring Sabu, Maria Montez, and Jon Hall. You may've missed John Qualen and Shemp Howard—but how can you forget Billy Gilbert as Ahmad, Thomas Gomez as Hakim the slave trader, or Charles Coleman as the eunuch?!!

See you in the movies!

TRAILER

While everyone else if filing out of the theater, look back over your shoulder and peer carefully at the star illustrations on the cover. Regardless of how you fared in the scoring, here's a chance to put yourself over the top—or, at least, to get a little more standing as a Buff. The following seven questions are all related to the cover illustrations—so knuckle down, and pick up a fast 100 points per question—or 700 more points for your total.

1. Though nominated *four* times, she never won an Oscar. She is _____ _____

2. The state of Iowa played an important part in the early lives of two of our players. One was born and raised in Dubuque—the other went to college at Grinnell. Name them: _____ _____ and _____ _____.

3. Jake Krantz was his real name—but filmgoers knew him as _____ _____.

4. Which of the two stars on the cover were once married to each other? _____ _____ and _____ _____.

5. She appeared in two memorable Marx Brothers films, but gained greater fame when she teamed with Patsy Kelly for a series of comedies. She died at an early age, and even today the mysterious circumstances of her death have never been fully explained. She is: _____ _____.

6. Two of the men pictured changed their names—from Austerlitz and Bickel to the names the American movie audience knows them by. Their first names are similar . . . but who are they?

7. Of the players pictured, three was born in foreign countries. Name the stars, and their respective birthplaces.

Bonus Points:_____

ANSWERS TO THE TRAILER

1. Rosalind Russell (top row, far left).
2. Margaret Lindsay, pictured with James Cagney (bottom row, second from right); and Gary Cooper (bottom row, second from left).
3. Ricardo Cortez, pictured with Mary Astor (middle row, far left).
4. Grant Withers, pictured with Mae West (top row, second from right), and Loretta Young (bottom row, far left).
5. Thelma Todd (middle row, second from left).

280

6. Fred Astaire (top row, far right) and Fredric March (middle row, second from right).
7. Errol Flynn, from Tasmania (top right, second from left); Marlene Dietrich, from Germany (middle row, far right); and Ray Milland, from Wales (bottom row, far right).

G'bye, now!